EVENWOOD

EVENWOOD REMEMBERS

KEVIN RICHARDSON

© Kevin Richardson 2010

Published by Evenwood Publishing

ISBN 978-0-9565428-0-9

All rights reserved. Reproduction of this book by photocopying or electronic means for non-commercial purposes is permitted. Otherwise, no part of this book may be reproduced, adapted, stored in a retrieval system or transmitted by any means, electronic, mechanical, photocopying, or otherwise without the prior written permission of the author.

Prepared by:

Pasttimes Publishing Ltd
64 Hallfield Road
Layerthorpe
York YO31 7ZQ
Tel: 01904 431213

Website: www.pasttimespublishing.co.uk

To my grandfather 12358 Private F. Richardson 10/DLI attested 8 August 1914, to France 21 May 1915, wounded probably 12 March 1916 and discharged 31 October 1916.

To those who returned and to those who did not.

Medals:
The 1914-15 Star, the British War Medal and the Victory Medal were awarded to 12358 Private F. Richardson but their whereabouts is unknown.

Note:
The above medals were awarded to 2315 Pte. A.E. Monk, 2/London Regiment and loaned to me by his daughter, Mrs Pat Hoy.

Union Jack "Remember" postcard

Thanks to:

Ian Collins, "An Illustrated History of the Embroided Silk Postcard"
gabrian@btinternet.com

-vi-

FOREWORD

"I have received a very charming card from Wilfred Howlett, with a silk Union Jack worked upon it and the word, "Remember". If he should read this letter of mine, he may take this message from me that I have not forgotten him and am not likely to do so."

Rev. G.J. Collis
Evenwood Parish Magazine, October 1915

39146, Private John Wilfred Howlett, 12/13 Northumberland Fusiliers was killed in action 18 September 1918, during the Battle of Epehy south west of Cambrai in northern France as the allied forces pushed for victory.

The prime purpose of this work is to pay tribute to 39146 Private John Wilfred Howlett and all of the 70 men born or resident in the Parish of Evenwood and Barony who lost their lives during the Great War. It is also intended to commemorate the losses of the forces of the British Dominions and dependencies overseas by including 3 men on the Hamsterley War Memorial, 2 served with the Australian Imperial Force and 1 with the Canadian Expeditionary Force. It is not for any sense of glory or nationalism but simply to remember the sacrifice of those many brave men who fought and died, so that those who paid the ultimate price will not be forgotten.

This work is not intended to be a comprehensive account of Evenwood and the Great War – readers are directed towards the publication "Evenwood's

Heyday: a colliery village 1895 – 1918". Neither is it a history of the Great War but rather it attempts to put the sacrifice of Evenwood's "fallen" into historic context and where possible draw upon information to verify those events surrounding their death. Arguably, work such as this can have no real conclusion. This is an ongoing project and hopefully further details will be made known as it progresses. There will always be questions. For instance G. Dowson is buried in Tyne Cot Cemetery near Zonnebeke, Belgium but his battalion was in fact serving about 50 miles to the south in the St. Quentin area of France. Why was he in Belgium? At some stage in the future, further information may be made available, questions may be answered and updates will be necessary. There may be some inaccuracies for which I apologise – only further research can eliminate errors. This is also an appeal for information. It is an open invitation for others to contribute and additions will be gratefully received. Any errors will be gladly amended upon receipt of accurate details. The author can be contacted at:

- 10 Alexandra Terrace, Evenwood, Bishop Auckland, Co. Durham DL14 9QN
- Tel: 01388 832060
- e-mail: kevinrichardson205@btinternet.com

Perhaps present day family links can be traced and if nothing else, a lost bond can be rekindled.

Remembering

A Man's destination is not his destiny,
Every country is home to one man
And exile to another.
Where a man died bravely
At one with his destiny, that soil is his.
Let his village remember.

From the Visitor Centre "the Beaumont-Hamel Newfoundland Memorial"
Veterens Affairs, Canada

LEST WE FORGET

ACKNOWLEDGEMENTS

The support, time and effort given by the following organisations and individuals is greatly appreciated:

- St. Paul's Parochial Church Council, Evenwood – the late Mr. Eric Proud unearthed the Parish Magazines which proved to be an invaluable source of information.
- The late Mrs. Kathleen MacMillan used these magazines as her primary source in writing about the Great War in "Evenwood's Heyday: a colliery village 1896 – 1918" – a publication written by a group of local historians supervised by the Department of Adult and Continuing Education of Durham University under the guidance of John Smith. This work is a continuation of Kathleen's endeavours. Kathleen and Eric, now sadly departed.
- The Green Howards' Museum, Richmond, North Yorkshire – Paul Cooper.
- Enniskilling Museum, Northern Ireland – Major Jack Dunlop.
- The Regimental Museum of the Border Regiment, Carlisle – Tony Goddard.
- Luftschiffmuseum Aeronauticum, Nordholz, Germany, – A. Cordes MA Head Archivist.
- The Thiepval Project Charity Fund, – Sir Frank Sanderson and Vincent Laude.
- The Trustees of the Durham Light Infantry Museum, Durham
- The King's Own Calgary Regiment, The Military Museums, Calgary, Alberta T2T 5J4, Canada – Al Judson, Military Archivist.

- Staff at Durham Cathedral, York Minster, Carlisle Cathedral and Lincoln Cathedral.
- Canon Neville Vine for granting permission to photograph the cross in St. Andrew's Church, South Church, Bishop Auckland.
- Mrs C Wolstenholme, St. John the Baptist, Hamsteels (Quebec)
- Brian Featherstone
- Tom Hutchinson
- Michael Sunderland
- John and Joyce Malcolm
- Joyce Robson
- Dr. J. Said
- Jim McTaggart
- Helen Smith
- Sibylle Moss
- Ann Crampton
- Pat Hoy
- Evenwood W.M.C Committee
- Clare Brayshaw

The following have been invaluable:
- The Commonwealth War Graves Commission
- "Soldiers Died in the Great War" C.D.
- www.ancestry.com
- national archives
- www.1914–1918.net-Chris Baker

Official records have been researched where possible but there is at least one major drawback – not all the D.L.I. War Diaries have been examined.

FAMILY CONTACTS AND HELPERS:

The support and assistance given by the following people has been generous and I give my whole hearted thanks.

DURHAM LIGHT INFANTRY

1. Cant T. 2nd John Cant, Ferryhill
2. Million W. 2nd Roy Million, Newton Aycliffe
3. Heaviside W. 2nd the late Mike Heaviside, Cockfield
4. Spence J. W. 2nd None
5. Baister D. 1/5th Roy Million, Newton Aycliffe
6. Brown A. 1/6th None
7. Cox G. T. 1/6th Malcolm Gallimore & Hilda Bell, Evenwood
8. Lee J.C. 6th None
9. Pinkney J.H. 1/6th None
10. Priestley G. 1/6th David Priestley, Staindrop, Colin Priestley, Lanehead
11. Rushford O. 1/6th – info provided by Lily Bainbridge, Cockfield
12. Simpson T. W. 1/6th Mrs. June Heslop, Ingleton & "Tot" Robson, Mrs. Clark, Evenwood
13. Snowball W. 6th Mr. Melvyn & Mrs. Edith McConnell, Bishop Auckland
14. Walling J. 1/6th Mrs. Mima Walling, Evenwood
15. Wardle J. A. 1/6th – Geoff Wardle, Pontefract
16. Graves J. C. 10th None
17. Dunn T. H. 11th Nelson Dunn, Evenwood
18. Applegarth T. W. 11th Mrs. Walker, Evenwood, Carol Gator & Diane McDougal
19. Maughan J.W. 12th Gloria Sowerby, Staindrop & Walter Maughan, Evenwood
20. Middlemas M. G. 12th Carole Kirby, Cockfield, John Middlemass, Notts, Ann Marshall, Ramshaw
21. Raine J. H. 13th John Caine, Newton Aycliffe
22. Wardle R. 14th Geoff Wardle, Pontefract
23. Maughan J. 14th John Maughan, West Auckland
24. Earl W. E. 14th Jean Earl, Evenwood

25. Metcalfe R.T. 15th None
26. Towers E. 15th None
27. Ellerker J.H. 15th Elsie Anderson, Evenwood
28. Featherstone W. 18th None
29. Million J. 18th Roy Million, Newton Aycliffe
30. Hirst F. 20th None
31. Dinsdale W. 22nd None

THE NORTHUMBERLAND FUSILIERS

32. Davis T. 1/4th None
33. Purvis F. 1/5th Brian Carter, Evenwood
34. Howlett J.W. 12th/13th. None
35. Cree C 21st (Tyneside Scottish) Mrs. Hewitt, Bishop Auckland & Dylis Caygill, Staindrop
36. Heaviside R. 22nd (Tyneside Scottish) the late Mike Heaviside, Cockfield

THE YORKSHIRE REGIMENT (THE GREEN HOWARDS)

37. Morley W. 4th Norma Garthwaite & the late Rhoda Stephenson Evenwood
38. Walton J. J. 6th None
39. Wilson R. 6th Malcolm Wilson, Ingleton & Judith Wright, Evenwood
40. Robinson E. 7th None
41. Simpson M. 9th None

WEST YORKSHIRE REGIMENT

42. Hewitt J. 2/6th Ann Mitchell
43. Conlon R. W. 2/6 – None
44. Oates J.J. 18th None
45. Raine M. T. 1/7th None

LINCOLNSHIRE REGIMENT

46. Arkless J. W. 2/5th Malcolm Galimore, Evenwood
47. Lowson C. H. 7th Barbara Crompton

ROYAL ENGINEERS

48. Atkinson A. K. 206th Field Co. None
49. Milburn J.T. 177th Tunnelling Company None
50. Rutter S. R. "Z" Special Coy. Doug Holland, Durham, Mrs. Sams, Bishop Auckland
51. Wardle H. 234th Field Coy. Geoff Wardle, Pontefract
Ken & Winnie Stannard, Barnard Castle

MACHINE GUN CORPS

52. Richardson J. J. – 6th Edith Wallace, Eggleston & Paul Simpson, Butterknowle
53. Skelhorn J. – 8th Rachael B

BORDER REGIMENT

54. Cooke E.J. 4th None
55. Dixon H. 5th Harry Carnell, Ramshaw, Barbara Gill, Crook

EAST YORKSHIRE REGIMENT

56. Marshall J. 8th None
57. Moses W.A. 7th None

AUSTRALIAN IMPERIAL FORCE

58. Marquis J.J. 28th Enid Clinton, Margaret Robertson, Sharon Spargo (Perth) Ainslee Evans (Katanning) Western Australia
59. Marquis F.W. 28th Enid Clinton, Margaret Robertson, Sharon Spargo (Perth)) Ainslee Evans (Katanning) Western Australia

MISCELLANEOUS REGIMENTS

60. Bryant G.W. – Royal Army Medical Corps None
61. Burrell A. Labour Corps None
62. Dowson G. 7/8th Royal Inniskilling Fusiliers – Barbara Nicholson & Julia McDonald
63. Gray W. Royal Field Artillery 52nd Battery 15th Brigade John and Mary Deighton, Raby Park, Staindrop

64. Heseltine J. 2nd York & Lancaster Regiment Joan Rutherford, Barnard Castle
65. Hutchinson J. 9th Manchester Regiment Fred Laverick, Evenwood
66. Oates A. 31st Batt. Canadian Infantry Sharon & Lorne Mercier, Calgary, Alberta, Canada
67. Parmley G. 1/4th King's Own Yorkshire Light Infantry Lynn Biggs, New Zealand & Jim Atkinson, Edmonton, Lily Bainbridge, Cockfield
68. Richards J. Royal Garrison Artillery (Pembroke Dock) None
69. Storey W.R. 1st The Loyal North Lancashire Regiment None
70. Smith W. 9th Bn., Lancashire Fusiliers None

ROYAL NAVY

71. Carrick W. RN HMS Ardent Mrs. Doris Kay, Evenwood, Janet Carrick, P. Murphy, Bill Carrick
72. Lynas A. RN HMS Ardent Vera Williams & Russell Place, Evenwood
73. Wren J. W. RN HMS Black Prince None

CONTENTS

Foreword   vii
Acknowledgements   ix

CHAPTER 1
Evenwood Remembers   1

CHAPTER 2
The Place and the People   8

CHAPTER 3
The Build up to War – In a Nutshell   22
The British Army   24
1914 Timeline   27
August 1914: Belgium and France   28

CHAPTER 4
1915 Timeline   36
    •   J.T. Cant   40
    •   W. Million   42
    •   J. Richards   44
    •   E. Towers   44
    •   H. Dixon   51

CHAPTER 5
1916 Timeline		54
•	C. Cree	57
•	J.T. Milburn	59
•	J. Marshall	61
•	J.H. Raine	62
The Battle of Jutland		64
•	J.W. Wren	66
•	W. Carrick	67
•	A. Lynas	67
The Battle of the Somme		70
•	T.R. Metcalfe	72
•	R.W. Conlon	76
•	A. Oates	78
•	J.C. Graves	80
•	W. Smith	83
•	W.E. Earl	84
•	F. Hirst	86
•	J.C. Lee	88
•	J.A. Wardle	88
•	R.W. Wilson	93
•	J. Maughan	96
•	G.T. Cox	98
•	A. Brown	101
•	J.J. Oates	102
•	T.H. Dunn	104
The Evenwood Zeppelin Raid		108

CHAPTER 6
1917 Timeline		117
•	W. Featherstone	121
•	J. Walling	123
•	J. Million	125
•	J.W. Arkless	128
The Battle of Arras		131
•	J.H. Pinkney	132

- J. Heseltine — 135
- R. Wardle — 138
- S.R. Rutter — 139
- E. Robinson — 141
- W.B. Heaviside — 144
- W.R. Storey — 147

The Third Battle of Ypres (Passchendaele) — 150
- H. Wardle — 151
- E.E.J. Cooke — 153
- J.J. Walton — 155
- W. Dinsdale — 157
- M.T. Raine — 159
- G. Parmley — 160
- G. Priestley — 165

The Battle of Cambrai — 168
- J.W. Spence — 169
- G. Bryant — 171

CHAPTER 7

1918 Timeline — 174
- J. Hewitt — 179

The German spring Offensive — 180
- G. Dowson — 182
- J. Hutchinson — 183
- T.W Simpson — 185
- J. Skelhorn — 188
- J.H. Ellerker — 191
- T.W. Applegarth — 194
- W. Morley — 199
- D. Baister — 201
- O. Rushford — 208
- J.J. Marquis — 212
- W.A. Moses — 214
- W. Gray — 215
- J.J. Richardson — 219

The Battle of Amiens – 100 Days to Victory		222
• C.H. Lowson		224
• W. Snowball		227
• A. Burrell		229
• F.W. Marquis		230
• R. Heaviside		234
• J.W. Howlett		235
• M. Simpson		237
• M.G. Middlemass		240
• T. Davis		243
The Armistice: 11 November 1918		246
• A.K. Atkinson		248
• F. Purvis		250
Spanish Flu		252
• Hamsterley P.O.W. Burials		254
1919 Timeline		257
• J.W. Maughan		257
Peace Terms		259

CHAPTER 8
Casualties	261
Demoblization	266

CHAPTER 9
Remembrance	281

CHAPTER 10
Rev. Collis	285

Appendices:
1:	The Toll: chronological order	292
2:	The Toll: by Regiment	306
3:	The Toll: Home Addresses	310
4:	The Roll	317
5:	Absent Voters List	323
6:	D.L.I. Casualties	331
Bibliography		335

CHAPTER ONE

EVENWOOD REMEMBERS

Those remembered in this work were born or lived within the Parish of Evenwood and Barony. The area includes the villages of Evenwood, Ramshaw and Evenwood Gate and the rural area which includes the settlements of High Lands, Low Lands, Morley and Windmill. It has been compiled having regard to:

1 St. Paul's Church, Evenwood: Comrades of the Great War – In Memoriam plaque
2 War Memorial for Evenwood, Lands and Morley located in Evenwood Cemetery
3 Evenwood W.M.C. Memorial
4 "Soldiers killed in the Great War" C.D. – those born in Evenwood
5 "Soldiers killed in the Great War" C.D. – those resident in Evenwood
6 Evenwood Parish Magazine
7 Information passed on by family members

Also included in this work are 3 soldiers who are commemorated on the Hamsterley War Memorial. They served in the Australian Imperial Force and the Canadian Expeditionary Force and are included as a tribute to the Commonwealth losses.

The full list of those recorded is as follows:

ST. PAUL'S CHURCH, EVENWOOD
COMRADES OF THE GREAT WAR – IN MEMORIAM:

1. 2/Lt. T. W. Applegarth
2. L/C J.W. Arkless
3. Sapper A.K. Atkinson M.M.
4. Pte. D. Baister
5. AB W. Carrick
6. Cpl. C.T. Cox
7. Pte. T. Davis
8. Cpl. H. Dixon
9. Pte. G. Dowson
10. Pte. T.H. Dunn
11. Pte. J. Ellerker
12. Gunner W. Gray
13. Pte. J. Heseltine
14. Pte. R. Heaviside
15. Pte. J. Hewitt
16. Pte. W. Howlett
17. Pte J. Hutchinson
18. AB A. Lynas
19. Pte. J. Maughan
20. Pte. J. Maughan
21. Pte. M. G. Middlemas
22. Pte. J. Million
23. Sgt. G. Parmley
24. Gunner F. Purvis
25. Pte. J.H. Raine
26. Pnr. S.R. Rutter
27. Sgt. T.W. Simpson M.M.
28. Pte J. Skelhorn
29. Pte. W. Snowball
30. Sgt. J.W. Spence
31. L/Cpl. W. Storey

32 Sgt. E. Towers
33 Pte. J. Walling
34 L/Cpl. J.W. Walton
35 Pte. R. Wardle
36 Pte. R. Wilson
37 AB J.W. Wren

Evenwood War Memorial – all of the above are included on the War Memorial. The additional names are:

38 G. Bryant
39 R.W. Conlin (note: name should read Conlon)
40 W.E. Earl
41 J.C. Graves
42 W. Morley
43 W. Moses
44 M.T. Raine
45 J.J. Richardson
46 O. Rushford
47 M. Simpson
48 H. Wardle

Evenwood W.M.C. – additional name:

49 W. Featherstone – commemorated on Etherley War Memorial

Those born in Evenwood, not on Evenwood memorials but commemorated elsewhere:

50 A. Brown - Staindrop
51 A. Burrell - Cockfield
52 J.T. Cant – Kirk Merrington
53 C. Cree - Cockfield
54 W. Dinsdale – Bishop Auckland
55 W. Heaviside – West Auckland
56 F. Hirst - Hamsteels
57 T.R. Metcalfe – Witton Park
58 J.T. Milburn – Shildon

59 W. Million - Etherley
60 J.J. Oates – Normanton, West Yorkshire
61 J.H. Pinkney – Stanley, Crook
62 G. Priestley - Cockfield
63 E. Robinson - Shildon

Those resident in Evenwood, not on Evenwood memorials but commemorated elsewhere:

64 J.C. Lee - Cockfield
65   C.H. Lowson – St. Helen Auckland & West Auckland
66 J. Richards – Etherley

Those resident in Evenwood, not on Evenwood memorials and not traced on a local memorial elsewhere:

67 E.J. Cooke

Those born in Evenwood, not on Evenwood memorials and not traced on a local memorial elsewhere:

68 J. Marshall
69 W. Smith
70 J.A. Wardle

Hamsterley War Memorial:

71 J.J. Marquis
72 F.W. Marquis
73 A. Oates

St. Paul's Church, Evenwood

Comrades of the Great War
In Memoriam

Evenwood War Memorial in the Cemetery, Oaks Bank, Evenwood

Evenwood Workmen's Club Memorial

CHAPTER TWO

THE PLACE AND THE PEOPLE

THE PLACE

The Parish of Evenwood and Barony is in south west Durham to the west of Bishop Auckland and to the north west of Darlington. The becks flow off the fells and moors above Woodland to form the river Gaunless which flows eastwards past the villages of Cockfield, Lands, Ramshaw, Evenwood and West Auckland then joins the river Wear to the north east

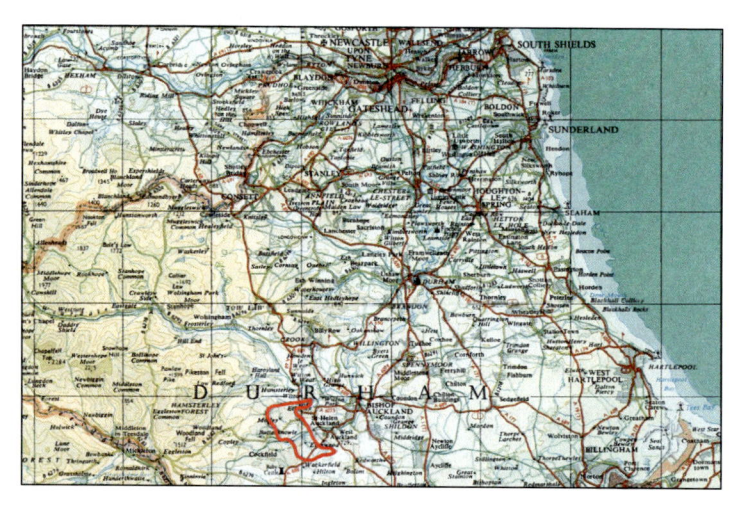

County Durham showing the Parish of Evenwood and Barony in relation to Bishop Auckland

of Bishop Auckland. From then on it meanders through the county to reach the North Sea at Sunderland.

The common factor to the area is coal. The Auckland Coalfield forms the southern part of the Great Northern Coalfield that dominated the counties of Durham and Northumberland. Evenwood and the other main settlements in the Parish – Ramshaw, Evenwood Gate and Lands Bank are pit villages. Low Lands, Morley and Windmill have rural roots but these hamlets also housed many coal miners who found work in the numerous drift mines which punctured the landscape in this part of the county. The modern world swept into the district following the opening up of the Auckland Coalfield via the Stockton and Darlington Railway and the Witton Park branch line in 1825. Coal had been worked in the locality for centuries but Lord Strathmore and the Rev. Luke Prattman wished to see the expansion of their mineral interests in the Gaunless Valley notably at Norwood Colliery (located to the east of modern day Lands Bank) and pits at Butterknowle and Copley. As a result, the Haggerleases Branch Railway was laid along a route following the river valley and it was opened for goods traffic in 1830. Coal was transported initially by horse draw chaldrons along iron rails and a stationary engine at Brussleton hauled them up the Incline to the top of the Brussleton Bank and onto Shildon, Darlington, Stockton-on-Tees and beyond. From 1856 following the construction of Shildon Tunnel, steam locomotives were used when the new railway line from Shildon to Bishop Auckland was opened.

Improved transportation resulted in large scale investment in the coal industry:
– Durham County Coal Company established pits in the Evenwood area such as the Norwood Colliery located at Ramshaw to the north of the Haggerleases branch railway, Evenwood Colliery located to the south and Cragg Wood Colliery (later called Storey Lodge Colliery) further to the west along the valley.
– Henry Stobart Co. Ltd owned the Jane Pit at Witton Park, the George Pit at Escomb together with pits at Chilton and Newton Cap, Bishop Auckland and this company expanded its interest into the Gaunless Valley from Lands to Ramshaw. In particular, a series of drift mines on Railey Fell ran into a bankhead at West Tees Colliery at the north end of Ramshaw.
– Thrushwood and Tees Hetton pits were sunk to the east of Evenwood,
– There were drifts at Ramshaw

- There were workings to the north at Carterthorne.
- The North Bitchburn Coal Company purchased Storey Lodge Colliery then bought the Evenwood and Thrushwood Collieries and in 1892 commenced a major undertaking – the sinking of Randolph Colliery at Evenwood. The following year, a new winning at Cockfield proved the Brockwell seam. In 1893, at Randolph, coal was drawn from the Brockwell and in 1895 the erection of 60 "Coppee" coke ovens was commenced. A second battery consisting of a further 20 ovens was completed by January 1897. By 1899, Randolph secured a daily output of 800 tons of coal and 500 men and boys were employed. In 1911 new by product coke ovens were built at Randolph.

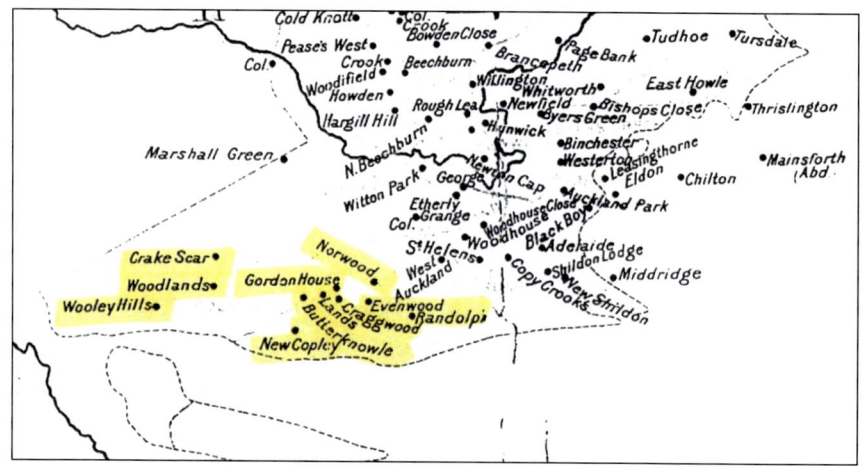

Gaunless Valley pits from Reid's Handy Guide c. 1914

Other mining enterprises in the Gaunless Valley included Woodland Collieries Co. Ltd. at Cow Close, Cowley, Woodland, Crake Scar and New Copley to the west of the district; Butterknowle Colliery Co. Ltd. at Diamond, Quarry, West Hutton and Salterburn, near Butterknowle; Lowson Bros. at the Black Horse, north of Wackerfield; H. Summerson at Millfield Grange to the north of Cockfield; H.H. Turnbull at Seven Sisters south of Cockfield; W. Teasdale at Old Copley; George Lowson at Pit Close near Windmill; H.J. Mein at Morley and Carterthorne collieries and George Bradford* at West Carterthorne on Railey Fell.

* *George Bradford* was the father of 4 remarkable sons – Thomas (1886-1966) served in the 8/DLI, was badly wounded at Ypres, was awarded the D.S.O. and was the only brother to survive the war; George (1887-1918) served in the Royal Navy and was awarded a posthumous V.C. for his bravery during the raid on Zeebrugge harbour, Belgium 23 April 1918; James (1890-1817) 18/DLI was awarded the Military Cross for his bravery near Gommecourt March 1917 and died of wounds 14 May 1917 and Roland (1892-1917) 2/DLI & 9/DLI was awarded the Military Cross and the Victoria Cross and was killed in action 30 November 1917.

As coal mining developed, the villages expanded – originally known as Gordon Lane, Ramshaw thrived. In 1865, the Ramshaw Colliery School built by Stobart & Co. was opened which later became the Railey Fell Miners' Institute; in 1870 the Ramshaw Primitive Methodist Chapel was opened; in 1884 Evenwood Station located at Ramshaw was opened.

At Evenwood, in 1865 the National School was opened; in 1866 St. Paul's Church was consecrated; in 1868 the vicarage was built – the first vicar being Charles Edward Palmer; in 1868 a fine house Brookside Cottage was erected; in 1876 the Wesleyan Chapel in Swan Street opened for worship; in 1885 the Jacob Wright Almshouses were built; in 1893 Evenwood School Infants moved into a new building; in 1897 the Randolph Institute was opened; in 1897 another fine house Victoria House was erected; in 1904 the Co-op opened for business; in 1906 the Congregational Chapel was built; in 1910 Ramshaw County School on Oaks Bank, Evenwood was opened; in 1912 the Primitive Methodists Chapel in Shirley Terrace was built and in 1914 the co-op extension opened for business.

Houses around the village green and those at Stones End appear to be the earliest built. Then the Oaks, Gordon Row, Copeland Row (formerly known as Tees-Hetton Row) and Chapel Street being the older terrace rows, were probably purpose built by the colliery companies to house miners. Smaller terraced blocks along South View, the Centre and around the Green, Manor Street, Jubilee Terrace, Raby Street, Victoria Street then sprung up. Randolph Terrace was the main access road into the colliery and would have been built after 1892. Building along the main road through the village took place – West View, Swan Street, Farncombe Terrace, Shirley Terrace and houses on Oaks Bank were probably built next. Following the opening of the co-op in 1904, it is assumed that the 4 red brick terraces behind it were built – Provident Terrace and Rochdale Street (both commemorating the co-operative movement). The origin of Delaware Avenue remains open to speculation! Accrington Terrace at Bank Top is believed to be named after the town which supplied the smooth red facing bricks. In 1910 Alexandra Terrace was commenced by private builders and provided housing for colliery officials.

Map of Evenwood & Barony Parish

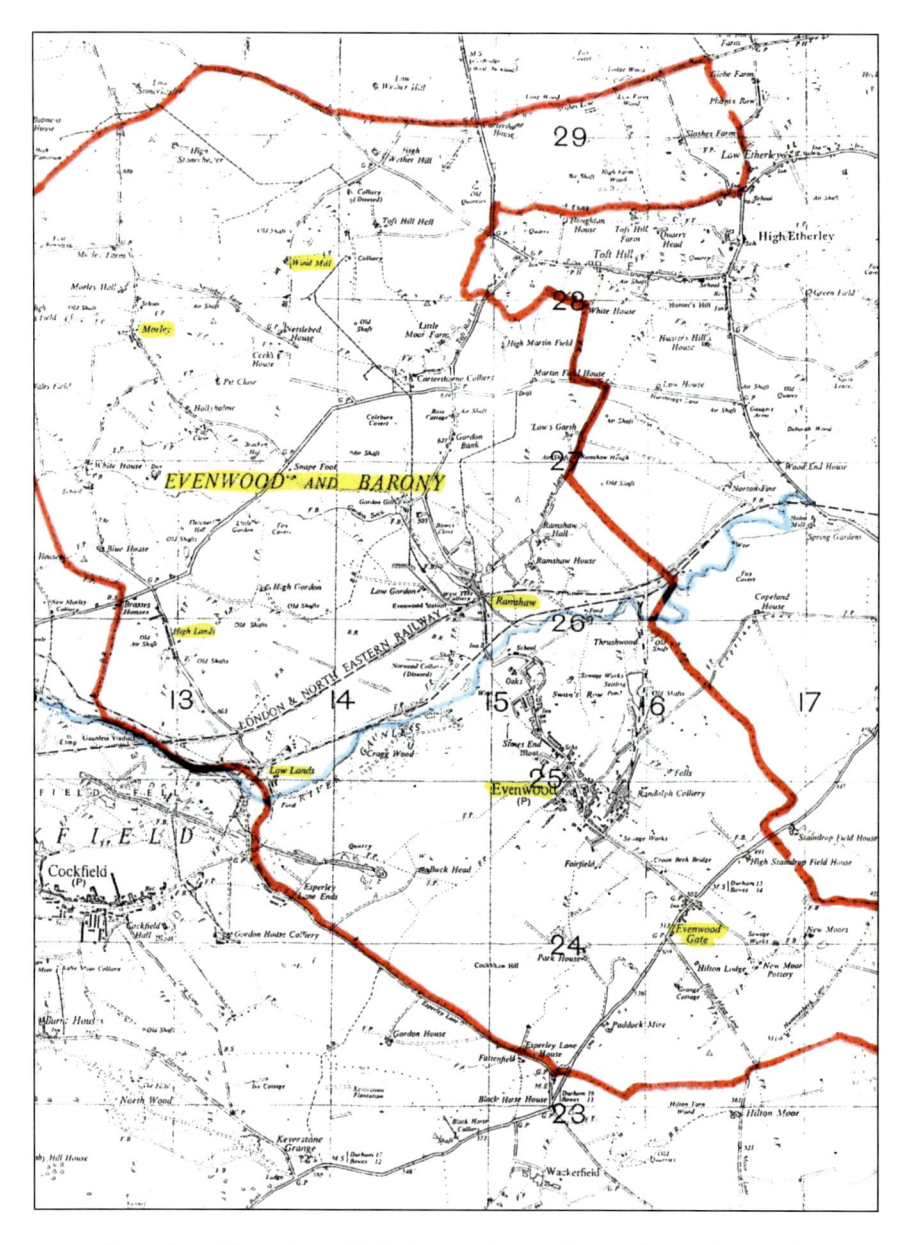

Reproduced from the 1950 Ordnance Survey Map © Crown Copyright

The Great War Years: Evenwood amd Ramshaw

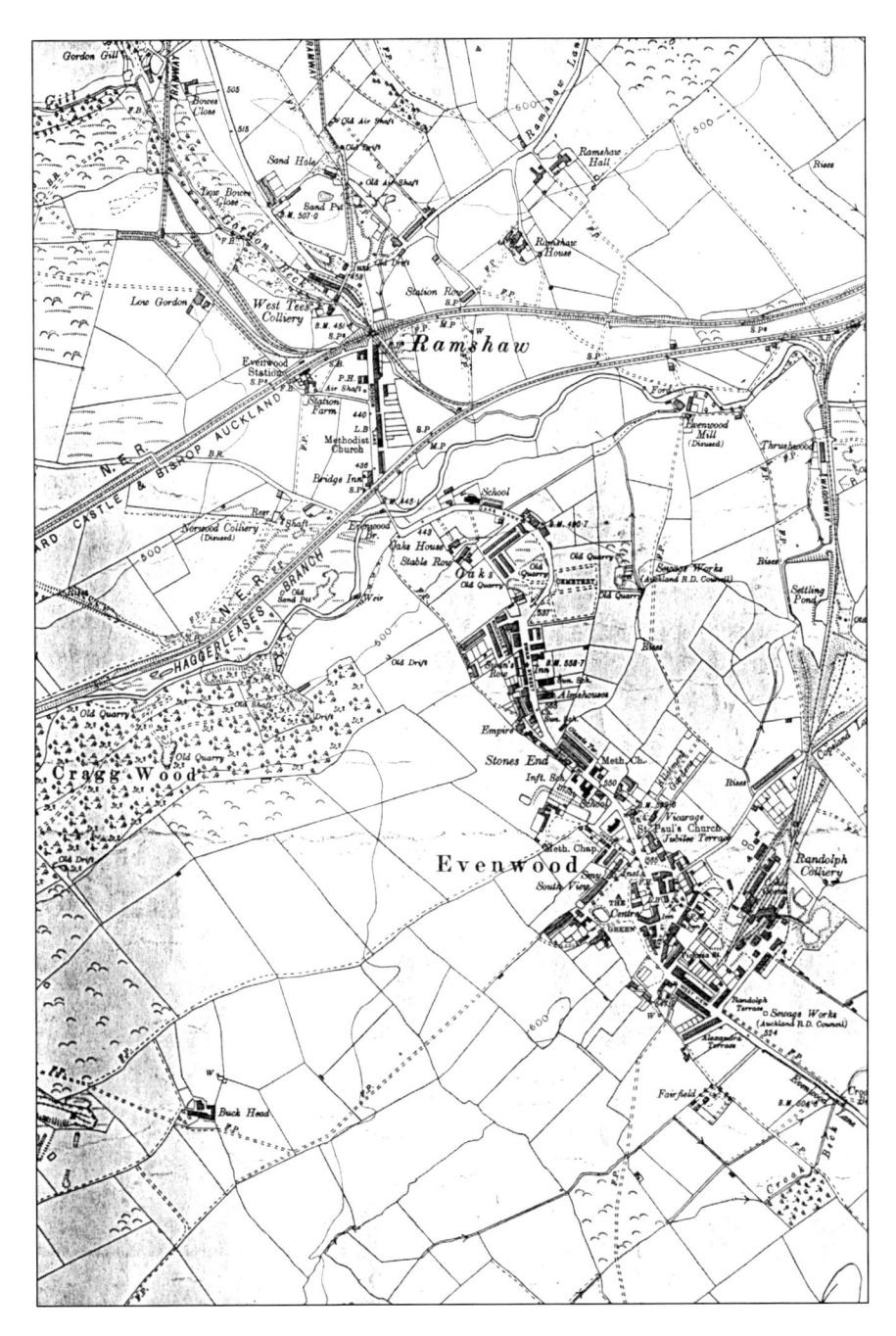

Reproduced from the 1921 Ordnance Survey Map © Crown Copyright
(3rd edition)

The Great War Years: High Lands otherwise known as Lands Bank

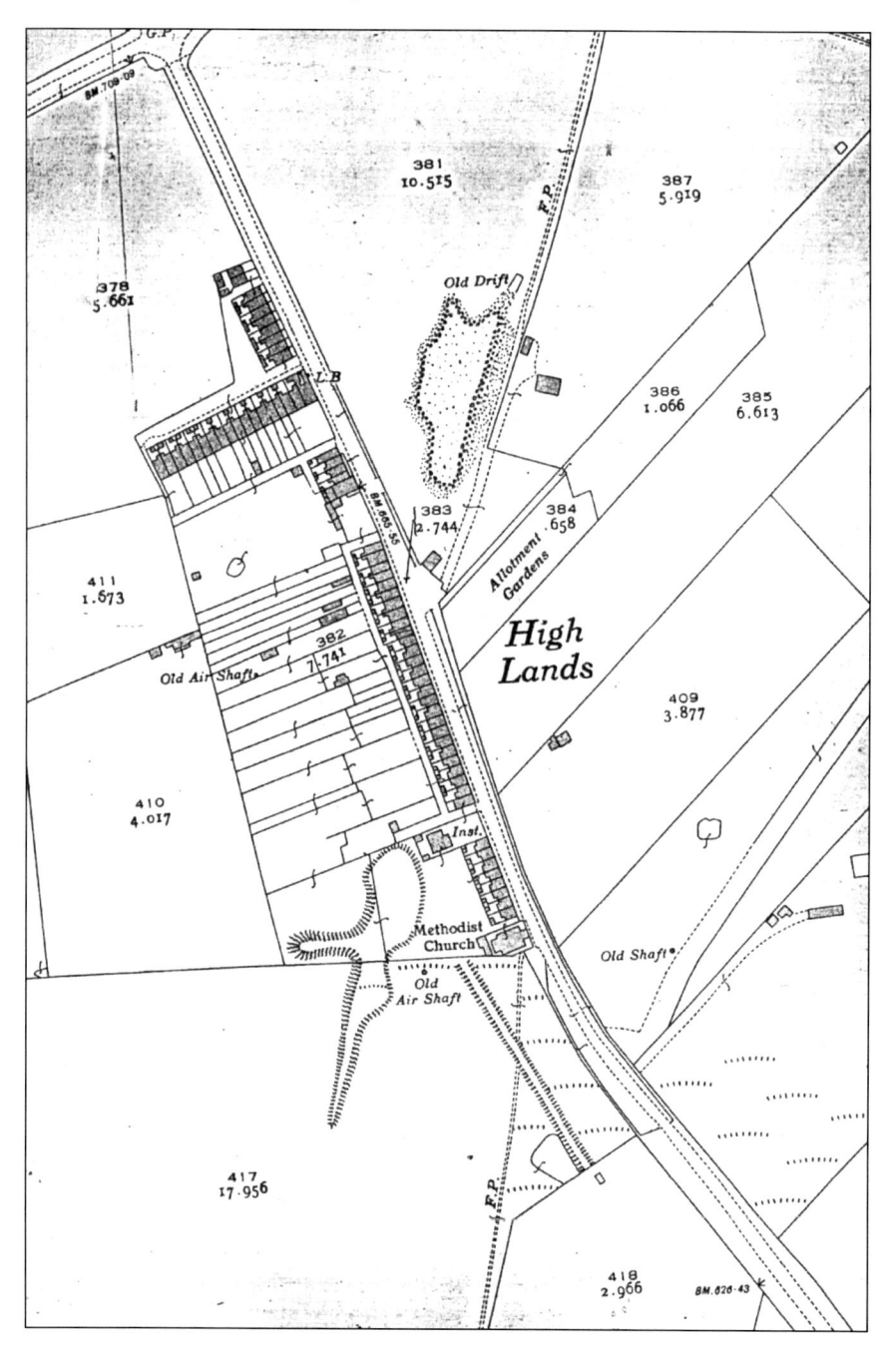

*Reproduced from the 1921 Ordnance Survey Map © Crown Copyright
(3rd edition)*

-14-

Further to the west, the small mining community known collectively as Lands (Low Lands, Lands Bank and High Lands) grew around a number of small drift mines sunk into the bank-sides of the valley of the river Gaunless. Many of the men and boys were employed at these drifts and a few terraced rows were built to house these families. Lands Chapel was built in 1876.

The hamlets of Morley and Wind Mill are located in the rural areas of the Barony so unsurprisingly, work was also found locally in farming. Coal reaches the surface along the Gaunless Valley and there were many drift mine workings in the fields over the whole area. Many farmers owned small scale drift mines and combined both aspects of work.

By the early Twentieth century, the villages within the Parish of Evenwood and Barony were in the form easily recognisable today and the population of the Parish was in the order of 5,000, most of whom lived at Evenwood.

THE PEOPLE

Evenwood, Ramshaw and Lands Bank were pit villages. An examination of the 1901 census pages confirms that over 89% of those in employment worked in the coal industry. Even employment in the rural district was dominated by coal mining where about 65% of those living in the Morley and Windmill areas worked in the pits.

The fledgling labour movement found support in the locality and the growth of the Durham Miners Association is hardly surprising. It is clear that the early Twentieth century witnessed the rise of a new political force in the area which threatened the old established order of Conservatives v Liberals.

The Conservatives had been in power nationally since 1895 and their local man was Lord Barnard whose seat was at Raby Castle, near Staindrop some 3 miles to the west. The Vane family were landowning aristocrats. The Liberal Party was generally seen as the party of the ordinary man. The Liberal Sir Joseph Whitwell Pease was the sitting M.P. for the Barnard Castle constituency which included the Parish of Evenwood and Barony. He was a Quaker industrialist with numerous commercial interests, an owner of coal and railway companies – hardly representative of the working classes!

With the rising influence of trade unions, the Independent Labour Party formed in 1893 began to attract local support. In 1898, the representatives of the Miners Lodges of Randolph, Norwood, Railey Fell and Storey Lodge collieries supported the candidature of David Carrick in the interests of Labour for the seat on the Auckland Rural District Council. David Carrick was a Primitive Methodist preacher and not without influence.

Following the death of the local Member of Parliament, Sir Joseph Whitwell Pease in 1903, a by-election was called for the Barnard Castle constituency. The constituency covered a huge area of west Durham including Weardale, Teesdale, the Gaunless Valley and the coal mining districts of Tow Law and Crook. This was to be the battleground for "associations" that represented the interests of "labour". Arthur Henderson, a Scotsman by birth, brought up in Newcastle-upon-Tyne, worked as a trade union official and his name was put forward as a candidate for the election. He stood as an Independent. The Barnard Castle Labour and Progressive Association was formed specifically to back his campaign. It consisted of disaffected Liberals, miners' representatives and I.L.P. members. All 3 sitting I.L.P. Members of Parliament, Kier Hardy, Shackleton and Crooks visited the constituency to support Henderson and they spoke to enthusiastic crowds. Henderson won by just 47 votes from Vane the Conservative. Following this landmark victory, Henderson addressed a "labour" meeting in Evenwood 24 November 1903. Given that there were 9,502 votes cast in the election and there were about 3,700 miners working in the Gaunless Valley area (not all would have the vote) it is fair to assume that the majority put their weight behind Henderson and were largely responsible for his narrow victory. He needed to thank them.

At this time, there were only 4 MPs with any "labour" interests. Henderson was re-elected in 1906 and held the seat until 1918 when the constituency was divided.

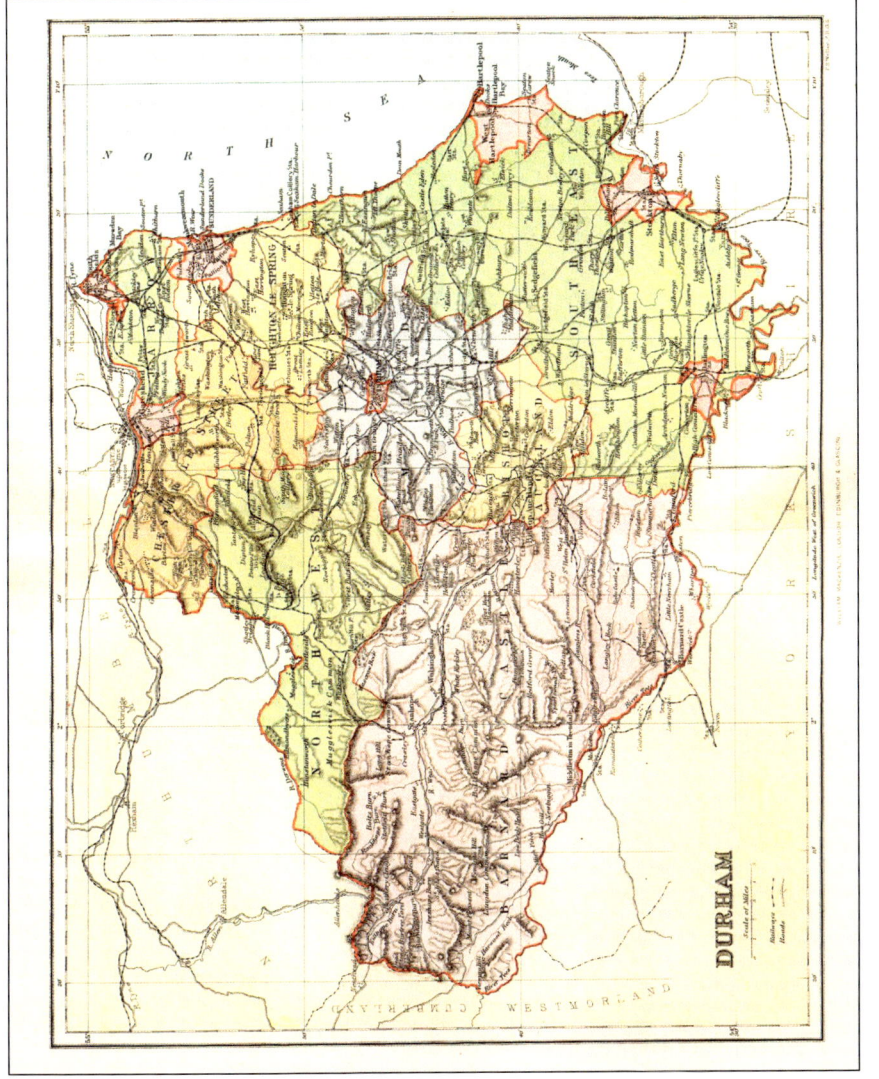

County Durham: Parliamentary Constituencies – Barnard Castle Constituency coloured mauve to the south west of the County

On 12 June 1909, Arthur Henderson was invited to Evenwood for the unveiling of the Randolph Durham Miners Union Lodge Banner. The unfurling ceremony took place on the village green outside the Miners' Institute. Other dignitaries present were Alderman William House J.P. and President of the Durham Miners Association, Mr. Thomas Summerbell M.P. for Sunderland and Mr. James Robson County Councillor for Bear Park. William House came from West Auckland just down the road where he had worked at the Town End Pit and was a union official. He had risen to be an influential figure in the politics of the County.

Randolph pitmen c.1910

A public meeting was held in the evening and the question of relations with Germany was on the minds of many. The Auckland Chronicle, Thursday 17 June 1909, reported as follows:

> "Answering the question as to why the members of the Labour Party visited Germany, Mr. Henderson said it was because of the ideals they held and the desires that actuated them....They went right through Germany and into the great centres and found that German people were not represented by the statements published in some newspapers of this country but that they were anxious to maintain those friendly relationships existing between two great countries...It

appeared to him that if they only talked long enough about a war with Germany they would get it. He wanted them to talk long enough about peace and they would keep peace. (Applause.)

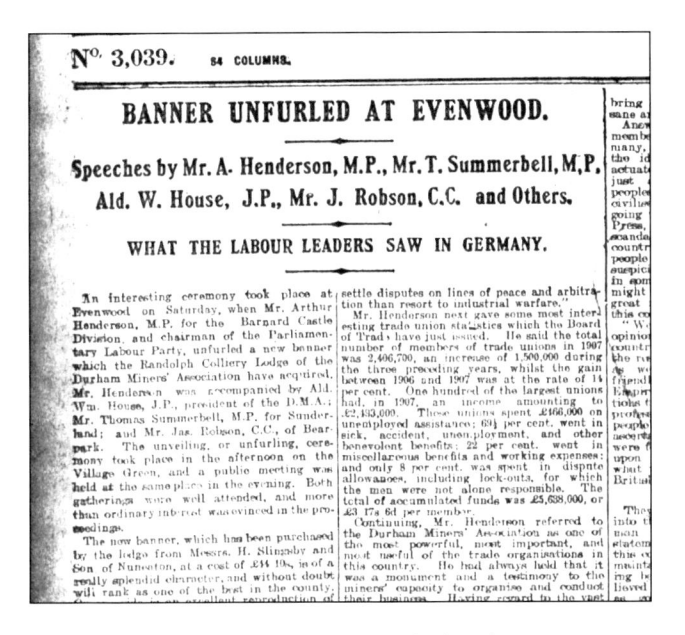

South Durham & Auckland Chronicle dated 17 June 1909: Randolph Miners' banner unfurled

Evidently, the world leaders did not "talk long enough about peace" and 5 years later communities across Europe and the wider world volunteered to take part in the industrial slaughter that would become known as the Great War.

Even though the matter was raised at this public meeting, it is probable that the great issues of the day such as the rivalry between Germany and Great Britain, the Irish situation, the Suffragettes, the fate of Captain Scott's expedition in the Antarctic were of little significance to the average Durham pitman. They had greater concerns – the dangers of work underground, the state of the coal industry, rates of pay, the next shift, a game of pitch and toss or handball may have been matters of more importance to the ordinary working man.

The men of the Parish were pitmen, first and foremost. Their job totally influenced their lives. Most knew no other work – if they did, they came from farming stock. They were born of pitmen to be a pitman. They married a pitman's daughter. She also would have been born into the life – the daily pattern of shift work; the range to be stoked up for hot water and cooking; meals on the table at specific times; hot water was needed for the bath, the tin bath in front of the range; looking after the children, usually born at yearly intervals, sometimes 2. In those days they had large families to care for, 8, 9, 10 children was not unusual. Monday was washing day. Sunday was a day of rest, if there was such a thing – church or chapel for some, the allotment garden, hens and rabbits, the pub or workingmen's club for others. The gamblers took in pitch and toss, the sportsmen football, cricket or handball – this was a popular game. It was akin to modern day squash but importantly, it cost nothing, just a small rubber ball and a gable end wall to play against, 2 competitors. In some villages, they had a special wall, the ball alley but not in Evenwood.

One great occasion did provoke great interest – the coronation of King George and Queen Mary in 1911. This was a good excuse for a celebration. The Evenwood Prize Silver Band led a procession for the children of the village and a sports day was held on the Gala Field to the south of Randolph Terrace. The men probably enjoyed a pint or two.

1911: The Bay Horse P.H. Coronation celebrations

Foreign affairs were reported in the press which undoubtedly influenced public opinion on Germany. There can be no doubt that Germany under the rule of Kaiser Wilhelm II was in the grip of fervent nationalism envious of older European powers and their vast empires and wealth. Germany looked to expand its influence throughout the world. The Kaiser was not very well received by the British press. Regardless of this, it is probable that foreign policy matters, spending on the military, unrest in the Balkan States were issues of secondary importance to the ordinary Durham pitman. He was determined to earn a decent living wage and support his family – that would have been at the forefront of his mind.

Foreign affairs were to come to the fore in the days after 28 June 1914 when 19 year old Gavrilo Princip assassinated Archduke Franz Ferdinand, the heir to the Austro-Hungarian throne. Apparently, the incident didn't matter too much to the British press – the Times didn't report the assassination until 3 weeks later on the 21 July when its consequences were beginning to reverberate around Europe. Initially, this event probably mattered little to the ordinary Durham pitman but its implications were far reaching and soon would affect every city, town, village and hamlet in Great Britain, Evenwood included.

Arthur Henderson would have been willing to "talk long enough about peace" in order to achieve peace but others had different ideas. Did Henderson support the war? Yes. Why? Patriotism.

The following account is provided by F.M. Leventhal:

> "Stirred by the violation of Belgian neutrality, he accepted Grey's rationalisations for British intervention. Despite his own pronouncements about Britain not being implicated in European quarrels, he could feel that the honour of the nation was involved in defending innocent Belgium. Whatever he had said in the past, there was now a higher duty as a British citizen which he could not evade. Nor was he surprised when his 3 sons joined the Honourable Artillery Company in September 1914."

Arthur Henderson
1863 – 1935
M.P. for Barnard Castle
1903 – 1918

CHAPTER THREE

THE BUILD UP TO WAR – IN A NUTSHELL

The main players were:
1. On the side of the Central Powers were Germany and Austria-Hungary. Italy was originally part of this group but took no part in the initial actions. In May 1915 Italy "changed sides" when she thought she had more to gain in terms of territory to the north and east by attacking Austria-Hungary. Turkey and Bulgaria allied themselves to the Central Powers.
2. On the side of the Allies were France, Russia and Great Britain. They enjoyed an understanding of mutual support should there be an attack by Germany and/or Austria-Hungary. Belgium by virtue of resisting German aggression was automatically part of the Allied powers. Serbia, Portugal, Italy, Romania, Greece and the U.S.A. joined the Allies over the course of the war.

Following the break up of the Ottoman Empire, various ethnic groups, including the Slavonic, Christian and Muslim peoples throughout the Balkan region sought self determination. The Austria-Hungarians extended their control to encompass the Balkans and although there was some form of local government for the various regions there was a burning desire for independence. Nationalism was a force throughout the Balkans. Russia saw herself as the protector of the Slavonic peoples of which there were many groups in the Balkans, including the Serbs. Thus Russia did not deter any unrest in the Balkans.

Once the Archduke was assassinated and Austria-Hungary declared war on Serbia then Russia mobilised her troops. Since Germany and Austria-Hungary were allies, Germany pledged to come to the aid of Austria-Hungary should Russia attack. Mobilisation of troops was interpreted as an aggressive act and Germany declared war on Russia 1 August 1914.

Anticipating that France would come to the aid of Russia, Germany mobilised her troops in readiness to attack France. Germany's military strategy was the "Schlieffen Plan", devised over a number of years but finally came to prominence under the "Great Memorandum" of December 1905. The German High Command considered Russia and France as the major threats to Germany in mainland Europe and it was seen to be necessary to deal with France first then concentrate on Russia. France had a line of major fortifications along her border with Germany. It was part of the Plan to by pass these fortifications altogether and attack to the north, sweeping through Belgium and northern France to capture the French capital Paris – all within 42 days. Victory completed in the west, Germany would then turn its attention to the east and inflict a crushing defeat on Russia.

Well, that was the theory of the Plan but there was a major problem – the neutrality of Belgium, guaranteed jointly by Britain, France and Prussia since 1839. Prussia was then a separate country but by 1914 was the driving force behind the new state of Germany. On 2 August, Belgium refused the German ultimatum demanding permission for her troops to cross through the country. Thus, Germany invaded Belgium and France on 3 & 4 August, declaring war on France on the 3rd and Belgium on the 4th. Since Germany had not respected Belgian neutrality Great Britain declared war on Germany on 4 August 1914 then Austria- Hungary on 12 August. On 2 November 1914 Serbia and Russia declared war on Turkey. 5 November 1914 France and Britain also declared war on Turkey. Bulgaria declared war on Serbia on 14 October 1915, Britain declared war on Bulgaria in October 1915, as did France and Russia. Italy joined the war against Austria-Hungary in May 1915, Turkey in August 1915, Bulgaria in October 1915 and finally Germany in August 1916. Germany and Austria-Hungary declared war on Portugal in March 1916 so she joined the Allies. Romania entered the war in August 1916 and Greece in June 1917. The U.S.A. joined the war on the side of the Allies after declaring war on Germany 6 April 1917, the first troops arrived in France 26 June 1917 and their first major battle wasn't until May 1918 but when they arrived in overwhelming numbers throughout the summer of 1918, Germany sought peace.

Eventually, 30 countries were involved – Austria-Hungary and parts of her Empire, Belgium and her Empire, Brazil, Bulgaria, China, Costa Rica, Cuba, France and her Empire, Germany and her Empire, Great Britain and the Empire, Greece, Guatemala, Haiti, Honduras, Italy, Japan, Liberia, Montenegro, Nicaragua, Panama, Portugal, Romania, Russia, San Marino, Serbia, Siam, Turkey and the USA. Uruguay and Peru severed relations with Germany.

THE BRITISH ARMY

Historically, Britain did not possess a large European, land based army, relying on protection of her interests overseas (the Empire) on a swift response from the Royal Navy and detachment of troops based at overseas garrisons. On 1 August 1914, whilst all forces of the British Army numbered almost one million men, the total Regular Army numbered only about 250,000 men. In reality, excluding the Regular Army, the greater proportion of the others were over age, unfit and only partially trained. The Army comprised the following units:

All Ranks	
Regular Army	247,432
Army Reserve	145,347
Special Reserve	63,933
Territorial Force	268,777
Territorial Force Reserve	2,082
Militia & Volunteers	5,943
National Reserve	215,451
Total	948,964

The British Expeditionary Force (B.E.F.) which went to the defence of France and Belgium consisted of one Cavalry Division and six Infantry Divisions, approx. 120,000 men.

By way of comparison, in 1914 France had 823,000 men in service and by the end of August they were reinforced by another 2,870,000 reservists. France could field 62 divisions, Germany 87 and Russia 114. Belgium had a larger army than Britain. The 7 British Divisions made little strategic difference.

It was obvious that Britain needed a larger Army so Parliament sanctioned an increase of some 500,000 men as demanded by Secretary of State for War, Lord Horatio Kitchener. The country underwent a massive wave of enthusiasm and patriotism and the response was overwhelming.

By the end of September over 750,000 men had enlisted and by January 1915, one million:

- 11 August 1914: the "Your King and Country need you. A call to arms" campaign called for 100,000 men to enlist and this figure was achieved within 2 weeks. These volunteers formed 6 new Divisions of Kitchener's Army, 9th to 14th Divisions.
- 28 August 1914: Kitchener asked for another 100,000 men to volunteer and they formed an additional 6 Divisions, 15th to 20th Divisions.
- A third 100,000 men were placed into another 6 Divisions, 21st to 26th Divisions.

The government demand for men continued unabated and after the first call for 500,000 men, another called for 3,500,000 before the year's end. This new army is often referred to as Kitchener's Army. Those recruited into the new army were used to form complete Battalions under existing British Army Regiments. These new battalions had titles of the form:

"xxth (Service) Battalion, *the regiment name*"
For example – 20th (Service) Battalion, the Durham Light Infantry

In theory a recruit was initially sent to his Regimental depot where he would receive his kit and be given an introduction to army discipline and training before being sent to the main training camps to join his battalion. In practice, no Regiment had enough equipment or the manpower to train the flood of recruits – old uniforms and emergency blue uniforms (Kitchener Blue) were issued. There was a lack of officers to train them and there was a shortage of weapons with no artillery pieces left in Britain. Not until early 1915, were problems overcome.

In 1914, the total available number of men of military age was 5,500,000 with around 500,000 more reaching the age each year. By late September 2,250,000 men had been enlisted and 1,500,000 were in reserved occupations such as coal mining, iron and steel production, railways, munitions. Of the rest, the recruiters discovered that almost 2 in every 5 volunteers were entirely unsuitable for military service due to poor health.

Kitchener's Recruitment Poster

1914

The first year of the war began as the war of movement but settled into stubborn trench warfare.

June 28	Assassination of Archduke Franz Ferdinand, heir to the throne of Austro-Hungarian empire, in Sarajevo, Bosnia
July 28	Austria-Hungary declares war on Serbia
July 29 – December 9	Austria-Hungary repeatedly invades Serbia but is repeatedly repulsed
August 1	Outbreak of war Germany declares war on Russia
August 3	Germany declares war on France
August 4	Germany invades neutral Belgium
August 4	**Britain declares war on Germany**
August 4	US President Woodrow Wilson declares policy of US neutrality
August 14	Battle of the Frontiers begins
August 17-19	Russia invades East Prussia
August 23	Japan declares war on Germany
August 23 – September 2	Austria-Hungary invades Russian Poland (Galicia)
August 26-30	Battle of Tannenberg, which Russia loses; Germany's greatest success of the war on Eastern Front
September 5-10	First Battle of Marne, halts German advance, resulting in stalemate and trench warfare
September 9-14	First Battle of Masurian Lakes, which Russia again loses
September 14	First Battle of Aisne begins
September 15 – November 24	The "race to the sea", trenches appear appear 15 September
September 17-28	Austro-German attack western Poland
October 14 – November 22	First Battle of Ypres
October 29	Turkey enters the war on the side of the Central Powers
December 8	Battle of the Falkland Islands
December 21	First German air raid on Britain
December 25	Unofficial Christmas truce declared by soldiers along the Western Front

AUGUST 1914: BELGIUM AND FRANCE

In August, the B.E.F. disembarked in France as German troops marched into Belgium and the French launched an all out offensive to recapture the provinces of Alsace and Lorraine, annexed by Germany after the war of 1870. The French action collapsed whist the German 1st and 2nd Armies swept through Belgium and into northern France intent on seizing Paris as intended by the Schlieffen Plan. The first major action involving the B.E.F. took place on 23 August at the Battle of Mons in Belgium when the outnumbered British regulars gave the German conscripts a bloody nose before withdrawing.

The first British casualty of the war is believed to be 20 year old L/14196 Private John Parr, 4th Battalion, Middlesex Regiment from North Finchley, London, a messenger shot off his bicycle near Mons, Belgium 21 August 1914.

On 26 August, the B.E.F. was involved in the epic rearguard action at Le Cateau which gained valuable time for the French to withdraw to the river Marne. General Joffre, the commander of the French forces, re-organised his troops for a counter strike and on 5 – 7 September, attacked the Germans on the approaches to Paris. The German forces had outrun their supply chain with grave consequences and they were driven back. The German Commander-in-Chief, General von Falkenhayn ordered a last attempt to break through to Dunkirk and Calais at the end of October but the attack was stopped by the British and French at the Belgian market town of Ypres. All along the front the Germans were able to pull back to occupy the higher ground and entrenched themselves into defensive positions. And so the brief period of mobile warfare had come to an end. Soldiers dug in along a 460 mile front that ran from the North Sea through Belgium into north and eastern France, down to the Swiss border.

EVENWOOD: WHAT HAPPENED?

The Evenwood Parish Magazine (EPM) is the prime source of information. There is no mention of any international tension until the edition of September 1914. Rev. G.J. Collis introduces the crisis by writing as follows:

"What a different outlook there is in the world since I wrote my last monthly letter to you. What has seemed incredible has come to pass and it seems today that a conflict such as we never thought to see in the course of the world is upon us. Great civilized nations, with their vast scientific modern engines of destruction, have let themselves loose in a gigantic slaughter of human life, the end of which we cannot for the moment foresee, although we feel pretty certain that as a result of it, somehow or other, the constitution of the world will be changed."

He comments on the local situation:

"We may not be called upon for the moment to take up arms by compulsion in defence of our homes but we certainly are called upon to suffer with the sufferers to some extent and to share voluntarily in the hardships and sacrifices of those who are enduring hardship and suffering for us at this time. As I go about, I feel somehow, that many of us in Evenwood do not quite grasp this fact at present. Perhaps Evenwood is one of the places in England where the changes, preparations and signs of our nation at war are scarcely apparent."

He mentions atrocities in Belgium and asks for sacrifice:

"Do we want to taste the experiences of the Belgian people with their burnt homes, their ruined crops, their devastated countryside and (according to many accounts) their kinsman, though not in battle, slaughtered before their eyes….The war will probably go on for a long time. I say then, do not let us be mere nonentities in the strife. The King and Country ask us, if we cannot take up arms in the cause, to redouble our efforts in sacrifices for the welfare and pray for the success of those who can."

The following month, in response to Kitchener's campaign, the village provided a number of volunteers:

"The National call to arms has not, thank God, found us in Evenwood, altogether unresponsive. Several of our brightest and best have offered themselves for service…I hope to publish later a list of names of our local "Roll of Honour" and I shall be exceedingly proud to do so."

Rev. Collis praised the efforts of the women of the Parish – the sewing meeting was "making various kinds of warm and comforting garments etc. for those at the front."

Reported in the November edition was the recruitment meeting which took place 8 October 1914 at the National School. It was addressed by Mr. Henderson M.P., Mr. Roberts M.P. for Norwich, Lord Barnard and Major Wilkinson from Bishop Auckland. Arthur Henderson by now was obviously convinced that there was little alternative to war and was joined on the platform by political opponents in a show of national unity. The EPM mentions three local recruits by name, Percy Brass and George Featherstone who were at Great Missenden, Buckinghamshire and Fred Neasham, cavalry barracks at Scarborough.

That month, Rev. Collis made his first report on a local casualty. Sir William and Lady Sybil Frances Eden of Windlestone Hall near Ferryhill lost of their eldest son, Lieutenant John Eden, 12th (Prince of Wales's Royal) Lancers on 17 October 1914 at Ypres, Belgium. He was the older brother of Anthony Eden who was to become Prime Minister of Great Britain from 1955 to 1957. Lady Eden was well known for her "religious and philanthropic efforts", the most well known being the Lady Eden Hospital at Bishop Auckland.

The drive for men continued and Rev. Collis informed his parishioners through the December edition of the EPM that he had received communications from the Government and the Bishop to use his "influence with the young men to get them to volunteer". The village held a Belgian Flag Day-buildings were decorated, the band paraded and "treated us to some excellent music", there was a social night in the school and a total of £26 was raised. Funds were also forwarded to H.R.H. Princes Mary towards providing each soldier and sailor with a gift on Christmas Day. Comforts were provided to the Durham Light Infantry. The men at Randolph agreed to a levy on their wages for "patriotic purposes".

Thus it is evident that there were volunteers and those at home did what they could to help the war effort and Belgian people.

THE GERMAN RAID ON NORTH EAST COASTAL TOWNS

On 16 December 1914, the First High Seas Fleet Scouting Group, commanded by Admiral Franz von Hipper, unleashed a bombardment of the North Sea ports of Hartlepool, West Hartlepool, Whitby and Scarborough. The raiding force of 5 battle cruisers, Seydlitz, Moltke, von der Tann, Derrflinger and Blucher plus accompanying light cruisers and destroyers was followed by the might of the German High Seas Fleet under Commander-in-Chief Frederich Ingenohl. The attack started at approximately 8.10 am and lasted until around 9.30 am, consisting of 1,150 shells resulted in 137 fatalities and 592 wounded. The 2 coastal defence batteries in Hartlepool, Heugh Battery and Lighthouse Battery, responded firing 143 shells and damaged 3 German ships including the heavy cruiser Blucher. The German High Command viewed the attack as legitimate since both Hartlepool and Scarborough were "fortified towns". The incident provoked outrage in the British press and the public at large which held the Royal Navy responsible for not affording adequate protection to these ports. Admiral von Hipper escaped the pursuit of Admiral Warrender's fleet which consisted of 6 battleships, 4 battle cruisers, 4 heavy cruisers, 6 light cruisers and 8 submarines and also evaded Admiral Beatty's attempted interception using 4 battle cruisers.

Rev. G.J. Collis wrote:

> "We have recently had the war brought very near to our own homes and in some cases right into our very midst. When on the morning of the 16th ult., Many of us in Evenwood heard the heavy booming of big guns we instinctively felt that something serious was happening somewhere. We were right. Something very serious was happening. When the news came through that Hartlepool, Scarborough and Whitby had been bombarded by German warships and that many English homes and innocent lives including a large proportion of women and children had been sacrificed it made our patriotic blood boil with indignation. We all, I fancy, had a consuming hope that the enemy who had done this thing in defiance it seems of all the rules of civilised warfare would be speedily caught and overwhelmed. In this, apparently, we were disappointed."

c.1914. Recruits outisde the Welcome P.H. Front Street, Cockfield

He then makes a patriotic appeal for volunteers for the war effort stating that:

"We cannot have a clearer call then the sound of the guns at Hartlepool."

The EPM provides details of recruitment. The majority of Evenwood men were Kitchener's volunteers. The February 1915 edition informs us that 43 men had enlisted. In April 1915, a more complete list provides details of 87 men (Appendix 4).

Some details of training are provided by Fred Prudhoe, writing from Edinburgh to Rev. G.J. Collis, vicar of St. Paul's Church, Evenwood:

"We are getting plenty of drill which we take in the following manner: 6.00am – reveille; 7.30 – breakfast; 8.40 – Swedish drill; 10.30 – Squad drill; 1.00pm – dinner; 2.10 – Squad drill; 5.00 – tea; 10.00 – lights out….A soldiers equipment is – 2 pairs of pants, 2 pairs boots, 3 pairs socks, 2 tunics, 2 pairs trousers, 1 cardigan jacket, 1 cap, 1 mess tin, blacking brush and blacking, hair brush and comb, shaving brush, tooth brush, knife, fork and spoon, needles, thread and buttons, rifle, 2 enamel plates, 1 enamel bowl and the pack which every soldier receives...Every Saturday our Regiment has to be prepared to fall in at a moment's notice at full strength and consequently all weekend leave is stopped...The first leave may prove to be my last as they are absolutely pushing bayonet drill down our throats. I have already passed out of the recruits' course and I expect to go through my musketry and bombing courses in a week or two. We are supposed to be perfectly fit for the front in 5 months and when we have finished all our courses, one never knows when one will be called up for the next draft...I can confidently say that I have never felt more fit then I do at the present moment."

Fred Prudhoe saw active service on the Somme in August 1916 and survived the war being demobilized about March 1919.

Northumberland Fusiliers at camp

1914: The First Battle of Ypres: an overview

The main body of the B.E.F. was fighting in Artois and the Flemish Hills having moved up from the Aisne. The 7th Division and the 3rd Cavalry Division was falling back westwards from Antwerp and Ghent and they met to form a continuous body of troops around the city of Ypres, Belgium. Field Marshal Sir John French, commander of the B.E.F. ordered the capture of Menin with a view towards advancing towards Courtai however the German Army attacked in force with the intention of breaking through to outflank the Allies on the River Yser. The Belgian Army held land to the north along the Yser on the British left and despite very heavy losses the defence held thus preventing the Germans from breaking the line, turn its flank to "roll up" the Allied forces and capture the Channel ports. The efforts of Von Beseler's Third Reserve Army and Falkenhayn's newly formed Fourth Army were thwarted – an enemy which turned out to be 5 times larger then the B.E.F. and even greater superiority of artillery. The British and Belgians defended against wave after wave of attack and were pushed back. Each village, wood and road junction saw heavy fighting. Names became immortalised – Zandvoorde, Gheluvelt, Langemarck, Zonnebeke, Hooge. There were 2 days of crisis – 31 October and 11 November 1914 when it seemed inevitable that the Germans would break through but enough courage was found to defeat the attack.

The defeat of the German offensive in Flanders ended with both sides entrenched along more than 400 miles of continuous front from the North Sea to Switzerland. The only way forward was by frontal attack against increasingly fortified trench systems. The Germans could afford to sit on their defences and the Allies had little choice but to carry out attacks. By the end of the battle both sides were exhausted. Britain had lost a considerable portion of its pre-war military strength and all but expended its ammunition stocks. B.E.F. casualties in this battle were approximately 54,100 including more than 700 officers – all experienced men of the Regular Army. For instance, between 14 October and 30 November 1914, the 7th Division lost 9,865 men of which 372 were officers. The total loss of the B.E.F. in France and Flanders from the commencement of the war to 30 November 1914 was approx. 86,000 men. The death in action of so many experienced officers and men would be a crippling loss. Ypres became an icon – its defence cost so many lives it became a symbol and could not be given up.

Ypres

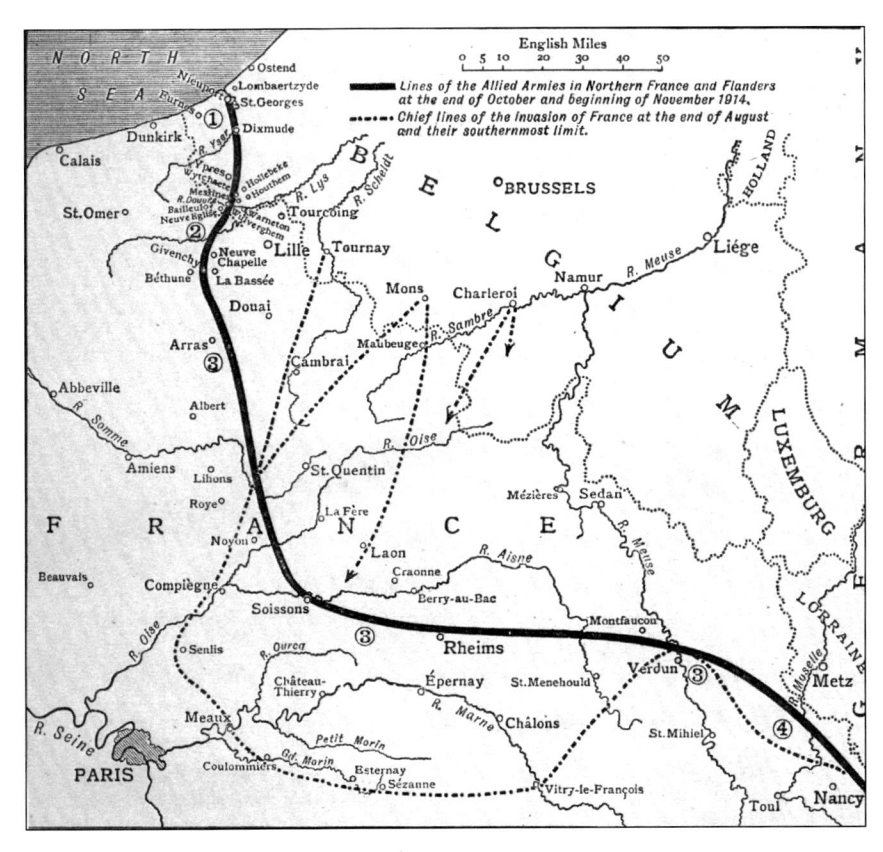

1914: The Western Front

CHAPTER FOUR

1915

The first full year of the war saw the Allies strive vainly to achieve a breakthrough on the Western Front while the Germans achieved numerous successes elsewhere. It was a disappointing year for the Allies and a positive one for the Central Powers.

January 1 – March 30	Allied offensive in Artois and Champagne
January 15	Japan's 21 demands on China
January 19-20	First German zeppelin attack on England
February 4	German U-boat attacks on Allied and neutral shipping; declares blockade of Britain
February 7-21	Russians suffer heavy losses at Second Battle of Masurian Lakes (also known as the Winter Battle)
February – April	Austro-Hungarian attack on Russian Poland (Galicia) collapses, with the Russians counterattacking
February 19-August	Allied amphibious attack on the Dardanelles and Gallipoli (initiated by Winston Churchill, who resigns as a consequence) ends with the Turkish siege of the Allied forces
March 1	First passenger ship sinks, the British liner *Falaba*

March 11	Britain announces blockade of German ports
April-June	Germans focus on Eastern Front, breaking through Gorlice-Tarnow and forcing Russia out of much of Poland
April 22 – May 25	First use of poison gas by Germany starts Second Battle of Ypres
April 25	Allied landing at Gallipoli
April 26	France, Russia, Italy and Britain conclude secret Treaty of London
May 2	Austro-German offensive on Galicia begins
May 7	U-boat sinks British liner *Lusitania* with the loss of American lives, creating a US-German diplomatic crisis
May 9	Second Battle of Artois begins
May 23	Ignoring treaty agreements with the Central Powers, Italy declares war on Austria-Hungary
May 25	British Prime Minister Asquith reorganises his Liberal government as a coalition of the parties
June 29 – December 2	Italians launch unsuccessful attack on Hungarians at 1st, 2nd, 3rd & 4th Battles of Isonzo; there are to be 12 in total
August 4	Germans capture Warsaw
September 5	Tsar Nicholas takes command of Russian armies
September 22	Second Battle of Champagne begins
September 25	Battle of Loos begins
October 3	Anglo-French force lands at Salonika in Greece
October – November	Austro-German-Bulgarian forces invade Serbia, expelling Serbian army from the country
December 19	Sir Douglas Haig replaces Sir John French as commander of British Expeditionary Force
December 28	Allies begin withdrawal of troops from Gallipoli

Throughout much of 1915, fighting continued on the "Western Front" in the Flanders region of Belgium around the market town of Ypres. It was not until September that the first major British offensive took place, some way to the south in northeast France around the village of Loos in the coalmining district of Lens.

The Western Front 1915

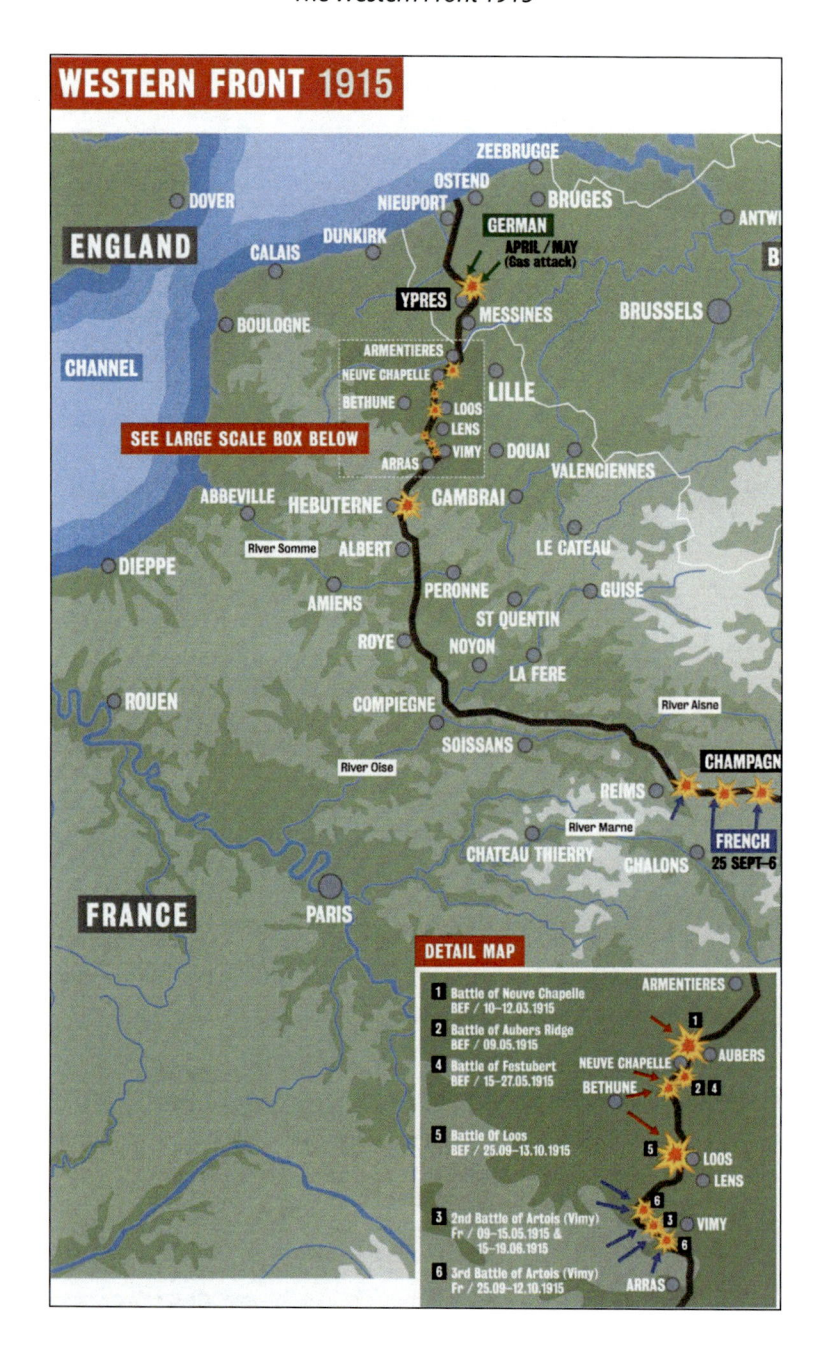

Map courtesy of the Thiepval Project Charity Fund

Between the months of April and December, another great offensive took place. A new front was opened in Turkey at Gallipoli. This was a tragic, bloody affair for both sides but particularly for the Australian troops. It is generally regarded that this was the defining moment in the formation of Australia as a nation with "national pride". There were no Evenwood fatalities in this theatre of warfare but 3 local men were killed at Gallipoli:
- 16381 Private R. Bagley, 6th Battalion, the Yorkshire Regiment, from West Auckland.
- Z/2000 Able Seaman H. Readman, Nelson Battalion, the R.N. Division, from Low Wham.
- 5115 (S) Sapper R.C. Yole, Royal Marines from South Side.

Five men with connections to Evenwood lost their lives during the year:
- Private Thomas Cant
- Private Wilson Million
- Acting Bombadier John Caleb Richards
- Corporal Herbert Dixon
- Serjeant Edgar Towers

The deaths of John Thomas Cant in June, Wilson Million in August and John Richards in September went unreported in the Parish Magazine. John Cant was born in Evenwood and lived at the Oaks for many years but moved to Kirk Merrington where he lived with his wife Jane and their young family. Thomas Cant would have known many in Evenwood and it is surprising that EPM carried no report of his death.

Wilson Million was born in Evenwood before moving to Byker near Newcastle-upon-Tyne. John Richards was born at Middlestone but reportedly lived at Evenwood. At some time, he and Wilson Million probably lived in the Morley/Wind Mill area which has closer ties with Toft Hill/Etherley than Evenwood thus it is not surprising to find that they are both commemorated on the Etherley War Memorial.

The EPM of November reported the first fatality when it was confirmed that Corporal Herbert Dixon died of wounds 4 October 1915. The second tragic news was that Serjeant Edgar Towers was "missing" after taking part in the offensive around Loos in September. It was not until a year later, September 1916 that his death was accepted by his family and a Memorial Service was held in St. Paul's Church.

Private JOHN THOMAS CANT 1882 – 1915

4/9455 Private John Thomas Cant, 2nd Battalion, the Durham Light Infantry was killed in action 11 June, 1915 and is buried at Potijze Burial Ground Cemetery, Belgium and commemorated on the Kirk Merrington War Memorial. He was 32 years old, born December 1882 at Evenwood to John and Hannah Cant and in 1901 was brother to William, Herbert, Hilda and Lily. The family lived at 16 the Oaks, Evenwood. By September 1914 he was married to Jane and they had 3 children Rose, Lily and John Thomas. They lived at Front Street, Kirk Merrington and he worked as a coal miner.

4/9455 Private John Thomas Cant, 2nd Battalion, The Durham Light Infantry

As a 19 year old, Thomas enlisted in 1902 into the Reserve Army (service no. 7782, 2/DLI) and served for 12 years. He was immediately called up for active duty at the outbreak of war and served in the 2/DLI.

The 2/DLI formed part of the 18th Brigade, 6th Division. The 6th Division landed at St. Nazaire 10 September 1914 and proceeded to the Western Front where it remained throughout

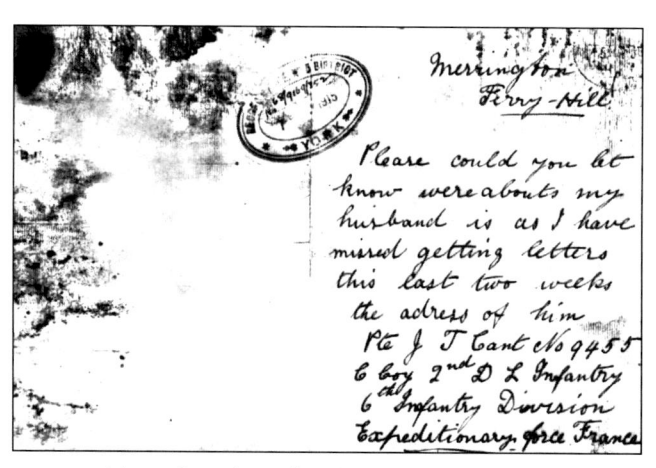

A letter from his wife asking his whereabouts

the war. It arrived in time to reinforce the B.E.F. on the Aisne before the whole army was moved north to Flanders. The Medal Roll indicates that 4/9455 Private John Thomas Cant entered France at a later date, 4 January 1915 so he did not see action on the Aisne or around Armentieres.

Probably, he was in the line on the night of 31 May/1 June 1915 when the Division took over its new position on the Ypres Salient. The Division stayed in this sector until the end of July 1916. Even though no active operations took place, trench casualties doubled immediately. Battle casualties during the whole period amounted to 10,938. At this time the 6th Division formed part of the 5th Corps of the Second Army and the First and Second Armies were bearing the brunt of the fighting along the British front but the coming of June 1915 brought a comparative lull along the southern British front until the middle of the month – a new German weapon, incendiary rifle ammunition was introduced.

> "These bullets were said to be filled with sulphur which ignited on discharge and continued to burn during flight. The clothes of soldiers lying between the lines had thus been set alight, the severity of any wound caused thereby being inevitably increased."

The 2/DLI was involved in operations at Hooge on 2 June 1915. Private John Thomas Cant was killed in action 11 June 1915. Also killed on this date were 3/9519 Private G. Munro and 20005 Private J.R. Wilson both serving with the 2/DLI. The service details of 4/9455 Private John Thomas Cant and the 2/DLI War Diary have not been researched but since there was no specific action on that date it is presumed that they were all victims of the usual violence of warfare – artillery shelling, machine gun or sniper fire.

Private John Thomas Cant was killed in action 11 June 1915

Potijze Cemetery is located to the north east of Ypres. The village was in Allied hands for practically the whole of the war but was subject to incessant shelling. Potijze Chateau contained an advanced dressing station and the burial ground was used from April 1915 to October 1918.

Private WILSON MILLION 1882 – 1915

11905 Private Wilson Million, 2nd Battalion, the Durham Light Infantry was killed in action 9 August 1915 at Hooge, Belgium. He has no known grave and is commemorated on the Ypres (Menin Gate) Memorial in Belgium and on the Etherley War Memorial. He was 32 years old, born c.1882 at Evenwood to Thomas and Mary Jane and was husband to Betsy Million living at Byker, Newcastle-upon-Tyne. The Medal Roll indicates that he entered France 5 January 1915, 1 day later than 4/9455 Private John Thomas Cant.

11905 Private Wilson Million, 2/DLI was killed in action 9 August 1915 at Hooge, Belgium. DLI officers commissioned the above painting of the action
Courtesy of the Trustees of the DLI Museum

Action at Hooge: 9 August 1915

The 2/DLI was involved in the action at Hooge and fought with distinction particularly on the 9 August 1915. The following passage pays tribute to the 2/DLI:

> "Where many units distinguished themselves it is perhaps invidious to single out one for special attention but it is impossible to record this episode in the epic of Hooge without emphasizing the part played by the magnificent battalion to whom fell the honour of assaulting the centre of the position about the crater across the Menin road, close to the ruins of the chateau….these men from Durham, miners and the very salt of the earth in the hour of danger, held on in the face of fearful losses. Twelve of their officers were killed or wounded before they were finally relieved. It is recorded that when at nightfall the order was sent for them to withdraw, the advance section of the battalion did not receive it, some 200 men with 4 surviving officers, clinging throughout the night to the ridge between the crater and the stables, where the struggle raged as furiously as anywhere."

Private W. Million was killed in action 9 August 1915

Casualties for the 9 August were:

Officers:
- Killed – Capt. A.H.M. Bowers, Capt. R.H. Leggard, 2/Lt. R. Gregg, 2/Lt. R.W. May, 2/Lt. J.D. Cartwright, 2/Lt. G.C. Holcroft
- Wounded: Capt. R. Turner, Lt. G. Sopwith, 2/Lt. G.M. Garland, 2/Lt. K. Storey, 2/Lt. R.K. Robson, 2/Lt. M. Coverdale

Other Ranks (O.R.'s):
- Killed: 92
- Wounded: 262
- Missing: 100

Total Casualties: 466

The battalion had gone to the trenches with some 650 men. Presumably, 11905 Private W. Million was one of those listed as "missing" and whose body was never found. He has no known grave and is commemorated on the Menin Gate Memorial.

The officers of 2/DLI commissioned a painting of this action at Hooge after the war, the only action of the whole conflict which they chose to remember in this way. It hung in the Officers Mess until the battalion was disbanded in the 1950's.

Acting Bombardier JOHN CALEB RICHARDS 1889 – 1915

54973 Acting Bombadier John Caleb Richards, 44th Company, the Royal Garrison Artillery died 18 September 1915. He and is buried at Pembroke Dock Military Cemetery and commemorated on the Etherley War Memorial. He was about 26 years old, born in 1889 at Middlestone to John and Mary Richards. It is probable that John Richards lived at Morley or Wind Mill. No details of his death are known.

Acting Bombadier John Caleb Richards died 18 September 1915

Serjeant EDGAR TOWERS 1893 – 1915

14525 Serjeant Edgar Towers, 15th Battalion, the Durham Light Infantry was killed in action 25 September 1915 at the Battle of Loos and is commemorated on the Loos Memorial, France and the Evenwood War Memorial. He was 22 years old, born at Etherley to Robert and Sarah Towers and by 1901 was brother to May and James and the family lived at the Oaks, Evenwood. He worked as a miner.

Edgar Towers enlisted 8 September 1914 and joined the 15/DLI. It was attached to the 64th Brigade of the 21st Division which was called to action in September 1915 at the Battle of Loos. News came home that Serjeant

Edgar Towers was missing. It was during this battle that Lieutenant J. Kipling, 2/Irish Guards, the son of Rudyard Kipling was also listed as missing. This sparked a crusade by Kipling to find his body and give it proper burial. They failed to locate him but since then the body of a serviceman has been identified to be Lieutenant J. Kipling although speculation remains. Such tragedy affected all sections of society whether pitman or poet, the slaughter knew no social boundaries.

The Battle of Loos 25 September – 8 October 1915

This battle formed a part of the wider Artois-Loos Offensive conducted by the French and British in autumn 1915, sometimes referred to as the Second Battle of Artois. This campaign comprised the major allied offensive on the Western Front during that year. French troops launched offensives at Champagne (the Second Battle of Champagne) and at Vimy Ridge near Arras. The strategy involved:

- A four day artillery bombardment of the German positions
- Full scale infantry attack in the area between Loos and the La Bassee Canal
- Diversionary attacks to the north at Bois Grenier and Pietre between Armentieres and La Bassee Canal.
- Once the German positions fell, reserves aided by cavalry, would pass through the gap and attack the German second line.

Two "New Army" Divisions, the 21st (which included the 15/DLI) and 24th were the reserve forces. They had recently arrived in France, had not seen the trenches and were untested in battle. The Divisions started moving from St. Omer 20 September with marches of over 20 miles throughout successive nights to reach the Loos Valley. Progress was slow and exhausting and the troops had been on the move constantly for several days. The ground was unfamiliar, roads and tracks were jammed with transport going in both directions and communication trenches were flooded and packed with men.

The Loos offensive began 25 September following a 4 day artillery bombardment in which 250,000 shells were fired including 140 tons of chlorine gas discharged from more than 5,000 cylinders. 75,000 British infantry made the initial attack.

The southern section of the attack, conducted by the IV Corps made significant progress, capturing Loos and forward towards Lens. However, the need for supplies and reinforcements brought the advance to a halt at the end of the first day. Delays whilst travelling meant that the reserves arrived at night time too late.

Fortunes on the first day of battle were mixed, to the north, the I Corps made less progress than the IV Corps but the 7th and 9th Divisions managed to establish a foothold on the Hohenzollern Redoubt.

There was some bad luck, for instance poison gas released with smoke into light winds before the infantry went forward, hung between the lines and in some places blew back at the British forces. Along the length of the front advancing masses of troops emerging from the smoke screen were met with devastating machine gun fire. Losses were appalling and the worst yet suffered by the British Expeditionary Force – there would be 8,500 dead by the end of the first day.

The delay in bringing up the reserves was a critical failure as the Germans were able to pour in their reserves and counter-attack the following day. Thus, any realistic chance of success had been lost on the first day.

14525 Serjeant Edgar Towers, 15th Battalion, the Durham Light Infantry

The 21st and 24th Divisions saw action in front of the formidable second line defences at Hulluch and Hill 70. The British infantry advanced without any preliminary artillery bombardment and were decimated by German machine gun fire. The inexperienced New Army divisions, already exhausted by their long march, fought hard but were driven back, the line only stabilising with the arrival of the Guards Division on the next day, 27 September. Thereafter the offensive disintegrated.

After several days of sporadic fighting, the British eventually were forced to retreat and Fosse 8 and the Hohenzollern Redoubt were lost in the following days.

The Loos attack was renewed 13 October when further heavy losses, more than 2,000 killed, combined with poor weather caused the offensive to be called off 19 October.

During the battle the British suffered 61,000 casualties, 20,000 dead – 50,000 of them in the action between Loos and Givenchy and the remainder in the subsidiary attacks. Many New Army units, rushed into the battle area for the first time only a matter of days after landing in France were devastated. German casualties were estimated at half the British total.

The 15/DLI: an account of its action.

On 11 September 1915, the 15/DLI sailed from Folkestone to Boulogne, France then entrained to the St. Omer district. Having marched throughout the night, on 25 September at 7.15pm, the 64th Brigade moved off through Mazingarbe and Vermelles, in support of the 63rd Brigade:

> "The men were wet, tired and hungry, for all had been sacrificed to get the division into battle with the least possible delay."

At 9.00pm, the 64th Brigade prepared for their advance into the line – unloading of Lewis guns, ammunition, bombs and tools. There was no time to reconnoitre the ground. At midnight, the 64th moved forward, the 14/DLI and 15/DLI leading the column.

26 September, 2.00am:

> "Now and then shells burst near….Patrols went out in search for the 63rd but could find no trace of them…The 15th settled down in a trench about a quarter of a mile in rear but there was not room for all of them so one company fell back to the la Basse road on the northern outskirts of Loos…The whereabouts of the enemy and the dispositions of the British troops in this portion of the field was as yet unknown.

Daylight: The congestion of traffic during the night was the cause of the delay and when the sun dispersed the morning mists the German shell fire stopped all movement on the road. The enemy batteries soon began to take their toll of the brigade, casualties including

Lieut. V.B. Odhams, of the 15th, who was mortally wounded about this time…Orders had been issued for an attack by the 21st and 24th Divisions.

11.00am – the 24th Division advanced …the 15th Battalion in support now linked up the right of the 63rd Brigade with the troops advancing from Loos…the Durhams were pulled round towards Hill 70 and suffered heavily through enfilade machine-gun fire from Chalk Pit Wood. Lieut.-Col. E.T. Logan had already fallen, mortally wounded, while gallantly leading the 15th…Soon the troops on the right of the Durhams began to retire."

By 12.30pm, the whole line was in retreat. At 2.00pm, there was another advance by the survivors of the DLI and the Kings Own Yorkshire Light Infantry:

"Heavily punished in flank by shrapnel and machine-gun bullets and unsupported by the British gunners…the infantry had no chance of success. The inevitable retreat was conducted under intense shell fire and the German bombardment continued till dusk…Many of the severely wounded had to remain where they fell. The exhausted survivors suffered torture from thirst – they had no chance of refilling their water bottles – remained in the old German trenches till they were relieved by the Guards in the early morning of September 27th.

The losses of the Durhams were very heavy…Besides the officers already mentioned Major R.B.Johnson; Capts L.A. de V. Carey, H. Wardell and G.T.Fitzgerald; Lieut. E.M. Carter; 2nd Lieuts J.W.L. Birbeck, E. Partridge, H.A.Boulton, C.H. Readman and O.de Putron wounded. There were no less than 450 casualties in the ranks."

Serjeant Edgar Towers was killed in action 25 September 1915

The 15/DLI did not enter the attack on German lines until 26 September. If the date of Sgt. Edgar Towers' death is correct then it was before the battalion was engaged in the actual attack. The advancing reserve battalions were subject to bombardment from the German artillery prior to taking up their position in the front line but this occurred on the early morning of the 26th. Possibly, he was the victim of sniper fire whilst on the way to the front on the 25th. Perhaps some unfortunate accident occurred during the night march of the 24th & 25th. Given the obvious chaos of the situation, perhaps there was an administrative error, perfectly understandable and Serjeant Edgar Towers was actually killed in action on the 26th. With so many casualties, killed, wounded and missing, was it possible to compile accurate reports? How many officers survived and who was fit enough or capable of filling in a report? The exact circumstances of Serjeant Edgar Towers' death are unknown.

The 15/DLI suffered 462 casualties including 22 officers. Lt-Col. E. T. Logan Officer-in-Command of the 15/DLI was killed on 26 September and is commemorated along with Sgt. Edgar Towers on the Loos Memorial to the Missing. Two other men local to the Gaunless Valley also lost their lives on 25 September 1915 and have no known grave. They are also commemorated on the Loos Memorial:

- 14554 Private William Brown, 15/DLI, of West Auckland, enlisted Bishop Auckland and commemorated on the Roll of Honour, West Auckland Memorial Hall.
- 20286 Private Fred Thompson, 15/DLI, of Butterknowle and commemorated on the Butterknowle War Memorial.

It is probable that these soldiers would have been known to each other

The New Army units had taken part in action for the first time and had suffered heavily – the typical attacking strength of a battalion at the time was 650-750 men thus casualties were approximately 66%.

The battle witnessed some significant "firsts":
- the first "Big Push."
- the first blooding of Kitchener's New Army.
- the first use of poison gas by the British army.

It had been a costly failure and consequently 10 December 1915, Field-Marshal Sir John French, Commander-in-Chief of the British Expeditionary Force resigned. General Sir Douglas Haig was appointed as his successor.

Sadly, little operational analysis was carried out and many lessons of the failure at Loos were not learned. Many mistakes were repeated with uncanny similarity on the first day of the Battle of the Somme 1 July 1916.

Reports of "Missing"

The Parish Magazine, November 1915 reported:

"I have also heard from Percy Brass, who with several others of our local lads, viz. G. Featherstone, J. Carling, E. Towers, A. Bainbridge, Lands and others who I cannot mention for certain, have taken part in a battle, probably the big battle began on September 25th, in the region of Loos... Edgar Towers is also believed to be wounded and has not been heard from (by his friends at home) for several weeks. However there has not I am told been any official confirmation of anything worse having befallen him. I trust and pray that Edgar's friends will soon have their anxieties relieved by hearing more cheering news of him."

No news was forthcoming and the following month, December 1915, the following update was given:

"Nothing, I am afraid, has been heard lately of Edgar Towers. He is known to have been wounded. The best that we can look for in his case, I think, is that he is a prisoner of war and that in due course he will return home again safe and sound. Uncertainty of course is dreadful but this at any rate is uncertainty which leaves room for hope."

The anguish for his family and friends continued and the April 1916 edition makes the following reference:

"Our sympathies and prayers must be with him (Joseph Bowman) and his people too. Also with Edgar Towers who has not been heard of since last September."

On Sunday 17 September 1916, the congregation of St. Paul's Church, Evenwood held a Memorial Service for Edgar Towers. It appears that his family were reluctant to accept the inevitable and a notice together with a photograph appeared in the Northern Echo 23 November 1916:

"Sergt. E. Towers (D.L.I) of 19 Rochdale Street, Evenwood missing. Any news of him will be welcomed by his parents."

Serjeant Edgar Towers is commemorated on the Loos Memorial at Panel 106 and 107. The Loos Memorial located in Loos-en-Gohelle, Pas de Calais forms the side and back of Dud Corner Cemetery. It commemorates over 20,000 officers and men who have no known grave who fell in the area from the River Lys to the old southern boundary of the First Army, east and west of Grenay. The name "Dud Corner" is believed to be due to the large number of unexploded enemy shells found in the neighbourhood after the Armistice. There are 20,597 identified casualties in this cemetery.

Corporal HERBERT DIXON 1884-1915

2130 Corporal Herbert Dixon, 5th Battalion, the Border Regiment died of wounds 4 October 1915 having been hit by sniper fire whilst serving in the Armentieres sector. He is buried at Houplines Communal Cemetery Extension, France and is commemorated on the Evenwood War Memorial.

He was 32 years old, born c.1884 at Workington, Cumberland to Tom and Jane Dixon. In 1901, he was brother to Sarah, Frederick and Edith. He married Rose Oldfield of Evenwood and they lived at 13 Shirley Terrace, Evenwood with their 2 sons Tom and Cresswell.

Corporal Herbert Dixon was a pre-war Territorial soldier and went to France in October 1914 with the 5th (Territorial) Battalion of the Border Regiment. This battalion was formed in Carlisle in August 1914 and attached to the East Lancs. Division. From 5 May 1915, the battalion was attached to the 149th Brigade of the 50th Division.

> 3rd - Nothing to report.
> 4th - O.C. 77 trench reports everything quiet. A piece of white paper was on a stick near the German bodies. This was shot off by one of our snipers. O.C. 75 Trench reports night quiet. Enemy's snipers are many and accurate opposite this trench. On the night of 4/10/15 clean shirts and socks were received from PONT de NIEPPE baths for the whole Battalion in the trenches.
> 5th - O.C. 75 trench has nothing special to report, except that enemy's sniping continues particularly accurate. Rifles are fixed, on parapets &c by day and accurate shooting takes place at

The Battalion's War Diary entry for 4th October confirms sniping activity

Although the 5/Borders was not involved in 1915 autumn offensive, the Battle of Loos, subsidiary operations took place to the immediate south of Armentieres at Bois Grenier on 25 September 1915. Fighting also took place to the north in the vicinity of Ypres at Bellewaarde Ridge and Hooge. There can be little doubt that hostilities were rife along the whole British sector during late September and early October 1915. Artillery bombardment, machine gun and sniper fire were all part of the daily routine and casualties were inevitable. Corporal Herbert Dixon was one of those casualties. The War Diary of the 5/Borders contains the following report:

> "4th O.C. 77 trench reports everything quiet. A piece of white paper was on a stick near the German bodies. This was shot off by one of our snipers.
>
> O.C. 75 Trench reports night quiet. Enemy's snipers are many and accurate opposite this trench…
>
> 5th O.C. 75 trench has nothing special to report, except that enemy's sniping continues particularly accurate.
>
> Rifles are fixed on parapets &c by day and accurate shooting takes place at night.
>
> O.C. 76 reports enemy very quiet.
>
> O.C. 77 ditto."

Enemy sniper action was reported on 4 October – the day when Corporal Herbert Dixon was hit and died. The War Diary contains no actual record of casualties for the first week of October 1915.

Corporal Herbert Dixon died of wounds 4 October 1915

Report of his Death

The Parish Magazine, November 1915 reported:

"Worst of all however, is the case of Herbert Dixon son-in-law of Mrs. Oldfield of Shirley Terrace. I suppose we all remember Herbert who used to be employed by Mr. Handley and afterwards by the Colliery Co., as a painter. He was killed on October 4th.

The following letter was published:

"Dear Mrs. Dixon – It is with deep regret that I have to inform you of your husband's death while on duty in the trenches. He was practically killed instantly, as he expired shortly after never regaining consciousness from the time he was hit. On behalf of the members of 5th Company I tender their deepest sympathy in the great loss you have sustained, which is ours as well, as he was respected by all he came in contact with and was always careful in his duties. He was buried in Houplines Cemetery near Armentieres, beside his other fallen comrades of the battalion."

Edward D. Birnie, C.Q-M. Sergt.

Corporal Herbert Dixon is buried at Houplines Communal Cemetery Extension. Houplines is to the east of Armentieres in the Nord region of France adjacent to the Belgian border. The writer of one of the letters of sympathy, Captain Edward D'Arcy Birnie D.S.O., M.C. of the 8/Borders was also to become a victim of the war. Aged 26 years, he died 23 March 1918 during the German spring offensive and is buried at Dernancourt Communal Cemetery Extension, south of the town of Albert in the region of the Somme, France.

CHAPTER FIVE

1916

The third year of the war saw the Germans attempt to "bleed France white" at Verdun whilst the British strived to breakthrough on the Somme. Both offensives were doomed to failure, both were titanic struggles with heavy losses. The Battle of Jutland took place in the North Sea off the northern tip of Denmark which resulted in a tactical victory for Germany but a strategic victory for the British. The Russians surprised everyone with impressive initial success in the Brusilov Offensive.

February 21 – December 18	German attack on Verdun in the longest battle of the war, ultimately defended by the French at great cost to both sides
March 11 – November 14	5th, 6th, 7th, 8th and 9th Battles of Isonzo between Italy and Austria-Hungary
April	British forces in Mesopotamia begin advance on Baghdad
March 9	Pancho Villa's raid on Columbus, New Mexico
March 24	French passenger ship, *Sussex*, torpedoed
April 24	Easter rebellion starts in Ireland
May 4	Germany renounces submarine policy
May 19	Britain and France conclude Sykes-Picot agreement

May 31 – June 1	Battle of Jutland, the biggest naval battle in history, ultimately without a clear victor
June – August	Turkish forces, led by Enver Pasha, are defeated by the Russians in the Caucasus
June 4 – September 20	Russian Brusilov offensive in Carpathia nearly knocks Austria-Hungary out of the war
June 5	With British support (led by T.E. Lawrence), Hussein, grand sherif of Mecca, lead an Arab revolt against the Turks in the Hejaz
July 1	Start of the Battle of the Somme, with the greatest number of casualties in British military history, 60,000
August – December	Romania enters the war with the Allies, but is quickly overrun by German forces
August 28	Italy declares war on Germany
August 31	Germany suspends submarine assaults
September 15	Tanks introduced for the first time on the Somme battlefield by the British
October 15	Germany resumes U-boat attacks
November 18	End of the Battle of the Somme
November 28	First German airplane (as opposed to zeppelin) air-raid on Britain
November 29	US occupation of Santa Domingo proclaimed
December 7	David Lloyd George replaces Asquith as British Prime Minister
December 12	Germany issues peace note suggesting compromise peace
December 18	US President Woodrow Wilson requests statements of war objectives from warring nations in peace note

The Western Front 1916
Map courtesy of the Thiepval Project Charity Fund

1916 saw 21 men with connections to Evenwood "fall" – 11 of whom are commemorated on the Evenwood War Memorial, 9 others who were either born or brought up in the village are commemorated elsewhere. Also Private John A. Wardle who was born and raised at Lands then lived at Aycliffe, north of Darlington but no local memorial has yet been traced for him. Private Anthony Oates of the Canadian Expeditionary Force is also honoured in this work.

The greatest naval engagement of the war, the Battle of Jutland saw 3 Evenwood men perish – John Wren and Andrew Lynas were lost at sea and are recorded on Naval Memorials, William Carrick was interned at Farsund in Norway.

The Battle of the Somme, the major British offensive that lasted from July to mid November witnessed 13 Evenwood casualties.

The following men have been researched:
- Private Christopher Cree
- Sapper John T. Milburn
- Private James Marshall
- Private John H. Raine

- Able Seaman John Wren
- Ordinary Seaman William Carrick
- Ordinary Seaman Andrew Lynas
- Private Richard T. Metcalfe
- Private Robert W. Conlon
- Private Anthony Oates
- Private John C. Graves
- Private Watkin Smith
- Private William E. Earl
- Private Fred Hirst
- Private Jeremiah C. Lee
- Pricate John A. Wardle
- Private Robert W. Wilson
- Private John Maughan
- Corporal George T. Cox
- Private Albert Brown
- Private John J. Oates
- Private Thomas H. Dunn

The great loss of life led to a shortage of men. The numbers of volunteers began to fall and measures were needed to provide more troops for the war effort. Conscription had been resisted until January 1916 following the introduction of the Military Services Bill which provided for the conscription of single men only. In May conscription was made universal although the government pledged not to send teenagers to the front line. Ireland was excluded from the scheme.

Private CHRISTOPHER CREE 1878-1916

21/1568 Private Christopher Cree, 21st (Tyneside Scottish) Battalion, the Northumberland Fusiliers died of wounds 2 February 1916 and is buried at Sailly-sur-la-Lys Canadian Cemetery, France and is commemorated on Cockfield War Memorial. He was 38 years old, born c.1878 to John and Elizabeth Cree at Toft Hill/Evenwood. He was the brother of Adam and Towers. Christopher married Elizabeth Ann Alderson and they had 5 children Patricia, Lydia, Laura, Edna and Ronald. They lived at Esperley Lane between Evenwood and Cockfield. He was a coal miner.

21/1568 Private Christopher Cree, 21st (Tyneside Scottish) Battalion, the Northumberland Fusiliers

Christopher Cree was one of 5 Evenwood men to fall whilst serving with the Northumberland Fusiliers. The others were Thomas Davis, Fred Purvis, Wilfred Howlett and Ralph Heaviside.

The 21st (Service) Battalion (2nd Tyneside Scottish) was formed at Newcastle 26 September 1914. In June 1915, it was attached to the 102nd Brigade, 34th Division. The Division moved to France in January 1916 and served with distinction on the Western Front throughout the war. Between the night of 25 January and the 28 January, the battalion proceeded into the line. At 12 noon on 29 January, the enemy shelled Battalion H.Q. and the Officers' Mess Cook. 21/1080 Private Johnson had his leg broken by shrapnel and became the battalion's first casualty – not in the trenches but behind the line. On 31 January, a very foggy night, the companies of the 21st Battalion rotated going into the line and the battalion's first fatality occurred the following morning when Private Cree was wounded by a machine gun bullet whilst on a working party. He died the following day. He had only been in France for 21 days.

Private Christopher Cree died of wounds 2 February 1916

Private Christopher Cree is buried at Sailly-sur-la-Lys Canadian Cemetery. The village of Sailly-sur-la-Lys is approx. 7km west of Armentieres, Pas de Calais, France. The cemetery was begun by Canadian units in March 1915 and used as a front line cemetery until July 1916. It contains 313 Commonwealth burials of the First World War.

Family photo of Christopher, wife Elizabeth and daughter Patricia c.1902

Sapper JOHN THOMAS MILBURN 1872 – 1916

102256 Sapper John Thomas Milburn, 177th Tunnelling Company, Royal Engineers, died of illness 31 March 1916. He is buried at Etaples Military Cemetery, France and is commemorated on Shildon War Memorial.

He was 44 years old, born c.1872 at Evenwood to William and Elizabeth Milburn and in 1891 was brother to Jane, Elizabeth, Ellen and Annie. He married Lizzie 31 December 1903 and they had 5 children, Elizabeth, William, Jane, Sydney and Thomas and lived at Hollands Hill, Shildon. He was a coal miner.

Shildon War Memorial.

102256 Sapper John Thomas Milburn joined the Royal Engineers, 3 June 1915 specifically as a "Tunneller's Mate" and entered France 8 June 1915. The 177th Tunnelling Company was formed that month at Lestrem then moved to the Wytschaete area. He joined the 177th Company on 18 June 1915 – it appears that Sapper John Thomas Milburn was one of the original recruits. In November 1915, the company moved to Railway Wood where it remained for 2 years. The Company was engaged in works for the Second Army, particularly:
- 1915 – July & August – Hooge
- 1915 – November – Wytschaete
- 1916 – June – Mount Sorrel

Sapper J. T. Milburn died on 31 March 1916

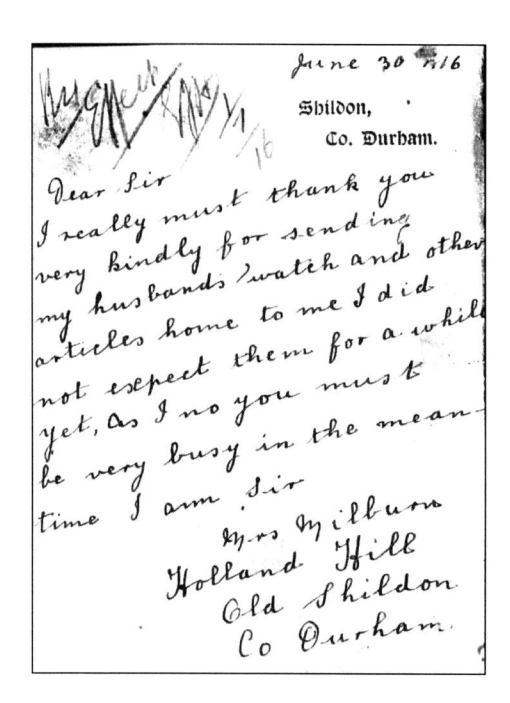

A letter from his wife dated 30 June 1916 to the "authorities" thanking them for returning his watch and other articles.

News of his Death

In July 1916, the Parish Magazine reported:

> "Another name I should like to mention among those who have given their lives for England is that of John Thomas Milburn, of the Royal Engineers. He wasn't actually a parishioner as he lived at Shildon where he leaves a widow and 5 children I am told. However he was brought up in Evenwood and his mother and sisters are well known and much respected members of our community...John Thomas Milburn did not actually fall on the battlefield. He died in hospital in France from ague contracted, I understand from the particular nature of his work on active service."

Sapper J.T. Milburn is buried at Etaples Military Cemetery. The area around Etaples was the scene of an immense concentration of reinforcement camps and hospitals. It was remote from attack other than aircraft and accessible by railway from the northern and southern battlefields. In 1917, 100,000 troops were camped among the sand dunes. The hospitals could deal with 22,000 wounded or sick. The cemetery contains 10,773 Commonwealth burials of the First World War.

Private JAMES MARSHALL 1888 – 1916

17196 Private James Marshall, 8th Battalion, the East Yorkshire Regiment was killed in action 31 March 1916. He has no known grave and is commemorated on the Ypres (Menin Gate) Memorial. He was 28 years old, born c.1888 at Evenwood to George and Margaret Marshall and in 1901 the family lived at Lindon Terrace, Chilton Lane, Ferryhill, Co. Durham. He was brother to Emily and Johnson and worked as a coal miner. He enlisted in Wallsend and lived at Fatfield near Washington when he joined up.

The Ypres (Menin Gate) Memorial

The 8th Battalion, the East Yorkshire Regiment was formed on 22 September 1914 and attached to the 21st Division as part of the 62nd Brigade. In September 1915, the Division saw action at the Battle of Loos suffering 3,800 casualties before 16 November 1915 being transferred to the 3rd Division, 8th Brigade. The 8th Brigade was involved in offensive operations at the Bluff between 14 February and 2 March 1916.

> "The Bluff is an artificial height created by the dumping of spoil when the Ypres-Comines Canal was excavated. In this low-lying area, and on the northern bank of the canal, it gave a considerable observation advantage to the troops occupying it. In the afternoon of 14th February, German infantry successfully attacked the British units holding the Bluff, after a very heavy bombardment with shells and trench mortars, and the blowing of some mines. Preparations were made to recover this important area, although they were slowed by severe weather. In the early morning of 2nd March, after a short bombardment which destroyed the enemy's defensive works, British infantry over-ran the position and consolidated it at a cost of 1,620 casualties. No further infantry actions were undertaken

by either side until June 1917, although violent mine warfare remained a feature of this troublesome spot."

Later in the month, 31 March 1916 Private James Marshall was killed. The circumstances of his death are unknown – he has no known grave.

Private James Marshall was killed in action 31 March 1916

Private James Marshall is commemorated on the Ypres Menin Gate Memorial. A local commemoration has not been traced.

Private JOHN HENRY RAINE 1888 -1916

24781 Private John Henry Raine, 13th Battalion, the Durham Light Infantry was killed in action 24 May 1916. He is buried at Bois-de-Noulette British Cemetery, Aix Noulette in France and commemorated on the Evenwood War Memorial. He was 28 years old, born on 8 February 1888 at Evenwood to Francis and Margeret Raine and lived at the Oaks, Evenwood. On 3 August 1911, John married Sarah Jane Dunn. By 1914, they lived at Osborne Terrace, Evenwood and had 2 children, Rachel Annie and Rhoda.

24781 Private John Henry Raine, 13th Batallion, the Durham Light Infantry

John enlisted 4 August 1914 at Darlington "for the duration of the war" leaving his job as a coal miner.

The 13th (Service) Battalion, the Durham Light Infantry was formed at Newcastle, September 1914 and was attached to the 68th Brigade of the 23rd Division. The Division landed in Boulogne, France in August 1915. 24781 Private John Henry Raine entered France 25 August 1915. A month later, as the Battle of Loos commenced, the 13/DLI stood to arms expecting a counter attack in the area around Pietre. The battalion was at the front over Christmas and into February 1916. On 17 March, the 13/DLI moved to trenches at Calonne when the Germans bombarded the lines. There were some casualties but overall, they were relatively light – in 7 months there were only 132 casualties. Few battalions serving on the Western Front had such light casualty figures.

During April, the Germans increased shelling the British trenches and following a spell of training at Reclinghem, the battalion returned to the line in the Souchez sector, 20 May 1916, described as follows:

Photograph of his wife Sarah and daughters Rachel and Rhoda c.1915

> "Ceaseless war was raged in these trenches with rifle grenades and trench mortars, the artillery of both sides joining in as occasion seemed to demand."

Private John Henry Raine was killed in action 24 May 1916.

The service details of 24781 Private John H. Raine have not been researched and the exact circumstances of his death are not known. Another 2 O.R.'s of the 13/DLI were killed in action on this date, 19697 Private J.E. Lee and 16704 Private F.G. Murray, both of whom are buried at Bois-de-Noulette British Cemetery, Aix-Noulette. All victims "as ceaseless war was raged in these trenches."

Report of his Death

The Parish Magazine, July 1916 reported:

> "one of our young men, John Henry Raine of 13th D.L.I., had been killed in action in France. John Henry Raine, in addition to a mother and father, brothers and sisters has a young wife and two small children to mourn his loss."

Private John Henry Raine is buried at Bois-de-Noulette British Cemetery, Aix-Noulette. The village is to the south of Bethune in the region of Pas-de-Calais, France. The Field Ambulance used the cemetery between April 1916 and May 1917 and there are 130 burials. The French National Cemetery of the Battles of Artois, Notre Dame de Lorette with the graves of 20,000 soldiers is located to the south and is visible from the approach road to the Bois-de-Noulette cemetery.

The BATTLE OF JUTLAND 31 May -1 June 1916

The Battle of Jutland was the most important naval encounter of the Great War. Evenwood lost 3 of her sons:
- Able Seaman John Wren, H.M.S. Black Prince
- Ordinary Seaman William Carrick, H.M.S. Ardent
- Ordinary Seaman Andrew Lynas, H.M.S. Ardent.

Naval rivalry between Britain and Germany was a major factor in the build up to the Great War. When the conflict began, the opposing admirals expected that the naval war would be settled by a massive clash between the 2 fleets of battleships. In reality, the fear of losing their ships meant that both fleets stayed in port for the first 2 years. Even when the great battle did come, it was indecisive.

On the morning of 31 May 1916 over 250 British and German warships were steaming on convergent courses to a rendezvous unanticipated by the Germans, off the Jutland coast of Denmark. Admiral Sir John Jellicoe was Commander of the British Grand Fleet which consisted of 28 Dreadnoughts, 9 battle cruisers, 8 armoured cruisers, 26 light cruisers, 78 destroyers, a seaplane and a minesweeper. Facing him was Admiral Reinhard Scheer commander of the German High Seas Fleet which consisted of 16 Dreadnoughts, 6 pre-Dreadnoughts, 5 battle cruisers, 11 light cruisers and 61 destroyers.

HMS Black Prince was part of the 1st Cruiser Squadron along with HMS Defence, HMS Warrior and HMS Duke of Edinburgh. HMS Ardent was part of the 4th Destroyer Flotilla along with another 18 destroyers. Both ships took part in the night battle of the 31 May-1 June. The Germans proved to be better equipped for night fighting with better co-ordination, star shells and searchlights The British destroyers were painted black, a bad colour for night fighting and after the battle they were repainted grey like their German counterparts. Whilst they attacked bravely their tactics were poor, usually approaching too close and launching their torpedoes at the wrong angles, enabling the Germans to fire first and avoid the torpedoes.

The 4th Destroyer Flotilla encountered the German van, including the 1st Battle Squadron. The "Westfalen" sunk HMS Tipperary, HMS Spitfire collided with "Nassau" and "Elbing" was accidentally rammed by "Posen" and sunk later. At 11.40pm HMS Broke challenged "Rostock" who opened fire causing her steering to jam and ram HMS Sparrowhawk. HMS Contest then ran into the back of HMS Sparrowhawk. "Rostock" was torpedoed and sunk for her troubles and "Westfalen" sank HMS Fortune. HMS Black Prince had been lost, arrived just after midnight and was blasted at close range by four battleships causing her to explode. All 857 men were lost. Moments later "Westfalen" sank HMS Ardent. There were only 2 survivors. Further engagements took place into the early hours of the morning but the German High Seas Fleet broke through and steamed for home. Jellicoe was unable to intercept the German fleet and it reached port by early afternoon. In terms of material losses, the outcome was:

- British losses: 3 battle cruisers – Indefatigable, Queen Mary & Invincible; 3 armoured cruisers – Black Prince, Defence & Warrior; 8 destroyers – Ardent, Fortune, Nestor, Nomad, Shark, Sparrowhawk, Tipperary, & Turbulent.
- 6,094 British sailors lost
- German losses: 1 battle cruiser – Lutzow; 1 armoured cruiser – Pommern; 4 light cruisers – Elbing, Frauenlob, Rostock & Wiesbaden; 5 destroyers – S35, V4, V27, V29 & V48.
- 2,551 German sailors lost.

Jutland was undoubtedly a material victory for the German High Seas Fleet whilst being a strategic victory for the British Grand Fleet. The Germans had inflicted heavier losses on the numerically superior Grand Fleet and had escaped near destruction but had failed to break the British blockade or control of the North Sea. The engagement had not altered the balance of power in any meaningful way. The relative strength, in favour of the British Fleet, was 28:16 before the battle and 24:10 afterwards. The Kaiser claimed victory, known to the Germans as "the Victory of the Skaggerak" but he would not release his High Seas Fleet to do battle again since he could not risk being defeated. Thus his navy stayed in port and submarine activity resumed in earnest. A German journalist described the action as:

"an assault on the gaoler, followed by a return to gaol."

Ultimately, the inactivity of the German sailors led to disorder beginning in August 1917 and full scale mutiny by November 1918. The naval war became one of blockade and new technology. The British swiftly put a stranglehold on all German overseas trade by blocking and stopping all ships steaming in and out of German ports. This policy gradually began to starve the country. The Germans responded by using their new weapon – the submarine, the U-boat. Early success was offset by the danger of provoking the USA into joining the Allies so the campaign was abandoned. A year later, Germany was desperate to bring Britain to its knees and gambled with the reintroduction of unrestricted submarine warfare. Success followed and hundreds of cargo ships bound for Britain were sunk. The British fought back by introducing the convoy system, airships and aircraft to spot the U-boats, depth charges were developed to attack them and ASDIC to detect them. The German gamble failed as the U.S.A. entered the war in 1917. The introduction of American troops, particularly from the summer of 1918 onwards turned the balance of power and ensured an Allied victory.

Able Seaman JOHN WILLIAM WREN 1893 – 1916

Tyneside Z/4043 Able Seaman John William Wren was lost at sea 31 May 1916 whilst serving aboard H.M.S. "Black Prince" and is commemorated on the Chatham Naval Memorial and Evenwood War Memorial. He was 23 years old, born c.1893 at Longhirst, Nothumberland to John and Elizabeth Wren. He enlisted prior to September 1915 and the family lived at 20 Copeland Row, Evenwood.

After the First World War, an appropriate way had to be found to commemorate those members of the Royal Navy who had no known grave, the majority of deaths having occurred at sea where no permanent memorial could be provided. An Admiralty

H.M.S. "Black Prince"

committee recommended that the three manning ports in Great Britain – Chatham, Plymouth and Portsmouth – each would have an identical memorial of unmistaken naval form, an obelisk, which would serve as a leading mark for shipping. Chatham Naval Memorial commemorates almost 8,500 sailors of the First World War.

Ordinary Seaman WILLIAM CARRICK 1894 – 1916

J/43920 Ordinary Seaman William Carrick served on H.M.S. "Ardent" and died 1 June 1916. He is buried at Farsund Cemetery, Norway and commemorated on the Evenwood War Memorial. He was 22 years old, born in 1894 at Evenwood to Joseph and Elizabeth Carrick and was brother to Margaret, Edmund, Ada, Florence, Barbara, Alice and Wilfred. The family lived at 13 South View. He enlisted 7 September 1915 with his friend, Andrew Lynas.

In October 1916, the Parish Magazine reported that the body of William Carrick had been recovered off the coast of Norway and 30 June 1916 interred by the Norwegian Government Authorities on Norwegian soil, at Farsund. Farsund is a small town in Southern Norway to the west of Kristiansand. He is buried at Farsund Cemetery where there are 9 First World War burials, 4 identified and 5 unidentified.

J/43920 Ordinary Seaman William Carrick

Ordinary Seaman ANDREW LYNAS 1896 – 1916

J/43919 Ordinary Seaman Andrew Lynas was lost at sea 1 June 1916 whilst serving aboard HMS "Ardent". He is commemorated on the Portsmouth Naval Memorial and Evenwood War Memorial. He was 20 years old, born in 1896 at Evenwood to James and Annie Lynas. He was brother to Margaret and step-brother to George Milburn Proud. The family lived at 18 Chapel Street, Evenwood. He enlisted 7 September 1915, trained at HMS "Victory" until 23 November 1915 before joining HMS "Ardent".

*J/43919 Ordinary Seaman
Andrew Lynas*

Andrew with his sister Margaret

Andrew Lynas is commemorated on the Portsmouth Naval Memorial that commemorates almost 10,000 sailors of the First World War.

Memorial Service

A Memorial Service was held 11 June 1916 in St. Paul's Church, Evenwood for the 3 seamen lost at the Battle of Jutland – Ordinary Seaman A. Lynas, Ordinary Seaman W. Carrick and Able Seaman J.W. Wren and also Private J.H. Raine who was killed in action in France.

Report of deaths

The Auckland Chronicle, 15 June 1916 reported:

"The Fallen Brave

In the North Sea naval battle Evenwood lost three of its lads. They were Wm. Carrick, son of Mr. and Mrs. Joseph Carrick, South View; Andrew Lynas, son of James Lynas Chapel, St. and John W. Wren, son of Mr. and Mrs. Wren Copeland Row. John H. Raine, son of Mr. and Mrs. Frank Raine and who was killed in France on 24 May, leaves a widow and two children. In honour of the fallen ones memorial services were held at St. Paul's Church on Sunday afternoon and at the Wesleyan Church at night. Both were overcrowded. The village band played "Lead, kindly light" and the Dead March in "Saul" and the Boy Scouts sounded the "Last Post"."

The July edition of the Parish Magazine contained the following account of the battle provided by Arthur Dunn aboard H.M.S. Birkenhead:

"Everybody who took part in the battle feels very certain that the whole of the German losses have not been published yet and when they are it will be a surprise to you all. When it began we had 4 battleships, 6 battle cruisers and 12 light cruisers which for nearly 3 hours fought the whole German fleet, we being included. How our ships got through it would be hard to say, for we were in the thick of it most of the time. We were with the "Invincible" which exploded just before the end. We had a narrow escape as a great number of shells fell between us just clear of both ships. I don't suppose any good news will have been heard of my 3 friends, seeing that their ships were sunk. The only thing that we are sore about is that we did not meet them earlier in the day. It was just beginning to turn dark when our main fleet arrived and as usual the Germans turned tail and ran. I shall never forget the brilliant flashes and the crashing of guns caused by our ships firing salvos or broadsides. One peculiar scene was the thousands of fishes floating on the water. They were of all kinds and sizes. I think they must have been stunned by the turmoil in the sea caused by the falling shells. I cannot explain what it was like in a letter so the main facts will have to wait the telling until I see you all again. I shall never forget it and feel thankful that I got through safely."

Another Evenwood lad, William Purdy, aboard H.M.S. Maidstone, was involved in the battle but his ship was in the main fleet so its part in it was mainly the pursuit.

The BATTLE OF THE SOMME 1 July – 18 November 1916

During the months of the Battle of the Somme, 13 men with Evenwood connections were killed, 6 of whom are commemorated on the Evenwood War Memorial and the others elsewhere at Witton Park, Hamsteels, Cockfield, Staindrop and Normanton. Private Anthony Oates, born at Hamsterley, lived in Alberta, Canada and served with the Canadian forces is mentioned here as tribute to the Canadian losses during the conflict. The casualties were:

- Private Richard T. Metcalfe
- Private Robert W. Conlon
- Private Anthony Oates
- Private John C. Graves
- Private Watkin Smith
- Private William E. Earl
- Private Fred Hirst
- Private John A. Wardle
- Private Jeremiah C. Lee
- Private Robert W. Wilson
- Private John Maughan
- Corporal George T. Cox
- Private Albert Brown
- Private Joseph J. Oates

The Battle of the Somme was viewed as a breakthrough battle, as a means of getting through the formidable German trench lines and into a war of movement. Political considerations and the demands of the French High Command influenced the timing of the battle. They demanded British diversionary action to occupy the German Army to relieve the hard pressed French troops at Verdun, to the south.

General Sir Douglas Haig, appointed Commander-in-Chief in December 1915, was responsible for the overall conduct of British Army operations in France and Belgium. The action on the Somme was to be the British Army's first major offensive on the Western Front in 1916 and it was entrusted to General Rawlinson's Fourth Army to deliver the resounding victory. The British Army included thousands of citizen volunteers, keen to take part in what was expected to be a great victory.

The main line of assault ran nearly 14 miles from Maricourt in the south to Serre to the north, with a diversionary attack at Gommecourt 2 miles further to the north. The first objective was to establish a new advanced line on the Montauban to Pozieres Ridge.

The first day, 1 July, was preceded by a weeklong artillery bombardment of the German positions. Just prior to zero-hour, the storm of British shells increased and merged with huge mine explosions to herald the infantry attack – at 7.30am on a clear midsummer's morning the British Infantry emerged from their trenches and advanced in extended lines at a slow steady pace over No Man's Land. They were met with a hail of machine gun and rifle fire from the surviving German defenders. Accurate German artillery barrages smashed into the infantry in No Man's Land and the crowded assembly trenches.

The British suffered enormous casualties:
- Officers killed 993
- Other Ranks killed: 18,247
- Total Killed: 19,240
- Total casualties (killed, wounded and missing): 57,470

In popular imagination, the Battle of the Somme has become a byword for military disaster. In the calamitous opening 24 hours the British Army suffered its highest number of casualties in a single day. The loss of great numbers of men from the same towns and villages had a profound impact on those at home. The first day was an abject failure and the following weeks and months of conflict assumed the nature of wearing-down warfare, a war of attrition, by the end of which both the attackers and defenders were totally exhausted.

The Battle of the Somme can be broken down into 12 offensive operations:
- Albert: 1 – 13 July
- Bazantin Ridge: 14 – 17 July
- Delville Wood: 15 July – 13 September
- Pozieres Ridge: 15 July – 3 September
- Guillemont: 23 July – 3 September
- Ginchy: 9 September
- Flers-Courcelette: 15 – 22 September

- Morval: 25 – 28 September
- Thiepval: 25 – 28 September
- Le Transloy: 1 – 18 October
- Ancre Heights: 1 October – 11 November
- Ancre: 13 – 18 November

Adverse weather conditions, the autumn rains and early winter sleet and snow turned the battlefield into morass of mud. Such intolerable physical conditions helped to bring to an end the Allied offensive operations after four and a half months of slaughter. The fighting brought no significant breakthrough. Territorial gain was a strip of land approximately 20 miles wide by 6 miles deep, made at enormous cost. British and Commonwealth casualties were 419,654 dead, wounded and missing of which some 131,000 were dead. French casualties amounted to 204,253. German casualties were estimated between 450,000 to 600,000. In the spring of 1917, the German forces fell back to their newly prepared defences, the Hindenburg Line, and there were no further significant engagements in the Somme sector until the Germans mounted their major offensive in March 1918.

Private RICHARD THOMAS METCALFE 1881 – 1916

14704 Private Richard Thomas Metcalfe, 15th Battalion, Durham Light Infantry, died of wounds 2 July 1916, and is buried at Mericourt-L'Abbe Communal Cemetery Extension, France and commemorated on Witton Park War Memorial. He was about 35 years old, born in Evenwood c.1881 to William and Hannah Metcalfe and in 1881 was brother to John, Joseph, Mary and William. By the time of his death he was married to Mrs E. Metcalfe of 4 Jackson Row, Woodside, Witton Park, Bishop Auckland. He enlisted at Bishop Auckland.

The 15th (Service) Battalion was formed at Newcastle in September 1914 and was attached to 64th Brigade, 21st Division. 14704 Private Richard Thomas Metcalfe entered France on 11 September 1915 with the 21st Division. Its first experience was truly appalling. Having been in France for only a few days and lengthy forced marches brought it into the reserve for the British assault at Loos in September 1915. The Division was sent into action on the second day, the 26th whereupon it suffered heavy casualties for very little gain – there were no less than 450 casualties in the ranks including 14525 Serjeant E. Towers from the Oaks, Evenwood.

The Battle of the Somme – 1 July 1916 – the First Day
The Battle of Albert – Fricourt and Mametz

The 21st Division formed part of the XV Corps was under the command of Lt-General Henry Horne. The Division faced the Fricourt and Mametz spurs which ran down from Pozieres Ridge. The terrain was ideal for defence and the Germans took full advantage.

The Allied Forces were helped by the detonation of three mines of 25,000lbs, 15,000 lbs and 9,000 lbs under the German lines opposite the small British salient, known as the Tambour. The mines were a pure diversion as the craters were not to be rushed and it was hoped that the lips thrown up around them would provide an interruption to the deadly flanking fire of the German machine guns.

Action of the 15/D.L.I.

1 July 03.00 a.m. – the 15/D.L.I. was ready to advance behind the 9th King's Own Yorkshire Light Infantry. Day broke and the German reply to the British gunfire was initially of no great strength. At 07.25 the heavy artillery lifted and the eager Yorkshiremen climbed out of their trenches and advanced into the smoke as the shrapnel barrage came down. The 15/DLI followed in their turn, with A and B companies in front. German machine guns hastily hoisted from deep dug-outs were little damaged by British barrage and opened up on the Durhams, who had covered 200 yards of "No Man's Land" and entered the shattered German line. Some Germans surrendered but others fought with bomb or bayonet. They resisted in shell craters and sectors of standing trench. The 15/DLI won their way until they joined the Yorkshiremen.

By 08.30 Crucifix Trench had been taken. The shrapnel barrage moved ahead, but the ground in front was swept by machine-gun fire from the right, where the Germans still held Fricourt, and from the left, where they lay in Birch Tree Wood. The sunken road and Crucifix Trench were put in a state of defence and in the road at the entrance to one of the dug-outs – now all filled with British and German wounded – headquarters were established. The brigade had gone far ahead of the troops on the flanks but with Lewis guns in Round Wood and Lozenge Wood all was in readiness for the German counter-attacks.

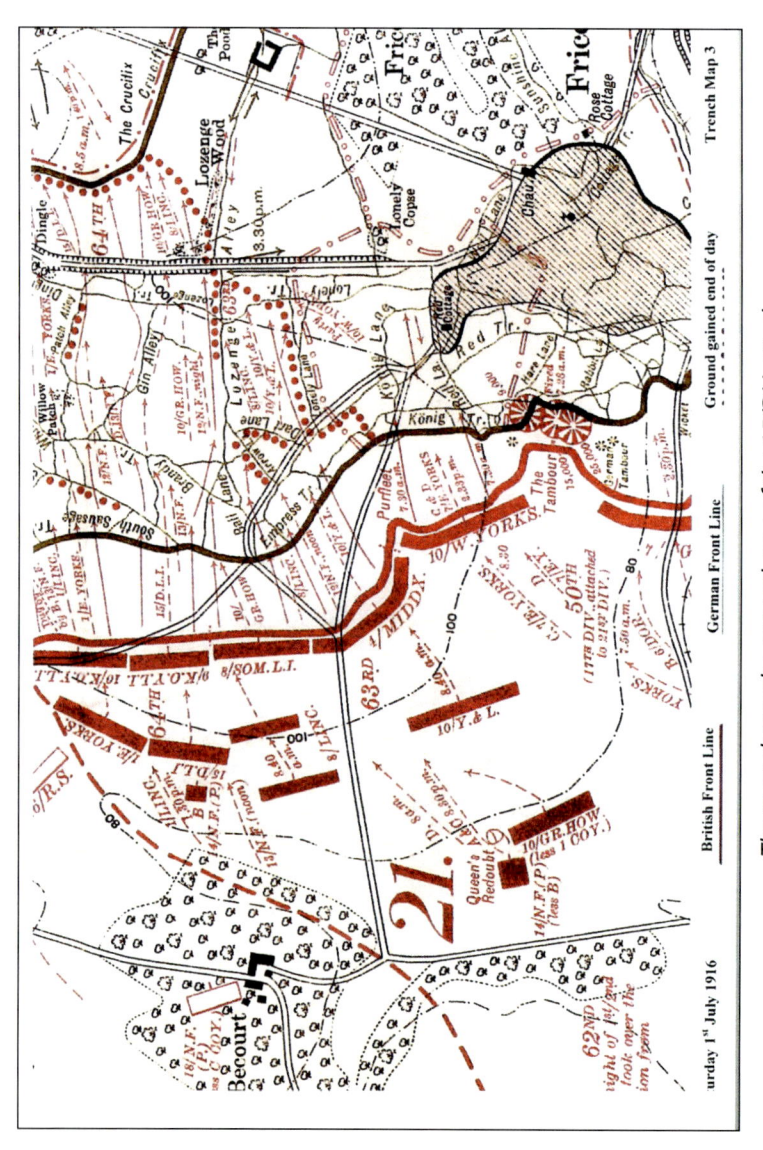

The map shows the general area of the 15/DLI attack

At 13.40 orders were received to attack Shelter Wood. A protective barrage came down 10 minutes early so that the action was carried out without artillery support. Fighting patrols advanced to 40 yards from the woods. In these positions the Durhams sniped at the enemy and, despite repeated attempts to dislodge them, held on until relieved eight hours later. As the afternoon wore on the area was heavily shelled and strafed by machine gun fire. At 17.00, the Germans were seen assembling near Birch Tree Wood and a party of 300 advanced but were dispersed with heavy loss by Lewis gunfire. In the evening two companies of the 10/Yorks. arrived in Crucifix Trench to establish touch with the 63rd Brigade upon the right. It was much later when the Lincolns and Middlesex appeared to take over the positions held by the 15/D.L.I., a long and difficult operation, not completed till dawn.

At 06.00 on 2 July, parties were still arriving in the original British front line, where the 15/DLI assembled under Major R.B. Johnson.

> "Grievous losses had been suffered. Among the other officers killed on July 1st were Capts. J. East and L.H. Sanger-Davies, and 2nd Lieuts. R.O. Cormack, C.S. Haynes, J.M. Jones and M.L. Huddlestone. Capt. F.P. Stamper was among the wounded and casualties in the ranks numbered 440. For their gallantry Sergts. E. Willison and T. Jones; Corpls. F. Connor and J.B. Lauder; and Ptes. J. Gray, J. Robinson, J.W. Robson, G. Tait and S.S. Dennis were awarded the Military Medal."

Private R.T. Metcalfe was one of the 440 casualties suffered by the 15/DLI – he died of wounds, 2 July 1916. In all 121 other ranks serving with the 15/DLI were killed in action or died of their wounds on 1 & 2 July 1916. The 21st Division suffered 4,256 casualties.

Private Richard Thomas Metcalfe died of wounds 2 July 1916

Private R.T. Metcalfe is buried at Mericourt-L'Abbe Communal Cemetery Extension. The village is about 6km south east of Albert on the road to Amiens. This cemetery used by field ambulances between August 1915 and July 1916.

Private ROBERT WILLIAM CONLON 1880 – 1916

31058 Private Robert William Conlon, 2nd Battalion, York and Lancaster Regiment died of wounds 13 September 1916. He is buried at Peronne Road Cemetery, Maricourt and is commemorated on the Evenwood War Memorial. He was 36 years old, born 1880 at Hamsterley.

Robert William Conlon joined up 23 February1916, aged 36 years leaving his job as a timber feller. He joined 3/8th D.L.I. but later was transferred to 2/Yorks & Lancs. Regiment (possibly 6 September 1916) which formed part of the 16th Brigade of the 6th Division.

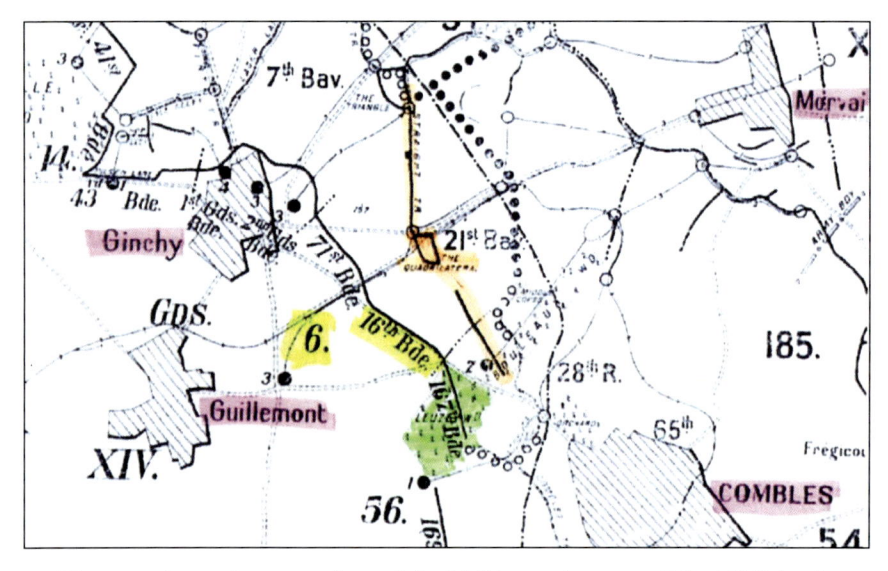

The map shows the general rea of the 2/Y&L attack – part of the 16th Brigade

August was spent on the Ancre on the front opposite Beaumont-Hamel. After a short period in reserve, between 6 – 8 September, the Division was moved to join the XIV Corps Fourth Army. On 9 September a successful attack captured Ginchy and Leuze Wood but the Germans held the high ground which formed a horseshoe between these 2 points. The trenches followed the shape of the spur and covered access was given to them by a sunken road leading back to the deep valley which runs north from Combles.

A strong point was positioned at the top of the spur – a 4 sided trench called the Quadrilateral, a parallelogram of some 300 x 150 yards. The Germans held up the advance of the Fourth Army. It was the task of the 6th Division to obliterate the horseshoe and straighten the line, in preparation for a general attack, 15 September.

Attacks by the 56th Division 12 September, to the south and the Guards to the north reduced the neck of the horseshoe to about 500 yards but the attack could not close it. The situation on the ground was undefined – the exact positions of the trenches in the Quadrilateral were unknown. Bad weather prevented observation by aircraft and bombardment had obliterated villages, roads and railways.

On the night 11/12 September the 71st Brigade relieved the Guards and the 16th Brigade relieved part of the 56th Division with orders to attack the next day and straighten the line by capturing the Quadrilateral. Artillery co-operation was weak, observation being difficult thus the northern attack could only advance 500 yards and the southern attack even less. Casualties from enemy artillery and machine gun fire were heavy. A second attack the same day at 6.00pm succeeded in bringing the line to within 250 yards from the Strong Point and joined up with the 16th Brigade.

Private Robert William Conlon died of wounds 13 September 1916.

Private Conlon received abdominal wounds and died on the way to the Advance Dressing Station. It appears that Private Conlon was with his battalion for only about 1 week.

Private Robert William Conlon is buried at Peronne Road Cemetery, Maricourt. At the beginning of the 1916 battle of the Somme, Maricourt was at the junction of the British and French forces within a short distance of the front line. It was originally known as Maricourt Military Cemetery no.3 and was begun by fighting units and Field Ambulances and used until August 1917. It was completed after the Armistice by concentrating graves from the battlefields in the immediate neighbourhood and from smaller burial grounds. There are now 1348 First World War casualties commemorated in the cemetery.

Private ANTHONY OATES 1888 – 1916

446121 Private Anthony Oates, 31st Battalion, the Canadian Infantry (Alberta Regiment) was killed in action 15 September 1916 at the Battle of Flers-Courcelette. He is commemorated on the Vimy Memorial in France and Hamsterley War Memorial. He was 28 years old, born 21 February 1888 in Hamsterley, County Durham and in 1911 emigrated to Canada. By 1915 he was married to Daisy and they had a daughter Frances. They lived in Calgary, Alberta. Anthony worked as a "teamster" for the City.

Anthony Oates enlisted 26 April 1915 in Calgary as recruitment took place throughout the Province of Alberta, Canada. The battalion arrived in England 28 May 1915. Its strength was 37 officers and 1122 other ranks. Then 4 months later, in September 1915, the battalion arrived in France as part of the 2nd Canadian Division, 6th Canadian Infantry Brigade.

The Battle of Flers-Courcelette

On 15 September 1916, the Canadian Corps (1st and 2nd Canadian Divisions) occupied positions to the north of the offensive line, opposite the German positions at Thiepval, Mouquet Farm and Martinpuich. The 6th Canadian Brigade was to the north of Pozieres in the vicinity of Mouquet Farm. The 2nd and 3rd Canadian Divisions of the Canadian Corps were in action near here. Private Anthony Oates served in "A" Company and the 31st Battalion War Diary provides the following report:

> "At 9-30 p.m. on the night of the 14th/15th, the Battalion Headquarters moved to dug-out, shared with 28th Battalion on CENTRE WAY, near Point 77, the remainder of the Battalion following;- A and B Companies taking their positions of assembly with the 27th Battalion and three platoons of "C" Company with the 28th Battalion……
>
> As my Battalion was very much scattered, I can only give an intelligible account by taking the various parties in detail.
>
>> A. Company (attached to 27th Battalion)
>> Three Platoons of this Company (Mopping-up Party) formed the 2nd Intermediate wave, following the first wave of the attached in at a distance of ten yards. The fourth platoon acting as Carrying Party and following the Reserve Company. The objective of this

446121 Private Anthony Oates, 31ˢᵗ Batallion, the Canadian Infantry (Alberta Regiment)

Company was the GERMAN FRONT LINE, where it was to mop-up and consolidate. This was carried out, a new trench being dug between 30 and 40 yards in front of the OLD GERMAN FRONT LINE. As Major H.M. Splane, the Officer Commanding Company was killed and all Company Officers either killed or wounded, very early in the operations, the Command of the Company fell to Company Serjeant Major G. LAWSON, who carried out the work in a highly creditable manner."

Battalion Orders No. 259 prepared by Lieut. Col. A.H. Bell Commanding 31ˢᵗ (Alberta) Battalion, C.E.F. for Sunday 17 September 1916 reported the casualties for 15 September 1916 – Killed in action, 7 officers and 56 O.R.'s, one of whom is recorded as 446121 Private A. Oates.

Private Anthony Oates was killed in action 15 September 1916.

Private A. Oates is commemorated on the Vimy Memorial which overlooks the Douai Plain from the highest point of Vimy Ridge, about 8 kilometres northeast of Arras. After the war, Vimy Ridge was chosen as the site of the great memorial to all Canadians who served their country in battle during the First World War, and particularly to the 60,000 who gave their lives in France. It also bears the names of 11,000 Canadian servicemen who died in France who have no known grave.

Thiepval Memorial to the Missing of the Somme

32120 Private John Charles Graves, 10th Battalion, Durham Light Infantry was killed in action, 16 September 1916

24048 Private Watkin Smith, 9th Batallion, the Lancashire Fusiliers was killed in action on 19 September 1916

18/1628 Private William Edwin Earl, 14th Battalion, Durham Light Infantry was killed in action, 27 September 1916

3914 Private John Alfred Wardle, 1/6 Batallion, Durham Light Infantry was killed in action 1 October 1916

Private JOHN CHARLES GRAVES 1883 – 1916

32120 Private John Charles Graves, 10th battalion, Durham Light Infantry was killed in action, 16 September 1916 and is commemorated on the Thiepval Memorial, France and Evenwood War Memorial. He was 33 years old, born in Yafforth, Yorkshire c.1883 to George and Mary Graves and brother to William Robert. He was a farm labourer and lived at Low Butterknowle Farm, Low Lands.

The 10/DLI formed part of the 43rd Brigade of the 14th (Light) Division. The 14th Division were called upon to share the attack of 15 September 1916, at Flers-Courcelette. 32120 Private John Charles Graves entered France on 25 August 1916 and on 4 September 1916 was posted from the 4/DLI to 10/DLI.

The Battles of Flers-Courcelette, Morval & Thiepval Ridge – an overview

The Battle of Flers-Courcelette commenced on 15 September 1916. The XV Corps were made up of the New Zealand Division, the 41st and 14th Divisions and were under the command of Lieutenant General Henry Horne. They were at the centre of the attack and were responsible for the capture of Flers. The 6th Somerset Light Infantry, 6th Duke of Cornwall's Light Infantry and the 6th King's Own Yorkshire Light Infantry joined the 10/DLI in the 43rd Brigade. The 43rd Brigade took up position between Delville Wood and the village of Ginchy. The 41st Division was to their left and the Guards to their right.

The offensive employed 12 Divisions and this battle is notable for the introduction of tanks, 49 were deployed and proved notoriously unreliable – only 15 rolled onto No Man's Land at the start of the attack. The B.E.F. and Canadian Corps made initial gains of some 2 kilometres within the first 3 days including the capture of the ruined villages of Martinpuich, Flers and Courcelette and much of the sought after High Wood. However a combination of poor weather and extensive German reinforcements halted the advance and the Allies again suffered high casualties. The attack was called off 22 September.

Haig renewed attacks in this area between 25 – 27 September in the Battle of Morval and the Battle of Thiepval Ridge. Advances were limited but positions were consolidated. The historian, Peter Hart concluded:

> "The pattern of the fighting on the Somme had now been clearly established. It was fundamentally a battle of artillery. The British could not advance without it: the Germans could not defend without it. The roar of guns was unceasing. It could grind away and erode the courage of all but the bravest."

The 10/DLI was involved in the action and at midnight of the 15/16 September, moved off in artillery formation and German shrapnel caused a few casualties. At dawn, there was considerable enemy movement near the village of Gueudecourt beyond Gird and Gird Support trenches. At 9.25am orders were received to attack with the objective to break through the Gird defences, clear Gueudecourt and establish a line beyond. A heavy bombardment accompanied the attack and the Durhams went forward at the appointed hour.

> "…as soon as they appeared in the open there came heavy machine gun fire from the front and from the right. On they went, paying dearly for every yard but when nearly a quarter of a mile had been gained the survivors had to seek cover in shell holes and stay there. Before mid-day parties of Germans were seen coming forward of the Gird line from the direction of le Transloy but no counter attack was attempted. The afternoon passed and then came orders for another attack to be delivered at 6.55pm. Colonel Morant collected about 100 men which included all employed at battalion HQ…The creeping barrage was again negligible and the German machine guns were as active as before. With no troops in immediate support and both flanks unprotected a withdrawal was inevitable and after dark the survivors of the battalion fell back and put Bull's Road in a state of defence. Many wounded were then brought in."

At dawn, 17 September, the 21st Division came up as relief and the 10/DLI handed over positions. A very weak battalion reached Pommiers Redoubt during the morning. Losses in killed, wounded and missing amounted to 381. The Battle of Flers-Courcelette raged on for another week and was regarded as a major success particularly when compared with the results of August and early September. A considerable stretch of the German front line had been captured and their second line system had been breached in the Flers sector. High Wood and the Bazentin Ridge had been captured and opened up an improved tactical position for the British – enhanced observation positions over the German lines. The Germans made a tactical retreat to the Le Transloy Ridge. The British casualties were atrocious and were comparable in percentage terms to the debacle of July. It was estimated that the Fourth Army suffered over 29,000 casualties. All

3 Divisions involved in the central push – the New Zealand, the 41st and the 14th all suffered severe casualties in achieving their objectives but significantly, there were no fresh reserve divisions behind them to surge forward and leapfrog onto victory.

In conclusion, the German line had been under immense pressure on 15 September 1916 but it held out. Their artillery struggled but had not been overwhelmed. German supplies were depleted but had not run out. German morale was failing but had not collapsed. Their resistance was still strong. The German nation was not ready for defeat!

Private John C. Graves was killed in action 16 September 1916.

3 officers and 136 O.R.'s of the 10/DLI were killed in action on 16 September 1916 including 32120 Private John Charles Graves. He had been in the Army for some 281 days but in France for only 24 days. Private John C. Graves is commemorated on the Thiepval Memorial, the Memorial to the Missing of the Somme. The Memorial bears the names of more than 72,000 officers and men of the UK and South African forces who died in the Somme sector before 20 March 1918 and have no known grave. Over 90% of those commemorated died between July and November 1916. It was designed by Sir Edwin Lutyens, built between 1928 and 1932 and unveiled by the Prince of Wales, in the presence of the President of France, 31 July 1932.

Private WATKIN SMITH 18?? – 1916

24048 Private Watkin Smith, 9th Battalion, the Lancashire Fusiliers was killed in action 17 September 1916 at the Battle of Flers-Courcelette. He has no known grave and is commemorated on the Thiepval Memorial, France. To date a local commemoration to him has not been traced. He was born in Evenwood, enlisted in York and lived at Forest Hall, Newcastle upon Tyne. He previously served with the 5th Cavalry Reserve, service number 15067. The service record of Private Watkin Smith has not been researched so the date he enlisted and was transferred to the 9th (Service) Battalion, the Lancashire Fusiliers is unknown. The battalion was formed 21 August 1914 and attached to the 34th Brigade of the 11th Division.

The Battle of Flers-Courcelette

The 11th Division formed part of the II Corps together with the 18th Division alongside the Canadian Corps (1st and 2nd Canadian Divisions). The II Corps occupied positions to the north of the offensive line, to the immediate south of Thiepval. The War Diary of the 9th Lancashire Fusiliers records the following movements:

> "2nd – 3rd Sept 1916 train from Frevent to Acheux;
> 3rd – 8th Puchevillers;
> 8th – 16th Bouzincourt;
> 17th – 18th Line, Mouquet Farm, Thiepval;
> 19th – 21st Bouzincourt;
> 21st – 22nd Ovillers-la-Boisselle;
> 22nd – 25th Mailly-Maillet;
> 25th Crucifix Corner, Aveluy; trenches, Mouqet Farm, Thiepval;
> 26th Attack, Mouqet Farm, Thiepval;
> 27th – 28th Zollern Trench, Thiepval;
> 29th Ovillers;
> 30th Varennes."

The 9/Lancs. was in the line opposite Mouquet Farm near Thiepval. 24048 Private Watkin Smith was killed in action during the same operation as 446121 Private Anthony Oates.

Private Watkin Smith was killed in action 17 September 1916

It is assumed that he was the victim of the usual violence of warfare – either machine gun fire, sniping or as most probable enemy artillery shelling. Private Watkin Smith is commemorated on the Thiepval Memorial, the Memorial to the Missing of the Somme.

Private WILLIAM EDWIN EARL 1897 – 1916

18/1628 Private William Edwin Earl, 14th Battalion, Durham Light Infantry was killed in action, 27 September 1916 during the Battle of Morval. He has no known grave and he is commemorated on the Thiepval Memorial, France and the Evenwood War Memorial. He was 19 years old, born c.1897, the son of William and Elizabeth Earl. By 1916, his mother lived at Buck Head, Evenwood. He enlisted at Darlington and Walworth was his recorded residence.

The 14th Battalion of the Durham Light Infantry formed part of the 18th Brigade of the 6th Division. The Division remained on the Western Front throughout the war and suffered a total of 53,740 battle casualties.

The Battle of Morval

The Battle of Morval took place in the days following 25 September. Morval is situated to the south of the British Fourth Army's sector to the north of the French 6th Army. The objective was to drive the Germans from their positions in the vicinity of Gueudecourt, Lesboeufs, Morval and Combles. The XIV Corps comprising the Guards, the 5th and 6th Divisions were faced with capturing the fortress villages of Lesboeufs and Morval.

The attack was launched at 12.35pm with the 16th Infantry Brigade on the right and gained the first objective. On the left the 2/DLI and the Essex captured their first objective and the West Yorks. and 2 companies of the 14/DLI captured their final objective. This was one of the most successful battles on the Somme – thanks to good weather and observation, a carefully arranged creeping barrage and a sound preliminary bombardment. The 14/DLI was involved on the evening, 26 September:

> "…the Durhams relieved the Yorkshiremen on the ground that had been won. All 4 companies were put in the front line which ran just east of the ruins of Lesboeufs and here the battalion remained until the early morning of September 29th when the 2nd Sherwood Foresters of the 71st Brigade took over the position. During this period German shell fire never ceased and losses amounted to 13 killed and 2nd Lieut. R.E. Bryant and 29 wounded."

On 29 September, the 14/DLI moved onto Meaulte and the focus of the Somme offensive moved to the north and the Battle of Thiepval. At the Battle of Morval, the tactic of "bite and hold" was successful in this instance due to the effective preliminary bombardment, the "creeping barrage" which provided cover for the infantry and the relatively weak German defences. Thus the British edged forward as the Germans edged back and prepared new lines of defence. During its time in the line, the Division suffered casualties amounting to 277 officers and 6,640 O.R.'s.

Private William E. Earl was killed in action 27 September 1916.

Private William E. Earl is commemorated on the Thiepval Memorial, the Memorial to the Missing of the Somme.

Private FRED HIRST 1893 -1916

30240 Private Fred Hirst, 20th Battalion, Durham Light Infantry died of wounds, 1 October 1916 probably inflicted in action at the Battle of Le Transloy and is buried at Heilly Station Cemetery, Mericourt-L'Abbe, France. He is commemorated on the War Memorial in St. John the Baptist, Hamsteels (Quebec) Parish Church, Co. Durham. He was 23 years old, born c1893 at Evenwood to Allen and Mary Hirst and was brother to William, Harriet, Hiram, Joseph, Robert, Sarah, Allen and Mary. The family lived at Quebec and he enlisted at his local Drill Hall 12 December 1915.

The 20th (Service) Battalion (Wearside) was formed at Sunderland 10 July 1915 and in January 1916 it was attached to the 123rd Brigade, 41st Division. The Division moved to France 6 May 1916 assembling near Steenwerck and getting familiar with trench warfare near Ploegsteert and the Douve Valley south of Ypres, Belgium. It remained there until August 1916 before moving south into the Somme, France. 30240 Private Fred Hirst arrived in France 5 May 1916. The 20/DLI took part in harassing action in the Armentieres sector before moving south to the Somme. The 20/D.L.I. was involved in a large scale raid on the night of 26 July 1916 in the sector north of the river Lys near Armentieres but the action was unsuccessful.

The War Memorial in St. John the Baptist, Hamsteels (Quebec) Parish Church, Co. Durham

"As nearly half the 140 men engaged were killed or wounded by the enemy barrage which broke up the assembly, the raid was doomed to failure."

Private Fred Hirst survived. On 16 August, the 41st Division was relieved handing over their billets to the13/D.L.I. A week later it entrained for the Somme region and carried out battle training at Yaucourt Busses. On 6 September, the 20/D.L.I. commenced their move to the Somme battle front.

Le Transloy

The Somme offensive raged on with battles at Morval and Thiepval and it was clear that fighting on the Somme was fundamentally a battle of the artillery. The roar of the guns was unceasing.

As the campaign moved into autumn, Haig was convinced that German resistance was weakening and he was determined that the offensive would not be abandoned. The plan was simple – to keep attacking culminating in another concerted attack all along the Somme front on 12 October.

In the meantime, on 1 October there was an attack on the villages of Eaucourt l'Abbaye and Le Sars in an attempt to eradicate a salient that bulged into the British lines. Haig wanted to keep hammering on to prevent the Germans reorganising their defences but the weather thwarted plans. That day a near continuous downpour started and it never ceased for 4 days. However, actions at Eaucourt l'Abbaye and Le Sars went ahead but the big show was postponed until 7 October. Regardless of the appalling weather, infantry attacks accompanied by artillery bombardment continued and actions such as those in which the 20/D.L.I. were involved to the east of Eaucourt l'Abbaye and north west of Gueudecourt were common place along the front.

Dawn 1 October found the 20/D.L.I. in the line northwest of Gueudecourt and in the afternoon patrols were pushed out to find the strength of the German trenches – they were in fact held in strength! Posts were dug within 200 yards of the enemy. Heavy shelling and machine gun fire resulted in 30 killed or wounded before the battalion withdrew to Pommiers Redoubt – 9 O.R.'s belonging to the 20/DLI were killed in action 1 October, 4

O.R.'s died of wounds that day including 30240 Private Fred Hirst who received a gun shot wound to the head.

Private Fred Hirst died of wounds on 1 October 1916

Private Fred Hirst is buried at Heilly Station Cemetery, Mericourt-L'Abbe. The 36th Casualty Clearing Station was at Heilly from April 1916 and the cemetery was begun in May 1916.

Peter Hart summarises the October offensive as follows:

> "The miserable month of October had in effect decided the outcome of the Battle of the Somme. The high hopes of a German collapse had dissipated in a quagmire of rain and blood. The threat posed by the British onslaught had been held. And yet the battle still dragged on."

Private JEREMIAH CAMERON LEE 1893-1916

3666 Private Jeremiah Cameron Lee, 6th battalion, Durham Light Infantry, died of wounds 1 October 1916 and is buried at Warlencourt British Cemetery, France and commemorated on Cockfield War Memorial.

He was 23 years old, born c.1893 at Cockfield to John and Elizabeth. In 1901 Elizabeth was a widow and mother to William, Laura, Emma, John, Jeremiah and Minnie. They lived at Main Street, Cockfield. By 1916 Jeremiah was married to Mary Jane and they lived at 13 Jubilee Terrace, Evenwood.

The 1/6th Battalion was formed in Bishop Auckland in August 1914 as part of the Durham Light Infantry Brigade, Northumbrian Division and in May 1915 became the 151st Brigade of the 50th Division. The Division arrived in France in April 1915 and served with distinction on the Western Front throughout the war.

Private JOHN ALFRED WARDLE 1881 – 1916

3914 Private John Alfred Wardle, 1/6/DLI was killed in action 1 October 1916. He has no known grave and is commemorated on the Thiepval Memorial to the Missing of the Somme.

3666 Private Jeremiah Cameron Lee, 6th Battalion, Durham Light Infantry, Medal Roll

He was 35 years old, born at Evenwood about 1881 and was the son of Edward and Mary Wardle. In 1901 he was brother to George, Elizabeth, and William and uncle to Fred and Herbert who lived with them at Blue House, Lands Bank.

John A. Wardle, together with Jeremiah Lee, James Holliday, Robert W. Wallace from Cockfield and Charles Lowther from Butterknowle lost their lives 1 October 1916 during the Battle of Le Transloy. The 6/D.L.I. took the village of Eaucourt L'Abbaye. They died in the same action as Private Oliver Rushford from the nearby hamlet of Wind Mill was awarded the Military Medal and his commanding officer Lieut.-Col. R. B. Bradford the Victoria Cross.

The Battle of Le Transloy

This offensive commenced 1 October 1916 and the village of Eaucourt L'Abbaye was captured:

"The preliminary bombardment commenced at 7.00am and continued till zero hour (3.15pm) when it changed to a barrage. Unfortunately there were some casualties from shells falling short, the total casualties for the day being about 40, including the Commanding

Officer wounded. Lieut.-Col. R. B. Bradford, now commanding the 9th Battalion, asked for and was given permission to take command of the 2 Battalions and for his subsequent work that day was awarded the V. C. He arrived at Battalion H.Q. at zero and at once went up to the front line.

The attack commenced at 3.15pm but partly on account of the failure of the 47th Division on the right and partly owing to the wire not being properly cut, the attackers were held up by machine gun fire and suffered heavy casualties. After considerable fighting with bombs and rifles 3 Lewis gun teams of X Company, under 2nd Lieut. T. Little and 2nd Lieut. C.L. Tyerman and one team of W Company under 2nd Lieut. Barnett succeeded in getting a footing in the first objective. During these operations Lieut.-Col. Bradford arrived on the scene and immediately took charge of the situation and under his direction and leadership the whole of the first objective was gained. A Company of the 9th Battalion then came up and using the new position as a starting point advanced and took the final objective after dark.

About dusk a counter-attack was attempted by the enemy on the front right. Advancing in extended order, about 20 of the enemy were challenged and they all cheered, shouting "Hooray". As they showed no further friendly signs they were fired on and driven off. During the night a further counter attack developed from the valley on the right but this was also repulsed.

The following day, by organised bombing, the whole of the final objective was captured and held and communication trenches were dug back to North Durham Street.

The casualties during the 2 days had been very heavy and included amongst the officers, in addition to those already mentioned 2nd Lieut. Peacock killed and 2nd Lieut. Lean, Capt. Peberdy, Lieut. Cotching, 2nd Lieut. Barnett and 2nd Lieut. Appleby wounded. Amongst the decorations gained were Military Medals awarded to Corporal Dixon and Privates Rushford and Atkinson, all signallers, and Private Turnbull of X Company. Good work was also done by Serjeants Gowland and Winslow.

On the night of the 2nd October Lieut.-Col. Bradford handed over the command of the Battalion to Lieut. Ebsworth, and it was relieved by the 7th Northumberland Fusiliers the night after."

The 6/DLI War Diary for October 1916 (Vol. 19) is brief on detail:

"Somme 1916 Oct.1 At 1am summer time altered back to normal by putting clock back 1 hour, this is to 12 midnight. 2Lieut Yaldwyn (Sniping Officer) attached to Y Company for duty. Commanding Officer saw all Company Commanders at 3am to talk over details of the attack. Completed jumping off trenches about dawn and occupied them in battle order by 6am. 60 men (draft and details) brought up from the Transport Lines to act as Carrying Party for the battalion. Artillery bombardment of German trenches from 7am to 3.15pm. 2Lieut. Yaldwyn wounded about noon. The Commanding Officer Major Wilkinson wounded about 1.30pm. Lt. Colonel Bradford of the 9th Durham L.I. took over command of the Battalion for the period of the operations.

3.15pm Assault delivered. 1st objective gained ?on the left later on the right also. 2nd Lieuts ? Cotching, Barnett & Appleby wounded.

Considerable amount of hostile Machine Gun fire from the right during the attack. German trenches not much damaged by Artillery fire. Block established on the right as troops on the right had not obtained their objective.

1   Company of the Durham L.I. sent up to re-inforce. About midnight 2nd objective was gained by combined assault.

2   German bombing attack on our 2nd line right repulsed in the early morning. Fairly quiet day but wet. During the night of the 2/3rd 6 Durham L.I. and 9 Durham L.I. relieved by 7 Northumberland Fusiliers.

3   Relief completed about 4-30am. Lt. Colonel Bradford ceased to be in command and Lieut. Ebworth assumed command of the battalion. Battalion moved to Starfish Line. At 1pm Battalion moved off bt platoons at 150 paces interval to BECOURT wood where it took up quarters it had previously occupied there

4   Wet morning – spent in packing up. Battalion moved at 11-45am by platoons to HENENCOURT WOOD, arriving about 4pm, having had dinners en route. Good camp. All battalion in tents."

Private Jeremiah Cameron Lee died of wounds and Private John Alfred Wardle was killed in action 1 October 1916.

The War Diary has no summary of casualties for the month of October. There was a total of 65 deaths for the period 1 – 3 October 1916:

- 1 October – 48 O.R.'s killed in action including 3914 Private John Alfred Wardle, 1 died of wounds 3666 Private Jeremiah Cameron Lee
- 2 October – 8 O.R.'s killed in action, 5 died of wounds
- 3 October – 1 O.R. died of wounds

In total 63 O.R. died and there were 2 officers killed in action:

- 1 October – 2/Lt William Little
- 2 October – 2/Lt David Ronald Peacock.

Private J. C. Lee is buried at Warlencourt British Cemetery. Warlencourt village is 5km south west of Bapaume, Pas de Calais, France. The cemetery was made late in 1919 when graves were brought in from 5 small cemeteries and the battlefields of Warlencourt and Le Sars. The cemetery now contains 3,505 Commonwealth burials and commemorations of the First World War. The cemetery holds 121 D.L.I. burials, soldiers who lost their lives in actions of October and November 1916 including:

- 4106 Private J. Holliday 1/6th Battalion, D.L.I., of Cockfield, enlisted Bishop Auckland and also commemorated on Cockfield War Memorial
- 3506 Private Robert William Gray, 1/6th Battalion, D.L.I. of Etherley Dene.

Other local men who died that day were:

- 4463 Lance Corporal Charles Lowther, 1/6th Battalion, D.L.I., of Butterknowle. He has no known grave and is commemorated on the Thiepval Memorial and Butterknowle War Memorial.
- 3974 Private Robert William Wallace, 1/6th Battalion, D.L.I., of Cockfield. He has no known grave and is commemorated on the Thiepval Memorial and Cockfield War Memorial.

It is highly probable that these service men would have been known to each other, coming from such tightly knit communities as they did.

Private ROBERT WILLIAM WILSON 1896-1916

16202 Private Robert William Wilson, 6th battalion, the Yorkshire Regiment died of wounds 3 October 1916 in Hampstead Hospital, England. He is buried in Evenwood Cemetery and commemorated on the Evenwood and Etherley War Memorials. He was 20 years old, born c.1896 at Evenwood to Moses and Elizabeth Wilson and in 1901 was brother to George, Frederick and Moses. At that time the family lived at Alpine Terrace. He enlisted 17 November 1914 at Bishop Auckland.

The 6th (Service) Battalion of the Yorkshire Regiment (Alexandra, Princess of Wales's Own) was formed at Richmond, 25 August 1914 and was attached to 32nd Brigade, 11th (Northern) Division.

The Battles of Flers-Courcelette, Morval & Thiepval Ridge

On 27 September orders were received to support the 34th Brigade in Ration and Sulphur trenches and orders given to attack Stuff Redoubt at 3.00p.m. The attack was postponed but commenced at 4.06p.m. There was continuous fighting until 30 September when the battalion was relieved by the 10th Cheshires. The following extracts are taken from 6th Green Howards Battalion War Diary:

> "27th – 4.6 p.m. – C & D Coys assaulted and took trench 91 – 45 afterwards gaining with WEST YORKSHIRES 45 – 18. WEST YORKSHIRES attacked on our right but failed to gain objective….
>
> 11.20p.m. – D Coy moved up to ZOLLERN & 1 Platoon A. to 91 – 45. Casualties amongst officers 2/Lt. A.H.B. SHIPLEY killed, 2/Lt. A.O. VICK, w 2/Lt. C.E. SOWERBY & Capt. K. HUTCHENCE wounded, 2/Lt. W.A. BOOT & 2/Lt. G.A. RICHARDSON missing.
>
> 28th –12.30a.m. Report received that we had twice got to 87 but could not hold it owing to heavy shell and machine gun fire. At dawn attack made on 38 but failed.

5.a.m. – 1 Coy. 8th WEST RIDING REGT. Sent to ZOLLERN and D. Coy to STUFF REDOUBT. Orders received that an attack would be made at 6.p.m. Task allotted to troops in STUFF REDOUBT was to bomb round enemy flanks. Attack was postponed but message did not get to STUFF REDOUBT. Troops there attacked at 7.42 p.m. and gained 38 & 87 but could not hold it owing to lack of ammunition and bombs…...

30th – Orders were received that attack would be made, object being to occupy whole of HESSIAN TRENCH from 21.d.99 – C.55. This was to be carried out by three bombing parties. First party to 97, second from 13 to 97, the third found from garrison of STUFF REDOUBT to bomb from 5 – 97. This was successfully carried out and captured ground was consolidated. Orders received that Battn. Would be relieved by 10th CHESHIRE REGT.

Total casualties. Officers 4 killed. Capt. N.P. SHEPHERD-TURNEHAM, 2/Lt. A.H.B. SHIPLEY, 2/Lt. H.C. Hurst, 2/Lt. G.F. STOUT. 3 missing. 2/Lt. W.A. BOOT, 2/Lt. G.H. RICHARDSON, 2/Lt. F.A. RUSHWORTH. 8 wounded Capt. K. HUTCHENCE, 2/Lt. H.O. VICK, 2/Lt. C.E. SOWERBT, 2/Lt. G.B. ANDREWS, 2/Lt. N.K. MACLEAN, 2/Lt. J.T. COLBERT, 2/Lt. L.A. GROSS, MAJOR W.B. SHANNON O.R. 381.

C.R. WHITE
Major Commanding 6th Yorkshire Regt."

Private Robert Wilson died of wounds 3 October 1916

The Green Howards Gazette of December 1916 states that Private Wilson was wounded and the edition of January 1917 reports that he had died of wounds.

News of his Death

The Auckland Chronicle, 12 October 1916 reported:

"**Military Funeral** The first funeral of a military character took place at Evenwood on Saturday when the remains of Pte. Robert Wilson were laid to rest. His death took place at Hampstead Hospital from wounds received at one of the battle fronts. He was a son of Mr. Moses Wilson, Ingleton late of Evenwood and the funeral took place from the house of his uncle and aunt Mr. and Mrs. William Hodgson, Chapel St. The cortège was a very large one nearly the whole village turning out to do honour to the fallen hero. Among other floral tributes was a large wreath sent by nurses of the hospital. An impressive service was conducted in the Wesleyan Church by Mr. John Cox who also read the last rites at the graveside."

The Parish Magazine reported his burial, 7 October 1916:

"Robert William Wilson aged 20 yrs., died at the Military Hospital, Hampstead, from wounds received in France."

Private Robert Wilson is buried in Evenwood Cemetery.

16202 Private Robert William Wilson, 6th Batallion, the Yorkshire Regiment commemorative plaque and medals

Private JOHN MAUGHAN 1893-1916

14633 Private John Maughan, 14th battalion, the Durham Light Infantry, died of wounds 16 October 1916, He was 23 years old and is buried at Grove Town Cemetery, Meaulte, France and is commemorated on the Evenwood War Memorial. He was born in 1893 at Evenwood to George and Sarah Maughan and in 1901 was brother to William, Ruth, Moses, George and Aaron. The family then lived at Copeland Farm. By 1915 they lived at 9 Clyde Terrace, Evenwood Gate. He enlisted prior to April 1915 at Bishop Auckland leaving his job as a coal miner.

14633 Private John Maughan, 14th batallion, the Durham Light Infantry

John was joined in His Majesty's Forces by 2 of his older brothers:
- 26/333 Private William Maughan, Northumberland Fusiliers
- 16593 Lance Corporal George Maughan, 3rd Dragoon Guards

And his cousin:
- Maughan Roxborough served with the D.L.I.

The 14/DLI was initially attached to the 64th Brigade, 23rd Division but 25 November 1915 was transferred to the 18th Brigade, 6th Division as part of the XIV Corps, Fourth Army.

Battle of Morval

The battalion moved to the front 7 October. Their bivouacs at Trones Wood came under heavy shell fire on the evening of the 10th – 17 men were killed and wounded. The next day, the battalion moved into assembly positions for the next attack – the objective was to capture Rainbow Trench and Shine Trench then advance to Cloudy Trench with the West Yorks.

The advance began 12 October at 2.05 pm with D Company on the right and C Company on the left. An enemy barrage commenced almost immediately. The advance kept going and Rainbow Trench was taken.

Shine Trench was also captured but the Germans defended the next objective with great resolve.

> "At the sunken road on the left the Fourteenth joined hands with troops of the 12th Division who had come forward on that flank. B Company had lost both officers – Capt. F. Hellier killed and 2nd Lieut. Gillot wounded – but before three o'clock the advance was resumed, bombers clearing the dug-outs in the sunken road. German shell and machine gun fire was still heavy but rifle grenadiers and Lewis gunners boldly handled, helped overcome the enemy resistance."

A and C Companies occupied Rainbow Trench with little loss though 2/Lieut. W.F. Swindell was killed and 2/Lieut. W.F. Dunn was wounded. Lieut. C.A.V. Newsome M.C. left A Company in the hands of his Serjeant-major to command B Company. Shine Trench was won, Lieut. Batty being wounded. D Company on the right was in touch with the West Yorks but could make no further progress due to heavy machine gun fire. A defensive flank was formed under the direction of Lieut. C.A.V. Newsome who was afterwards awarded a bar to his Military Cross. He was wounded the following day, 13 October when the Germans persistently shelled the lost trenches. 14633 Private John Maughan was also wounded 13 October and taken to 2/2 London Casualty Clearing Station.

By dawn, 14 October, the 14/DLI handed over to the 11/Essex and retired to a position south of Gueudecourt. On 15 October, the Brigade attacked again but without success. By the evening, the 14/DLI was only 200 strong and relieved the Essex men in Rainbow and Shine Trenches. Just after midnight Rainbow Trench was heavily bombarded. On 16 October, British gunners were busy but many of their shells fell short hitting Shine Trench. The 14/DLI was relieved that night and moved back to Montauban, where a draft of 185 men of the 2/1st Derbyshire Yeomanry was absorbed.

Private John Maughan died of wounds 16 October 1916

During the October fighting the battalion lost 7 officers and 182 men. Private John Maughan died in hospital 16 October 1916 having received fatal gun shot wounds 3 days before. One other O.R. serving in the 14/DLI died of wounds on the same day – 42792 Private G.A. Wink formerly

25023 Suffolk Regiment. Casualties 12 October 22 men lost, 19 killed in action and 3 died of wounds. The following day a further 6 men died, 5 killed in action and 1 died of wounds and another 2 men on the 15th. Two officers were lost in the same period.

Report of his death

The Parish Magazine (November 1916 edition) reported:

> "I have heard that the war has taken toll of another of our Evenwood lads, John Maughan who has died in hospital after being grievously wounded on the battlefield."

A Memorial Service was held on the Sunday, 5 November 1916. The Auckland Chronicle, 16 November 1916, reported:

> "Pte. J. Maughan D.L.I. son of Mrs. S. Maughan 9 Clyde Terr., Evenwood has died from wounds. Prior to enlistment he was a miner at Randolph Colliery. He was well respected by all in the locality. Mrs. Maughan has also 2 sons on active service."

Private John Maughan is buried at Grove Town Cemetery, Meaulte, south of Albert. In September 1916, the 34th and 2/2nd London Casualty Clearing Stations were established at this point, known to the troops as Grove Town, to deal with casualties from the Somme battlefields. They were moved in April 1917 and, except for a few burials in August and September 1918, the cemetery was closed. Grove Town Cemetery contains 1,395 First World War burials.

Corporal GEORGE THOMAS COX 1888 – 1916

3472 Corporal George Thomas Cox, 1/6th battalion, the Durham Light Infantry was killed in action 5 November, 1916 at the Butte de Warlencourt. He has no known grave and is commemorated on the Thiepval Memorial, France and Evenwood War Memorial. He was 29 years old, born in 1888 at Evenwood to John and Annie Cox and in 1901 was brother of Elizabeth, Florence, Alice, John, Margaret and June. The family lived at the Oaks, Evenwood. He enlisted at Bishop Auckland prior to April 1915.

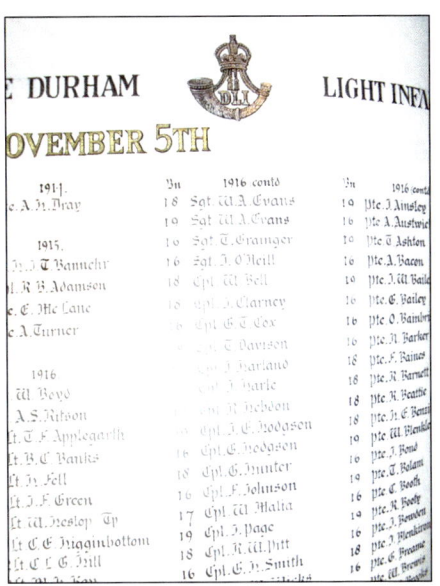

DLI memorial cross in Durham Cathedral and The Roll of Honour

The Butte de Warlencourt

The 1/6th Battalion of the Durham Light Infantry was to see action at the Butte de Warlencourt, an ancient burial mound, located between the towns of Albert and Bapaume in northern France. Bapaume was occupied by German troops. The British front line had advanced from a few miles north east of Albert in the direction of Bapaume to the feature known as the Butte de Warlencourt. The Butte stood about 50 feet higher than the surrounding land and in theory provided a useful observation point for the Germans particularly towards High Wood and Martinpuich. The Butte was honeycombed with tunnels and dugouts which provided shelter for the German garrison. It had already resisted numerous British attacks over the previous month of October. In November 1916, it was the turn of the 151st (Durham) Brigade who moved into line as part of the 50th (Northumbrian) Division.

The 1/9th DLI was charged with capturing the Butte and a quarry beside its west face. The 1/6 and 1/8th DLI were to seize the Gird Trench and Gird Support Trenches. The 28th Australian Division was to attack alongside the 8th battalion. In support, to the right were the 1/4th Northumberland

Fusiliers, to the left, the 1/6th N.Fs. and the 1/5th Border Regiment were in reserve. Zero hour was set for 0910 Sunday 5 November. In the early hours of Sunday morning, the companies moved forward to man the front line trench. The weather was dreadful – heavy rain, a howling gale, it was bitterly cold and there were rumours that men had drowned in the mud. Owing to the boggy ground, progress was extremely slow. The trench was in a deplorable condition and the men had to march along the parados to reach their allocated places. Unfortunately, they were in full view of the enemy – shell, machine gun and rifle fire were thrown at them. The Durhams went over the top – with mud high above their knees, wading, slipping, stumbling and falling forward, laden with the usual infantry equipment necessary for such an attack (rifle, packs, grenades, entrenching tool, pick, Lewis gun drums) – it was worse than they could ever have imagined.

The Germans were not caught by surprise and with such a narrow frontal attack they could concentrate all their machine gun fire on a devastating onslaught on the hapless Durhams. The British artillery failed to eliminate the German batteries. They opened up a barrage of shells all along the sector. They succeeded in isolating the British front line and cut off the assaulting troops from any reserves. The Durhams were isolated and fought the battle on their own. On the right the 1/8th was badly hit by a combination of both German shell fire and British shells dropping short. They were even hit from behind by their own long range machine gun barrage that was meant to be supporting them! Many men had difficulty getting out of the trench and needed assistance from their mates – all under heavy fire. Despite this, the left of the line managed to get within 30 yards of the Butte before they were overwhelmed. The few survivors fell back in disarray to their original front line.

Meanwhile, the 1/6th Durhams were dying one by one as they found themselves marooned between the lines. The wounded were left scattered around No Man's Land, marooned in shell holes and slowly sinking down. Many who were too weak to save themselves must have slowly drowned.

Corporal George T. Cox was killed in action 5 November 1916.

Report of his Death

The Auckland Chronicle dated 17 December 1917 reported:

> "News has reached Mrs. Cox, 8 Oaks Bank, Evenwood that her son Cpl. G. T. Cox who was reported missing on the 5th November 1916 is supposed to have died on that date."

Corporal George T. Cox is commemorated on the Thiepval Memorial, the Memorial to the Missing.

The following casualties have been estimated:
- The 1/6th D.L.I – 11 officers killed, wounded or missing; 34 other ranks dead; 114 wounded and 111 missing.
- The 1/8th D.L.I – 9 officers killed, wounded or missing; 38 other ranks dead; 100 wounded and 83 missing.
- The 1/9th D.L.I – 17 officers killed, wounded or missing; 30 other ranks dead; 250 wounded and 111 missing.
- The 151st Machine Gun Company – 3 dead; 20 wounded and 8 missing.

With almost 1000 casualties, misery was brought to many Durham homes. There are 10 officers and 264 other ranks of the above DLI Battalions with 5 November 1916 recorded as their date of death. Other local men serving with the 6/DLI to lose their lives that day were:
- 1672 Private Alfred Brown, born Evenwood, enlisted at Staindrop.
- 3429 Private Fred Brunskill of High Etherley, enlisted Bishop Auckland
- 2211 Corporal Ralph Hebdon, born Barnard Castle, enlisted Bishop Auckland
- 2264 Corporal George Henry Smith, born Barnard Castle, enlisted Bishop Auckland.
- 3124 Private Robert Wilson of West Auckland, enlisted Bishop Auckland.

Private ALFRED BROWN 1894 -1916

1672 Private Alfred Brown, 1/6th battalion, the Durham Light Infantry was killed in action 5 November 1916 at the Butte de Warlencourt. He is buried at Warlencourt British Cemetery, France and is commemorated on St. Mary's Church War Memorial, Staindrop. He was 22 years old, born c.1894 at Evenwood to James and Annie Brown and in 1901 was brother to Joseph and George. At that time the family lived at Morley. He enlisted at Staindrop.

Private Albert Brown was killed in action 5 November 1916

DLI memorial cross in St. Andrew's Church, Bishop Auckland

Warlencourt is a village about 5km south west of Bapaume, Somme, France. The cemetery was made late in 1919 when graves were brought in from 5 small cemeteries and the battlefields of Warlencourt and Le Sars. The cemetery now contains 3,505 Commonwealth burials and commemorations of the First World War. There are 1,682 identified graves and 1,823 unidentified burials and special memorials for those known or believed to be, buried in the cemetery.

Private JOHN JOSEPH OATES 1865 – 1916

40797 Private John J. Oates, 18th Battalion, the West Yorkshire Regiment died of wounds 24 November 1916 at the Battle of Ancre. He is buried at Etaples Military Cemetery, France and is commemorated on the War Memorial in Normanton, West Yorkshire. John Oates served in the Kings Royal Rifles (service number 28982) prior to the 18th West Yorkshire

Regiment. He was 41 years of age, born c.1865 at Evenwood to Edward and Sarah Oates. By 1916 was married to Lily and lived at 48 Castleford Road, Normanton in the West Riding of Yorkshire.

The 18th (Service) Battalion, (2nd Bradford), the West Riding Regiment was commonly known as the Second Bradford Pals and was formed in February 1915. It was attached to the 93rd Brigade of the 31st Division.

The Battle of Ancre 13 – 19 November 1916

The 31st Division of the XIII Corps was required to cover the left flank of the V Corps near the village of Serre. Its task was to provide a defensive flank to cover the advance of the 3rd Division.

The 92nd and 93rd Brigades were in the line and the 13th and 12th East Yorkshires actually did rather well, capturing the German front line and establishing a strong post in the old mine crater. The failure of the 3rd Division left them hopelessly isolated and the German counter-attacks pounded away at their positions. Enemy shells rained down on No Man's Land and cut them off from all support. There was no hope of maintaining the isolated salient and that night the Yorkshiremen ended the day back in the British front line.

As night fell, 13 November the situation was mixed. The V Corps were ordered to move forward again on a front stretching between Beaucourt and the Ten Tree Alley Trench, which ran across Redan Ridge about 500 yards south of the village of Serre. The situation lay in the balance as the British reorganised for the next push and the German reserves moved forward to bolster their line. The 190th Brigade of the Royal Naval Division was ordered to attack Beaucourt at 0745 – it fell at 1030pm that day.

War Memorial, Normanton, West Yorkshire

Gough wanted to resume the attack on the 15th but Haig intervened then after consultation ordered a further attack 18 November. This proved to be the last attack of the Battle of the Somme. The 31st Division was not involved. The II Corps (18th, 19th and the 4th Canadian Division) and the V Corps (32nd and 37th Divisions) took the offensive to the Germans but the attack represented "the epitome of suffering."

Private John Joseph Oates died of wounds 24 November 1916

It is assumed that he died of wounds received during the action of 12 November. Private John Joseph Oates is buried at Etaples Military Cemetery.

Private THOMAS HENRY DUNN 1893 – 1916

36618 Private Thomas Henry Dunn, 11th battalion, the Durham Light Infantry died of wounds 26 December 1916 whilst serving in the Guillemont area. He is buried at St. Sever Cemetery Extension, Rouen, France and commemorated on the Evenwood War Memorial. He was 24 years old, born in 1893 at Evenwood to William and Hannah Dunn and in 1901 was brother to Christopher, Bella, William, Arthur, Albert, James, Frederick and Nelson. At that time they lived at Chapel Street but by 1916 lived at 4 Randolph Terrace.

36618 Private Thomas Henry Dunn, 11th Battalion, the Durham Light Infantry

Three of his brothers were also on active service:

- M12236, Arthur James Dunn, HMS Birkenhead
- Frederick Dunn, Durham Light Infantry (awarded the Military Medal)
- 40500 L/Cpl. Nelson Dunn, 1st Bn., Worcester Regt.

The 11th (Service) Battalion (Pioneers) D.L.I. was attached to the 61st Brigade, 20th (Light) Division and became known as the Pioneer Battalion to the 20th Division from 6 January 1915.

Thomas Henry Dunn worked as a coal miner, a reserved occupation. It was not until 1916 when conscription came into force that he was one of many needed to reinforce the DLI battalions following heavy losses on the Somme. He joined up 28 February 1916 and Private Thomas Henry Dunn entered France 11 October 1916 finally being posted to the 11/DLI. His will stated:

> "In the event of My Death I give the whole of my property & effects to my Mother Mrs Hannah Dunn 4 Randolph Terrace Evenwood near Bishop Auckland County Durham.
>
> Thomas Henry Dunn
>
> 3rd Durham Light Infantry"(note: 3/DLI not 11/DLI)

At the opening of the Battle of the Somme, 1 July 1916, the 11/DLI was still in Flanders working in the Ypres salient behind Wieltje. The battalion entrained to Doullen, France 25 July and next day marched to Couin relieving the 38th Division in the Colincamps-Hebuterne sector. The 11/DLI was employed repairing the support trenches following the havoc of the opening days of the battle and building deep dug-outs whilst also manning the support trenches. Then 20 August, the 11/DLI moved to the Candes-Murlancourt sector in the Somme area and 18 October, the battalion moved to the Citadel at Carnoy. By 1 November it was at Saleux. Thomas wrote a letter dated 4 November to his brother and sister when billeted at Bourdon on the river Somme enjoying a little comfort and relaxation. The letter is reproduced below:

> *"Dear brother & sister Nov 4th*
> *I am writing to tell you that I am in the pink and hope you are both the same. I am sorry that I have not been able to get hold of anything for the bairns yet but I will look out for something for them without fail. I am at a very pleasant place here within sound of the big guns but I can still sleep alright. I was sorry that our Nelson & Matty could not get with us. I'm enclosing a photograph which you can give to mother. It is of a pal of mine from Etherley. You can send a few Woodbines if you like. We cannot get them here, that is the only*

drawback here. I think that this is all at present, promising to write again soon. I will close with best love & hoping to see you all again soon. From your young brother Tommy

Pte. T. H. Dunn 36618
6th Platoon B. Company
11th D.L.I. (Pioneers)
20TH Division
B.E.F. France"

The battalion then moved to Picquigny and Corbie before marching onto the Citadel in heavy rain. It was noted that:

> "The camp was deep in mud and there was little protection from the weather nor were better quarters found when the battalion moved to Montauban…Then parties were provided to carry up rations, water and trench boards to the line and the cellars of Ginchy, Lesboeufs and Morval were explored and cleared. Two main communication trenches called Ozone and Flank Avenue were put in hand…The trench became a drain and the Pioneers spent much of their time pulling out infantrymen and helping the stretcher bearers, whose task was indescribably difficult. One of the wounded died after being 32 hours on the way from the front trenches to the Lesboeufs-Morval road.
>
> On December 20th, when the division were relieved, the Pioneers remained at work. The extensions of a light railway for the gunners, well beyond Guillemont, entailed the removal of piles of German dead. Weather conditions were as awful as they could be.
>
> All ranks were becoming thoroughly tired out and unfit and the climax was reached on December 29th when heavy rain flooded the camp at Montauban. As a result of the medical officer's representation the 11th were moved back to Ville next day."

The conditions were clearly miserable and the battalion worked under constant threat from enemy snipers and artillery barrages. Whilst the exact circumstances leading to the death of Private T.H. Dunn remain unknown, his Medical Report states that on 12 December he was hit in the thigh by gun shot. He was taken for treatment at one of the military hospitals in Rouen. He succumbed to his wounds 2 weeks later.

Private Thomas Henry Dunn died of wounds 26 December 1916.

Private Thomas H. Dunn is buried at St. Sever Cemetery Extension, Rouen. During the First World War, Commonwealth camps and hospitals were stationed on the southern outskirts of Rouen. Almost all of the hospitals at Rouen remained there for practically the whole of the war. They included 8 general, 5 stationary, 1 British Red Cross and 1 labour hospital and No. 2 Convalescent Depot. The great majority of the dead from these hospitals were buried at the city cemetery of St. Sever but in September 1916, it was necessary to build an extension. There are 8,346 Commonwealth burials from the First World War.

News of his Death

The Parish Magazine of December 1916 reported:

> "News has just reached us of the death from wounds, in France, of Pte. Tom Dunn, D.L.I., son of Mr. and Mrs. Dunn of Randolph Terrace. Our deepest sympathies are with his family and relatives at this sad hour."

On Sunday 14 January 1917, a Memorial Service took place at St. Paul's Church, Evenwood.

THE EVENWOOD ZEPPELIN RAID & OBERLEUTNANT ZUR SEE WERNER PETERSON

Werner Peterson was in command of the naval airship L16 when Evenwood was bombed 5 April 1916. He was killed about 6 months later 24 September 1916, when shot down over Essex whilst commanding the airship L32. He is buried in Cannock Chase German Military Cemetery, Staffordshire.

Oberleutnant zur See Werner Peterson

From December 1914 onwards, Zeppelins crossed the North Sea to hit targets in northern England. For instance 15 June 1915 Wallsend marine engineering works, Cookson's antimony works and Pachin's chemical works at Willington Quay, Palmer's engine construction department at Jarrow and collieries in the vicinity of South Shields were bombed causing damage and many casualties and to the south of the region, 8 September 1915 Skinningrove iron works in North Yorkshire was hit.

The official history states that such attacks caused considerable disruption to industrial output and interrupted vital war work as trains were stopped and blast furnaces were dowsed. During 1916, 13 weeks of Zeppelin alarms caused a loss of 390,000 tons of pig iron which represented about 1/6th of total annual output. Such raids forced the diversion of considerable resources to the defence of the country and possibly as important, there was a detrimental effect on public morale. This situation was not overlooked by Evenwood's vicar, Rev. G.J. Collis and he commented:

> "The Zeppelin peril it seems is with us. Not only here, where we are not so very far from the coast but even in towns right in the centre of the country the strictest lighting precautions are being taken. Heavy fines are being imposed upon those who by carelessness

or any cause expose themselves and their neighbours to danger by exhibiting too much artificial light. The Zeppelins, being so far purely night raiders, are dependent upon such lights for their guidance in their cowardly attacks….This dastardly unseen foe of the night which from the safe distance up above the clouds seeks to murder men, women and children in their beds is something we English people hardly ever thought possible in civilised races…And then we read of the German people praising and applauding these things and also the almost equally cowardly work of the submarines which torpedo passenger ships and leave their occupants to drown; when we think of the spies and agents who while they receive the hospitality and friendship of our communities are all the while plotting in darkness to destroy us. "

On the night of 5 & 6 April 1916, the war came to communities of south west Durham when there was indiscriminate bombing of Evenwood and Eldon Lane by the German Zeppelin L16.

5 & 6 April 1916: The Raid on Evenwood and Eldon Lane

On Wednesday, 5 April 1916, the naval airship L16 under the command of Oberleutnant zur See Werner Peterson left its base at Nordholz in North West Germany heading for northern England.

The crew of the naval airship L16

The mission was a night attack on Leeds. Peterson intended to cross the English coast over Scarborough then cruise westwards to bomb Leeds. At about 23.30, the L16 actually crossed the English coast to the north of Hartlepool and headed inland towards the coal mining area around Bishop Auckland. Probably deceived by the fiery glow of the many pit heaps and smoke from the numerous coke works and collieries, believing that he was over Leeds, at about midnight 23 bombs were dropped over targets below. It is stated that 15 miners cottages were wrecked, another 70 damaged in the Evenwood area and Ramshaw School also suffered damage. Casualties were light, only one man and a child were injured.

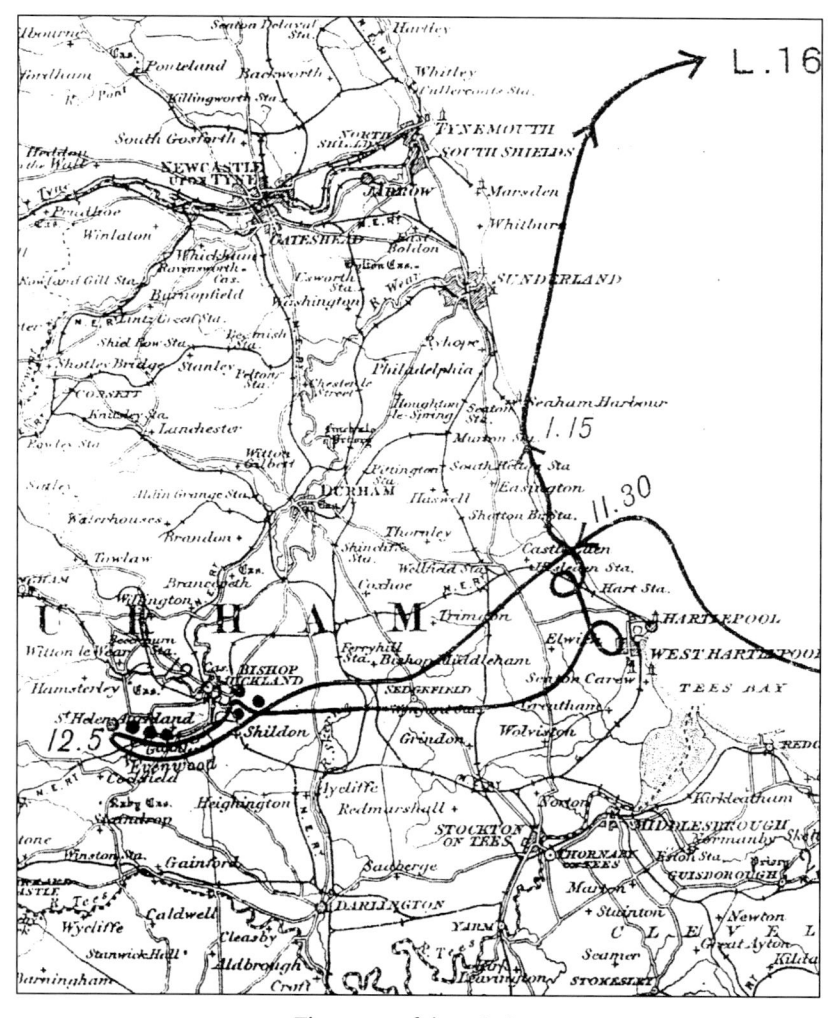

The route of the mission

The L16 turned for home dropping another 27 bombs on the Gurney Valley area, to the east of Bishop Auckland where there was another concentration of collieries and coke works at Auckland Park and Eldon. Eldon Lane School, buildings in Gibson Street at Close House, the Co-op, the Friends' Meeting House and several other houses were damaged. Tragically, one child was killed when a house in Close House was hit by an incendiary bomb.

The airship then headed for the coast, flew north eastwards over Seaham Harbour at about 01.15 and escaped the attention of 5 defence sorties. Aircraft were despatched from Cramlington, Beverley and Scarborough but failed to spot the L16. One R.F.C. pilot Captain J. Nichol crashed his plane into a house and was killed outright. The Commonwealth War Graves Commission confirms that Captain John Nichol of the Royal Flying Corps (secondary regiment 1st Battalion, Royal Scots Fusiliers) aged 22 was killed 5 April 1916. He was the son of Dr. F.E. and A. L. Nichol, of 1 Ethelbert Crescent, Margate, Kent. He is buried in Margate Cemetery alongside his brother Edward who also died on active service.

Destroyers from the Tyne and the Humber also drew a blank in their search for the zeppelin.

Back in Evenwood and Ramshaw, it is reported that many children spent the night in the open air in the fields and most were absent from school the following day. Local tales inform us that many spent subsequent nights sheltering in "Snecker's Drift", a small coal drift located in the pit field just to the southwest of the road bridge over the river Gaunless. This drift fed into Norwood Colliery. Ramshaw School was closed for 2 weeks for repair works but when it opened not all the windows had been replaced and the weather was extremely cold – only 50% of the roll was present. Rev. G.J. Collis wrote:

> "This last has indeed been an eventful month and one which many of us will long remember. One has to be very careful what one puts in print about Zeppelin raids but at least we all know the locality of one of these ruffianly monsters which visited the North Eastern County region on the night of the 5th and the early morning of 6th ult. We know all about it, where it went and what it did. One little boy killed in bed by an incendiary bomb was the sole satisfaction that these

miserable night warriors achieved as the result of at least 40 attempts upon a purely civilian population, mostly in bed at the time. It is true that they did a certain amount of material damage but not much considering the immense power of the explosives used. One would hardly think it possible that such a rain of destruction could do so little harm. Great gaping holes in the land, broken windows, roofs partially unslated, doors and in some case furniture damaged was really a small price to pay as the result of such a visitation…But the prevailing feeling is one of thankfulness."

There were no reports in the local press. The national press was heavily censored but on 6 April "The Times" reported:

"Immediately the dirigible appeared over the town the searchlights had no difficulty in locating it and anti-aircraft guns were speedily in action. Heavy fire was directed on the Zeppelin and the aim appeared to be very good on the part of the gunners."

The town was unnamed. On Friday, 7 April, The War Office statement appeared in "The Times" and this confirmed the attack of 3 Zeppelins – the first dropped 5 bombs and there were no casualties, the second dropped no bombs and the third dropped several bombs causing only slight material damage. 24 explosive bombs and 24 incendiary bombs had been dropped causing injury to 2 men, 1 woman and 5 children. One child had been killed. On 8 April "The Times" reported that the inquest on the child had been held in the village inn and:

"The verdict was returned that the child was killed by an incendiary bomb dropped from an enemy aircraft."

The official German communiqué appeared in "The Times" on the Saturday via Reuters Agency and stated:

"Naval Airships on the night of April 5 destroyed large ironworks near Whitby and extensive buildings with blast furnaces after previously pelting with explosive bombs and placing out of action a battery north of Hull.

Furthermore, factories at Leeds and the environs and a number of railway stations in the industrial district were attacked. Very good effects were observed. The airships were heavily bombarded. All landed undamaged."

The L16 was wrecked when landing at Nordholz 19 October 1917. It made a total of 132 flights of which 16 were raids. Many of the flights were under the command of Oberleutnant zur See Werner Peterson.

AIRSHIP DEVELOPMENT

As the war progressed, the both German Navy and Army built their own airship fleets. The navy airships were usually made of aluminium by the Zeppelin Company and the army used the wooden Shutte-Lanz or "SL" airships. By 1916, there were 2 generations of German airship employed in combat and both forces operated bombing missions over England.

THE LATE SUMMER OFFENSIVE OF 1916

In the summer of 1916, the new L30 class airships were delivered to the German Navy. The Leader of Airships, Peter Strasser orchestrated an all out offensive against England for late summer. Ineffective raids took place on the 31 July, 2, 18 & 24 August but the mission of 2 September was the largest zeppelin raid of the war. London was the target. The raiding fleet consisted of 16 airships, 12 naval (L11, L13, L14, L16, L17, L21, L22, L23, L24, L30, L32 & SL8) and 4 army (LZ90, LZ97, LZ98 & SL11). SL11 was attacked by 2 aircraft and shot down and the crew was afforded a discrete military funeral since such attacks on civilian populations were roundly condemned by the press and public feeling ran high.

23 September 1916: Oberleutnant zur See Werner Peterson took part in another attack when he commanded the L32 on a raid over southern England. The L32 circled over the River Thames, possibly with engine trouble. He was cruising with L31. The cloud cover above the Thames broke and the L32 was spotted immediately by searchlights from London's eastern defences and attacked by anti-aircraft fire. Peterson dropped his payload near Purfleet, Essex and turned towards the sea heading for home and trying to gain altitude. R.F.C. First Lieutenant Frederick Sowery, aged 23, flying his British built BE2c4112 biplane was on routine night patrol and sometime after 1.00am intercepted L32. He fired 2 drums of Brock-Pomeroy ammunition (note elsewhere quoted as "firing three drums of

incendiary ammunition into the body of the airship.") L32 soon caught fire and with her hydrogen blowing off like a blow torch, she dropped slowly to the ground near Snail's Hall Farm, South Green, Great Burstead near Billericay, killing all 22 crew on board.

Officers from the Naval Intelligence Division were first to the scene and despite the heat, filtered through the wreckage. They were rewarded with a copy of the German Navy Cipher Book which Peterson must have taken on board against regulations. Its capture was a boon to Royal Navy code breakers.

One witness described how in the night sky he saw a pink glare which turned to coppery red, then a ball of flame emerged which changed its shape to a perpendicular cylindrical mass of flame. By 3 o'clock that night, not only had the local people rushed to see the wreckage but cars full of Londoners started to arrive to view the wreckage of twisted and broken aluminium struts. Access to the area was limited by a narrow country lane and by 8 o'clock it was reported that the lane was blocked with "motor cars, motor-cycles, bicycles, traps, tradesmen's carts, and pedestrians, all jammed together". By far the most popular transport was bicycles with hundreds laid abandoned on the fields. Souvenir hunting was prevented by a cordon of soldiers armed with fixed bayonets, and police, but this did not deter the souvenir hunters who scoured nearby potato fields looking for debris. Even lemonade sellers set up their stalls in an attempt to profit on the spectacle. First Lieutenant F. Sowrey was later awarded the DSO. A few days later Oberleutnant zur See Werner Peterson and his crew were buried at Great Burstead Churchyard.

The next raid took place 1 October – L31 was commanded by Heinrich Mathy who made an audacious attack on Portsmouth but on his return his vessel was hit by gunfire from an aeroplane flown by Second Lieutenant W.J. Tempest. The zeppelin came down at Potter's Bar, killing all crew members. In total 11 airships took part in this raid but only 2 managed an attack. The loss of 3 ships, L31, L32 and L33 was a serious blow and 2 experienced officers including their L3O class leader Heinrich Mathy. Captain Alois Bocker had been captured. Captain Ganzel was dismissed – his nerves were wrecked. Many crew members were dead or captured. This had a major debilitating effect on German morale.

Back in Evenwood, Rev. G.J. Collis remained vigilant, offering advice to his parishioners:

> "The lighting regulations are now so strict and it is almost impossible to prevent a considerable amount of illumination escaping from our windows…we do not desire to give the Zeppelins more assistance than we need if they should unfortunately happen to find their way into our neighbourhood…neither do we wish to be fined by the public authorities for infringing their necessary precautions."

And then:

> "We are all patriots now-a-days I trust. Let it be seen that we do not mean to be inconvenienced more than need be by the Zeppelin menace. We shall be glad to resume the old conditions when the time comes."

Then in January 1917, he wrote, gleefully!

> "Verily we are living in historic times! Of things which have recently passed perhaps the most exciting to us here was the burning Zeppelin which fell off our coast plainly seen by very many of us on the night of the 4th ult. That was a wonderful night and the story of it will be told and retold and listened to with interest for very many years to come."

There is no record of a Zeppelin raid on Hartlepool for that date. However, a week earlier 28 November 1916, the German airship L34 was intercepted and destroyed by British pilot 2/Lt. Ian Pyott in his BE2c2738 off the coast of Hartlepool. Pyott was so close that his face was scorched. This must be the incident to which Rev. Collis referred.

In 1916, there were 23 airship raids in which 125 tons of ordnance were dropped killing 293 people and injuring 691. Anti-aircraft defences were becoming tougher and new zeppelins were introduced which increased their operating altitude from 1,800m to 3,750m (6,000 ft. to 12,375 ft.) Throughout 1916 anti-aircraft equipment improved and strategies were developed to combat the threat from the airships. In view of the mounting losses, Germany turned to other technologies particularly the development of the Gotha, a large plane specifically designed for bombing to replace the airships. The naval airship division was slowly relegated to the status of reconnaissance arm of the fleet. The threat of the zeppelin was over. The Leader of Airships, Peter Strasser continued his push for their use throughout the war but he was killed 5 August 1918 while leading the last zeppelin raid. A total of 84 Zeppelins were built during the war. Over 60 were lost, roughly evenly divided between accident and enemy action. 51 raids were undertaken in which 5,806 bombs were dropped, killing 557 people and injuring 1,358. It has been argued that the raids were effective far beyond material damage in diverting 12 fighter squadrons and over 10,000 personnel to air defences and hampering wartime production.

CANNOCK CHASE GERMAN MILITARY CEMETERY

The German Military Cemetery was established in 1959 and contains 2,143 war dead from the Great War including the crews of 4 zeppelins shot down over England. Their remains were brought from their original burial places at Potters Bar, Great Burstead and Therberton. Oberleutnant zur See Werner Peterson and the crew of L32 are laid to rest here.

Cannock Chase cemetery plaque

CHAPTER SIX

1917

The fourth year of the war saw the German High Command re-introduce the policy of unrestricted submarine warfare which proved a disastrous decision in the long term since it brought about America's entry into the war which ultimately, contributed to Germany's defeat. America declared war on Germany in April 1917.

In late February, German forces pulled back to the Siegfried-Stellung, a defensive line using every lesson learnt in the previous 2 years of warfare. This was known to the British as the "Hindenburg Line".

In April, the British attacked Arras with the Canadians capturing Vimy Ridge and then the French launched an offensive on the Chemin des Dames which ended in failure and wholesale mutiny of the French forces.

Britain led the campaign against Germany and between July and November launched a major offensive in Belgium along the Ypres Salient at Messines then Passchendaele. This proved to be another costly affair.

Finally in November, Britain attacked at Cambrai.

Internal turmoil and revolution in Russia resulted in a peace pact with Germany

January 10	Allies state peace objectives in response to US President Woodrow Wilson's December 1916 peace note
January 31	Germany announces unrestricted submarine warfare
February 1	Germany resumes unrestricted submarine warfare
February 3	US severs diplomatic ties with Germany
February 23 – April 5	German forces begin withdrawal to strong positions on the Hindenburg Line
February 24	Zimmermann Telegram is passed to the US by Britain, detailing alleged German proposal of an alliance with Mexico against the US
February 26	US President Woodrow Wilson requests permission from Congress to arm US merchantmen
March 1	Zimmermann Telegram published in US press
March 11	British capture Baghdad
March 12	US President Woodrow Wilson announces arming of US merchantmen by executive order after failing to win approval from Congress
March 15	Tsar Nicholas II abdicates as a consequence of Russian Revolution
March 20	US President Woodrow Wilson's war cabinet votes unanimously in favour of declaring war on Germany
April 2	US President Woodrow Wilson delivers war address to Congress
April 6	US declares war on Germany
April 9-20	Nivelle Offensive (Second Battle of Aisne, Third Battle of Champagne) ends in French failure
April 9	Canadian success at the Battle of Vimy Ridge
April 16	Lenin arrives in Russia
April 29 – May 20	Mutiny breaks out among French army
May 12 – October 24	10th, 11th and 12th Battles of Isonzo fought, ending in Italian failure
May 28	Pershing leaves New York for France

June 7	British explode 19 large mines under the Messines Ridge
June 15	US Espionage Act passed
June 26	First US troops arrive in France, 1st Division
June 27	Greece enters the war on the side of the Allies
July 2	Pershing makes first request for army of 1,000,000 men
July 6	T.E. Lawrence and the Arabs capture Aquaba
July 11	Pershing revises army request figures upwards to 3,000,000
July 16	Third Battles of Ypres (Passchendaele) begins
July 31	Major British offensive launched at Ypres.
September 1	Germany takes the northernmost end of the Russian front in the Riga offensive
October 24	Austria-Germany breakthrough at Caporetto on Italian front
November 7	Bolshevik Revolution in Russia results in Communist government under Lenin taking office
November 20	British launch surprise tank attack at Cambrai
December 7	US declares war on Austria-Hungary
December 9	Jerusalem falls to Britain
December 22	Russia opens separate peace negotiations with Germany (Brest-Litovsk)

The men of Evenwood saw action in all the major theatres of warfare and the death toll increased. 1917 saw 20 men with Evenwood connections lose their lives, all on the "Western Front". The Evenwood War Memorial commemorates 13 casualties. Those researched are:
- Private Wallace Featherstone
- Private John Walling
- Private Joseph Million
- Lance Corporal John W. Arkless
- Private John H. Pinkney
- Private James Heseltine

Western Front 1917
Courtesy of Thiepval Project Charity Fund

- Bugler Ralph Wardle
- Pioneer Sidney R. Rutter
- Private Ernest Robinson
- Private William Heaviside
- Corporal William R. Storey
- Sapper Herbert Wardle
- Private Edgar E.J. Cooke
- Lance Corporal John J. Walton
- Private Walter Dinsdale
- Serjrant Gordon Priestley
- Rifleman Mathew T. Raine
- Corporal George Parmley
- Serjeant James W. Spence
- Private George W. Bryant

The Battle of Arras saw 3 men with connections to Evenwood die – J.H. Pinkney, R. Wardle and E. Robinson. The tragic episode, the Third Battle of Ypres more commonly known as Passchendaele took another 7 lives – H. Wardle M.M., E.J. Cooke, J.J. Walton, W. Dinsdale, M.T. Raine, G. Parmley and G. Priestley. The action at Cambrai accounted for J.W. Spence and G. W. Bryant.

Private WALLACE FEATHERSTONE c1883 – 1917

18/65 Private Wallace Featherstone, 18th battalion, Durham Light Infantry was killed in action 1 March 1917* whist serving in the Hebuterne sector. He is buried at Gommercourt British Cemetery No. 2, Hebuterne, France and commemorated on both the Etherley War Memorial and the Evenwood W.M.C. Memorial. He was about 34 years old, born c.1883 to Wallace and Margaret Featherstone and in 1901 was one of 8 children.

By the time of Wallace's death, his mother was a widow and lived at Cox House Farm, Windmill near Morley. His older brother Jonathan is believed to have contracted typhoid fever and died in hospital in France whilst on active service. He also is commemorated on Etherley War Memorial.

18/65 Private Wallace Featherstone, 18th Batallion, Durham Light Infantry

Wallace Featherstone enlisted at Darlington but his date of attestation is unknown. The 18/DLI was attached to the 93rd Brigade of the 31st Division. The battalion was stationed at Hartlepool from October 1914 and was the first DLI battalion to come under fire when Hartlepool was bombarded by

---

* The Commonwealth War Graves Commission provides 1 February 1917 as the date of death for Private Wallace Featherstone but this does not appear to be correct. Both the "Soldiers Died in the Great War" CD and "Durham Pals – 18th, 19th & 22nd Battalions of the Durham Light Infantry in the Great War" by John Sheen provide a date of 1 March 1917. The account of the battalion movements and action suggests that the later date is correct. It therefore seems reasonable to assume that Private Wallace Featherstone lost his life during the action of 1 – 4 March 1917.

a German squadron of warships, Derfflinger, Von Der Tann and Blucher 16 December 1914 when the battalion lost 5 men killed and 11 were wounded.

The battalion was the only DLI battalion to see service in the Middle East. In December 1915, it left Liverpool aboard SS EMPRESS OF BRITAIN bound for Egypt. The Medal Roll confirms that 18/65 Private Wallace Featherstone entered Egypt 22 December 1915. After 3 months guarding the Suez Canal, on 5 March 1916, the 18/DLI embarked upon SS IVERNIA and headed for Marseilles, France. By 30 March, the 18/DLI was in the trenches north-west of Beaumont Hammel in the region of the Somme, north-west France.

Trench Warfare

On 26 February 1917, the 18/DLI took over from the 7/Loyal Regt. of the 19th Division. The German artillery pounded the British lines and No Man' Land. On 27 February, the area was occupied then handed over to the 4/Leicesters. By 7.30 the whole MOTLKE GRABEN was occupied from CRUCIFIX CORNER to GOMMECOURT CEMETERY.

> "The battalion now commenced attacking the FIRST GRADE STELLUNG, B Company sent a platoon up the ROM GRABEN on the left but a strong German bombing party assisted by 2 machine guns strenuously resisted all attempts by the Durhams to force their way into the main positions. Two enemy communication trenches on the right were practically obliterated and 2 platoons that tried to use them got lost in the darkness. The battalion kept trying all night and most of 1st March to enter the enemy position but that afternoon a patrol from D Company reported that FIRST GARDE STELLUNG was strongly held by many Germans armed with several machine guns. It wasn't until 0200 hours on the 3rd March when 18/West Yorks got into ROSSIGNOL WOOD that the Durhams were able to make progress."

The action continued throughout 3 – 4 March when the battalion was relieved by the 12/York & Lancaster Regiment. The 18/DLI made their way to Rossignol Farm for a well earned rest. The battalion's losses were:

"Casualties amounted to 15 killed, 28 wounded and 3 missing. The battalion received the congratulations of the First Army commander and the Distinguished Service Order was conferred upon 2nd Lieut. H.E. Hitchen M.M., 2nd Lieut. J.B. Bradford received the Military Cross and the Military Medal was awarded to Lance-Corpls T. Rigg, H.W. Lawler, Laskey, Hutchinson and Fraser and to Pte. Vocknock."

Private Wallace Featherstone was killed in action 1 March 1917

Private W. Featherstone is buried at Gommecourt British Cemetery No. 2, Hebuterne. The cemetery contains 1,357 First World War burials and commemorations of which 675 are identified casualties and 682 are unidentified. The 18/DLI incurred the following casualties:

- 1 March 1917 – 7 O.R,'s killed in action including Private Wallace Featherstone
- 2 March 1917 – 1 O.R. died of wounds
- 3 March 1917 – 5 O.R.'s killed in action, 1 O.R. died of wounds

Private JOHN WALLING 1890 – 1917

250188 Private John Walling, 1/6th battalion, the Durham Light Infantry died of wounds on 8 March 1917. He is buried at St. Sever cemetery extension, Rouen, France and is commemorated on the Evenwood War Memorial. He was 27 years old, born 15 June 1889 at Evenwood to William and Sarah Walling and in 1901 was brother to William, Isabella, Margaret, Thomas, Frances and Robert. John married Isabelle 29 January 1910 and they lived at the Oaks, Evenwood with their son Edgar.

John Walling was one of the first from Evenwood to enlist and it is probable that he saw action during the infamous attack on the Butte de Warlencourt when Corporal George T. Cox and Private Alfred Brown lost their lives.

On New Year's Day 1917, the 1/6 DLI was in the line near Flers. It was relieved by the 1st Australian Division on 24 January. The Division then moved south into a sector hitherto held by the French, south of Peronne. The Battalion was in the village of Foucaucourt as Divisional Reserve. The village was "nothing but ruins". The Battalion moved up the line to relieve the 5/Yorkshires.

250188 Private John Walling, 1/6th Battalion, the Durham Light Infantry. Family bible

"Following on the methods adopted by the French the relief took place through very long communication trenches running from Estrees through Berny to the line in front of Misery. These trenches as a result of the thaw were everywhere knee deep in mud and usually waist deep and men arrived in the line without boots and in a few cases without trousers, having lost them in the mud. The experiences of X Company were perhaps the worst. Leaving camp at about 5pm then 130 strong they were met by guides who lost their way and eventually arrived in the front line at dawn having lost over 10 men stuck in the mud. The relief was not reported complete til 4pm the next day. The front line trenches were worse if possible than the communication trenches and the days that followed were most unpleasant. There was very little cover from enemy snipers who were pretty active and there were several casualties from fishtail trench mortars. One night was marked by a very intense strafe for a short time with rifle grenades and trench mortars. It afterwards appeared that this was the enemy's parting shot for soon after the Division was relieved the enemy's extensive retirement on this sector took place. After 2 tours in the front line, one in support in trenches round Berny and one in reserve at Foucacourt, the Battalion was relieved early in March by the 2/5th South Staffordshire Regiment (59th Division) who had just come from Ireland and had not previously seen any fighting in France. On relief the Battalion returned to Foucaucourt."

Private John Walling died of wounds 8 March 1917.

The circumstances of his death remain unknown but it is assumed that he received wounds while on duty in the front line – possibly as a result of sniper activity, rifle grenades or trench mortar shelling.

Report of his Death

The April edition of the Parish Magazine reported:

> "Lastly, I have to record the death on active service of 2 more of our local young men viz. Pte. J. Walling whose people live at Oaks House and Pte. J. Million of South View. The former died of wounds and the latter from pneumonia contracted in the trenches."

Private John Walling is buried at St. Sever Cemetery Extension, Rouen – the same cemetery as Private Thomas Dunn.

Private JOSEPH MILLION 1891-1917

36621 Private Joseph Million, 18th Battalion, Durham Light Infantry died of pneumonia 17 March 1917 and is buried in Varennes Military Cemetery, France and is commemorated on Evenwood War Memorial. He was 27 years old, born c.1891 at Evenwood to Richard and Mary Million. He married Ellen Mary (nee Smurthwaite) in January 1917, they had a son Harold and lived at South View, Evenwood however it is understood that during the war she lived at the "Wheatsheaf Inn" Staindrop. Joseph Million served in the 18/D.L.I. otherwise known as the "Durham Pals". 18/65 Private Wallace Featherstone is another from the Parish to lose his life whilst serving with this battalion.

Reports from October and March clearly indicate the miserable conditions the troops had to endure. Illness in the trenches was rife and flu laid low many soldiers:

> "The misery of the men was compounded by the inevitable outbreaks of flu, respiratory infections, gas gangrene – caused by bacteria from the faecal matter in the soil – dysentery and trench foot, though some welcomed even that horrific condition, often accompanied by the loss of several toes, as a way out of the nightmare of mud and earth."

36621 Private Joseph Million landed in France 20 February 1917 and joined the 18/DLI 11 March. Within 25 days of landing in France, he had contracted pneumonia and died. Notes from his medical history indicate that Joseph Million was admitted to hospital with breathlessness and right sided chest pain. He was also found to have bronchial breathing. These are classical signs of a lung infection. Unfortunately, due to the lack of antibiotics he succumbed to the infection. It appears from the report that shortly after admission he became cyanosed (turned blue due to lack of oxygen from lung failure) and died shortly after. Clearly the infection must have been quite severe and advanced for this to have happened. A poor immune system due to malnourishment would have contributed to this sad demise. The report gives a time of death as 10.30am but it is not clear how long he had been in hospital. It also states that the infection is as a result of exposure. However, the last words of the report cannot be deciphered. It is clear that he suffered a comparatively short but intensely uncomfortable time at the front.

Private J. Million died of pneumonia 17 March 1917.

36621 Private Joseph Million, 18th Battalion, Durham Light Infantry. Field Service report form

Report of his Death

The Parish Magazine reported:

> "Lastly, I have to record the death on active service of 2 more of our local young men viz. Pte. J. Walling whose people live at Oaks House and Pte. J. Million of South View. The former died of wounds and the latter from pneumonia contracted in the trenches."

Private J. Million is buried at Varennes Military Cemetery. Varennes is a village located between Albert and Amiens. The cemetery was laid out by the 39th Casualty Clearing Station in August 1916 following the Battle of the Somme. It was then used by the 4th, 11th and 47th Casualty Clearing Stations. There are 1,219 burials.

The personal effects of 36621 Private Joseph Million, 18/DLI were forwarded to his wife Ellen who was living at the "Wheatsheaf Inn" at Staindrop in July 1917. They consisted of:

> "Correspondence, photos, religious cross and book, pair of gloves, bracelets, metal cigarette case, locket and chain, razor in case, gold ring, metal watch, 2 keys, belt, knife, 2 discs."

A pension was awarded to Ellen for herself and one child to take effect from 15 October 1917. The commemorative plaque and scroll was forwarded to Mrs. Million some time later. By September 1919, Ellen Mary had remarried, now called Mrs. Jepson and lived at Mill Wynd, Staindrop.

The GERMAN RETREAT to the HINDENBURG LINE
14 March – 5 April 1917

The devastating nature of the British offensive of the Battle of the Somme caused a serious re-assessment by the German High Command. British offensive operations continued through the winter, notably actions on the Ancre. The German army created a formidable new line some miles to the rear and they executed a withdrawal to it in March 1917. The German withdrawal was pursued and the British encountered a veritable fortress – known to the Allies as the Hindenburg Line and the Germans, the Seigfried Line.

Lance Corporal JOHN WILLIAM ARKLESS 1898 -1917

24/784 Lance Corporal John William Arkless 2/5th Battalion, the Lincolnshire Regiment was killed in action 11 April 1917 as the Germans retreated to the Hindenburg Line. He has no known grave and is commemorated on the Thiepval Memorial, France and Evenwood War Memorial. He was 19 years old, born c.1898 at Evenwood to Benjamin and Hannah Arkless and in 1901 was brother to Henry, Margaret, Thomas, George and Mabel. At that time the family lived at 8 Bowes Hill.

24/784 Lance Corporal John William Arkless 2/5th Batallion, the Lincolnshire Regiment. John William with his mother and sister Mabel (left)

The 2/5th Lincolns was formed at Grimsby in February 1915 and in July 1915 it was attached to the 177th Brigade of the 59th Division. The Division was stationed in Ireland and involved in actions against the Republican Uprising of Easter 1916 and returned to England in January 1917. In February 1917 it landed in France and spent the remainder of the war on the Western Front.

The 2/5 Lincoln Regt. War Diary confirms that it was stationed at Roisel from 6 April 1917 preparing for an attack on German positions. The battalion marched to Templeux 9 April and took over new positions along the east side of Hargicourt towards Malakoff Farm. However the German trench was only 2 ft. deep and heavy enemy fire from a position known as the Quarry made it impossible to hold. A new position was established and this too was heavily shelled during the night. Noon 10 April, an attempt to bomb down the German trench to Malakoff Farm was frustrated by enemy machine gun fire from Cologne Farm and the Quarry. At 6.00pm information was received that the 7/Worcesters to the left "would advance its posts to the Sunken Cross Roads in F29b, which was strongly held by the enemy." Orders were received at the same time:

"to take any advantage of their advance and to push our posts forward, to bomb down the enemy trench from HARIGOURT to MALAKOFF FARM and to capture the QUARRY and L.5d and COLOGNE FARM en route."

On the ground, it was decided that no attempt would be made on Malakoff Farm until both the Quarry and Cologne Farm were in British hands. Following liaison with 7/Worcesters arrangements were made with 295th Brigade Royal Field Artillery for artillery support. At 11.00pm, information was received that the Germans were reported to be returning to the Hindenburg Line. At 3.00 am 11 April, patrols reported that the Quarry and ground in the vicinity of Cologne Farm was clear of the enemy. The artillery support was cancelled and orders for the attack were issued. The War Diary continues:

"HARGICOURT 11.4.17
3.00am. A heavy engagement ensued as these places were found to be strongly held. An account of the battle is found in Appendix XIII.
4.30am. The attacking troops returned to the original line held.
Casualties.
Officer killed. Capt. T. Bryant
Officers wounded. Lieut. J.S. Simons
................................Lieut. J.H. Shrewsbury
Officer wounded & captured. Lieut. R.W. Alston
Officer wounded & missing. Lieut. J.W. Walker
Other ranks Killed, wounded and missing 254
8.30pm. Inter company reliefs. A Coy by D Coy. C Coy by B Coy. A & C Coys. Suffered most casualties in the attack and were formed into a composite company in reserve.
9.00pm. Situation unchanged. Our lines were continuously shelled by the enemy by Field Artillery and also by 15cm. Howitzers. We suffered a few casualties. 1 man, 5 wounded. Attempts to establish a post at L.5.c.5.1. were met by heavy m.g. and rifle fire. A German post at L.5.a.9.5. was found to be strongly wired and held."

Lance Corporal John W. Arkless was killed in action 11 April 1917.

Losses on 11 April were heavy and it is evident that the report received at 11.00pm on 10 April 1917 informing "that the Germans were reported to be retiring on the Hindenburg Line" was clearly wrong and the decision to cancel the artillery support was a gross error. The battle continued into the 12 April with the German snipers causing great problems – Lieut. F. Wright was killed and 4 OR's were wounded while on patrol. 2/4 Leicesters were to the right and 7/Worcesters to the left. By 8.00am on 13 April, sniping posts were established in Hargicourt and enemy activity was "considerably reduced." At 8.00am. 14 April, the situation was unchanged, the British lines and HQ were shelled intermittently. By 8.30pm. A & C Companies were relieved by B Company. D Company being stronger arranged its own reliefs within the company. By 16 April, the situation was still unchanged with the Quarry and Cologne Farm being held by the Germans. The Germans were clearly putting up stout resistance as they organised their retreat to the Hindenburg Line. On 11 April 1917 the following casualties were suffered by the 5/Lincs – 3 Officers and 60 O.R.'s were killed in action.

Reports of "Missing"

The Auckland Chronicle dated 17 May 1917 reported:

> "Mrs. Arkless, Gordon Bank, has received intimation that her son Pte. John Wm. Arkless is missing. Pte. Arkless was a son of the late Mr. Ben Arkless and before joining the colours was employed in the grocery department of Evenwood branch of the Bishop Auckland Co-operative Stores."

Notification of his Death

The Parish Magazine, over a year later, August 1918 reported:

> "Then there are Ptes. Arkless, D.L.I and W.R. Storey, (nephew of our good friend and sidesman Mr. J. Brass) both of them once reported missing, now officially notified as dead."

Lance Corporal John William Arkless is commemorated on the Thiepval Memorial, the Memorial to the Missing of the Somme.

The BATTLE OF ARRAS 9 April – 16 June 1917: an overview

The new French Commander in Chief, Robert Nivelle prepared a Master Plan for a new offensive against the German lines:

> "He would attack at the shoulders of the great German salient on either side of the Somme. The French would take the southern Aisne sector, the Chemin des Dames, as their front of assault, while the British, by inter-Allied agreement would reopen an offensive on the northern shoulder of the Somme salient, at Arras and against Vimy Ridge."

The objective of the British and Canadian Corps was to capture Vimy Ridge which would lead the way into the Douai Plain and (it was hoped) the un-entrenched German rear. Then a rapid advance by the cavalry would link up with the French forces which would have broken through at Chemin des Dames, 80 miles to the south.

The British Army launched a large scale attack at Arras. Although initially successful, it soon bogged down and became another costly affair. The battle was composed of the following phases:

- 9 -14 April 1917 – The Battle of Vimy, The First Battle of the Scarpe
- 23 – 24 April 1917 – The Second Battle of the Scarpe
- 3 -4 May 1917 – The Third Battle of the Scarpe
- 11 April – 16 June 1917 – Flanking Operations around Bullecourt.

The infantry was able to shelter in the great subterranean quarries at Arras and they were brought to the front line through tunnels dug by the Army's tunnelling companies. Similar tunnels had been dug at Vimy Ridge for the Canadian troops. Such preparation did not arouse suspicion amongst the Germans and von Falkenhausen, commander of the Sixth Army kept his Reserves 15 miles behind the front.

The German defences were bombarded by 2,879 guns, one for every 9 yards of the front, which delivered 2,687,000 shells – shorter in duration but double the weight of that delivered before the Battle of the Somme the previous July.

The first day of the battle 9 April 1917, was a triumph for the Allied forces. In a few hours the German front had been penetrated to a depth of between 1 and 3 miles, 9,000 prisoners were taken, few casualties suffered and a way forward was (apparently) cleared. The success of the Canadians at Vimy Ridge was sensational! But the usual inflexibility in the plan prevented further progress – a pause of 2 hours after objectives had been gained, the day was shortening and the impetus ran out allowing the Germans to bring up their reserves 10 and 11 April.

The April weather was atrocious – rain, sleet, snow, low temperatures and the shelling had turned the chalky surface into gluey mud. The attacking troops were exhausted, a halt was called to allow casualties to be replaced and the troops to recover – losses totalled nearly 20,000 (1/3rd of casualties suffered at the first day of the Somme).

23 April – hostilities recommenced, the Germans had reorganised and were reinforced so could counter-attack and as a result, a month of attrition set in bringing a further 130,000 casualties for no additional gain of ground.

On the southern front, whilst the Germans were caught by surprise on the Vimy-Arras sector, they were not on the French sector, Chemin-des-Dames. Security failures had alerted the Germans to the proposed attack so their forces were prepared. After 5 days of intensive fighting when the French suffered 130,000 casualties including 29,000 killed, the offensive was effectively abandoned. There had been a penetration of 4 miles over the 16 mile front but German defences remained intact. There had been no breakthrough.

The aftermath of the Nivelle's offensive had major repercussions on the French army. The offensive was judged to be a failure and on 29 April 1917, Nivelle was replaced by Petain. In addition, the failure punctured the French fighting spirit and precipitated what historians called "the mutinies of 1917."

Private JOHN HENRY PINKNEY 1897 – 1917

202546 Private George Henry Pinkney, 1/6th Battalion, the Durham Light Infantry was killed in action 14 April 1917 at the Battle of Arras. He has no known grave. He is commemorated on the Arras Memorial and on the Stanley (Crook) War Memorial.

He was 20 years old, born c.1897 at Evenwood to J.G. and Mary Pinkney and by 1917 the family lived at 8 Chapel Row, Stanley, Crook. He may actually have been born at Esh near Durham.

9 -14 April 1917: The Battle of Vimy, The First Battle of the Scarpe

The following account describes in more detail the involvement of the 6/DLI and the action of 14 April:

> "At 1 am on the 14th April the men moved to the assembly position in the dry bed of the Cojeul River with the 8th Battalion in support and the 5th Border Regiment in reserve, the 9th Battalion being already in a line just south of Guemappe. The original orders had now been considerably altered and zero hour arrived before fresh orders had been circulated to the companies. The result was that at 4.30am after moving in file from the assembly position to a bank some 200 yards in front, the Battalion advanced under a barrage in 4 waves of companies W being front Z in rear, with no orders except a rough indication of the direction.
>
> As they advanced they were met by very heavy machine gun fire from the front and from Guemappe in their left rear. W and X companies reached the ridge 500 yards from the starting point and passing down the other side were not seen again during the day. Y and Z companies also reached the ridge but could get no further. Later they were joined by the 8th Battalion which was also held up.
>
> The fighting then died down but apart from one brief message from X company no trace could be found of the 2 front companies and the casualties in the remaining 2 were very heavy. To add to the confusion, the 56th Division on the right had lost direction and men of the London Regiment were everywhere mixed with those of the 50th Division.
>
> At dusk orders were received that the line on the ridge would be taken over by the London Rifle Brigade. A soon as the light permitted search was made for W and X companies. Eventually the remnants consisting of 4 officers and about 20 men were discovered. Having reached a small system of trenches they had organised their defence

and successfully beaten off determined attempts to surround them. About 80 men were finally assembled after the relief and more joined the Battalion during the next few days but the casualties amounted to over 200 or more than 50% of the total fighting strength. The officers killed were Capt. Brock, Lieut. Richardson and 2/Lieuts. Greene, Payne and Newton whilst many were wounded Capts. R.S. Johnson and H. Walton, commanding W and X companies were subsequently awarded the Military Cross and Corporal Betts the D.C.M. and Croix de Guerre.

After burying as many bodies as could be recovered the remnants of the Battalion moved back to dug-outs in the Hindenburg Line on Telegraph Hill which were reached after a roundabout march at dawn."

Private John Henry Pinkney was killed in action 14 April 1917.

On 14 April, the 6/DLI incurred the following casualties. 4 Officers were killed in action – Capt. A.L. Brock, 2/Lt. H. Greener, 2/Lt. J.W. Payne and Lt. W.H. Richardson and 51 O.R.'s. Between 15 – 21 April, a further 5 O.R.'s died of wounds.

Private John Henry Pinkney is commemorated on the Arras Memorial which

The Arras Memorial

202546 Private George Henry Pinkney, 1/6th Batallion, the Durham Light Infantry was killed in action on 14 April 1917

39208 Private Ernest Robinson, 7th Batallion, the Yorkshire Regiment, was killed in action 13 May 1917

stands in the Faubourg-d'Amiens Cemetery in Arras. It commemorates 35,000 servicemen from Britain, South Africa and New Zealand who died in the Arras sector between spring 1916 and August 1918 who have no known grave. It was unveiled in 1932.

Private JAMES HESELTINE 1892 – 1917

31149 Private James Heseltine, 2nd Battalion, York and Lancaster Regiment, was killed in action 22 April 1917. He is buried at St. Patrick's Cemetery, Loos, France and is commemorated on the Evenwood War Memorial. He was 25 years old, born c1892 at Evenwood to Frank and Elizabeth Heseltine and in 1901 was brother to Robert, Benjamin and Sarah. The family lived in the Sloat, Evenwood. James was married to Amy (Griffiths) and lived in the Oaks, Evenwood.

James Heseltine enlisted 3 March 1915 into the DLI (service no. 3487) and was promoted to Lance Corporal 30 October 1915 and posted abroad with the 1/6 DLI on 7 July 1916. On 3 September 1916, L/Corporal James Heseltine was transferred to the 4th Battalion, York and Lancaster then 6 September 1916 joined the 2/Y&Lancs. This battalion was part of the 16th Brigade, 6th Division which landed in France in September 1914 and reinforced the hard pressed British Expeditionary Force on the Aisne before the whole army moved north to Flanders. It remained on the Western Front throughout the war and in September 1916, saw action at Flers, nearing the end of the Battle of the Somme. Private James Heseltine was admitted to hospital 5 October 1916 with boils which was then diagnosed as eczema and returned to England for treatment. On 15 January 1917, Private James Heseltine was back in France with the 2/Y&Lancs.

31149 Private James Heseltine, 2nd Batallion, York and Lancaster Regiment

The Loos Salient

Over the winter of 1916 into the spring of 1917, the 6th Division occupied positions at the La Bassee sector and on the Loos Salient. The month of March and the first weeks of April 1917 were notable for raids and counter-raids, considerable artillery and trench mortar activity which:

> "gave place to more or less continuous fighting consequent on the withdrawal of the enemy opposite the right of the Division after the successful attack by the Canadians at Vimy."

The 6th Division details are:

> "April 12th – 2nd York and Lancasters raid (2 officers and 80 other ranks under Capt. Hardy) – got into enemy trenches and killed 16 Germans.
> 13th – Enemy withdrew from Railway Triangle closely followed by 2nd York and Lancasters, who entered enemy dug-outs before candles had burnt out. 24th Division on our right also advancing line. System of bombardment followed by pauses during which patrols went out and occupied what they could.
> 14th – enemy small raid on 1st West Yorks. – driven off.
> 15th – a certain amount of ground gained in the face of increasing opposition – Buffs and York and Lancasters advanced a bit."

It is clear that from the 13 April 1917, the Division pressurised the enemy during its withdrawal and the attacks continued:

> "By this time continuous fighting, under very trying weather conditions had exhausted the 16th Infantry Brigade.... During 10 days the Division had been engaged in continuous fighting on the front of one brigade, whilst holding with the other two a front of approximately 7,000 yards. Four battalions from other brigades, in addition to its own four, had passed through the hands of the 16th Infantry Brigade which was conducting the fighting. Battalions relieved from the fighting front one night were put straight into the line elsewhere on the following night and battalions which had already done a long continuous tour in the trenches were relieved one night, put into the fighting front on the following night and 24 hours later had to deliver an attack. The enemy concerned about the fate of Hill 70, concentrated a very formidable artillery on the

narrow front involved and bombardments and barrages on the front of attack were of exceptional severity."

Private James Heseltine killed in action 22 April 1917

On 22 April 1917, 20 men of the 2/Y&L were killed in action. There are 6 men of the Y&L Regiment buried with Private James Heseltine at St. Patrick's cemetery, Loos with the same date of death and 4 other burials for 19 April 1917. It is possible that they were all victims of German shelling or possibly they were killed as the British attacked the retreating German positions the previous week. The 2/Y&L are known to have been involved in the fighting at that time. The Battalion war diary has not been examined but Appendix 1 of the Divisional History states that there were 4,884 casualties between 2 March – 25 July 1917 at Loos as a result of "Raids and attacks, Hill 70."

News of his Death

The Auckland Chronicle reported:

"The latest victims claimed by the war are Pte. Ralph Wardle, son of Mr. & Mrs. Ralph Wardle, Evenwood Gate killed and Pte. James Heseltine, son of Mrs. Heseltine and the late Frank Heseltine, Sloat, killed. Both prior to their enlistment were workmen at Randolph Colliery."

The Parish Magazine reported:

"Two more of our boys have fallen in action recently – Ralph Wardle of Evenwood Gate and James Heseltine, whose parents live at the Centre, Evenwood. Both of them fell, I understand in France."

Private James Heseltine is buried at St. Patrick's Cemetery, Loos. This cemetery was begun during the Battle of Loos and then used in 1916 and closed in June 1918 but then a small number of graves were brought in from the battlefields between Loos and Hulloch. There are 595 burials.

Private RALPH WARDLE 1895-1917

14526 Private Ralph Wardle, 14th Battalion, the Durham Light Infantry died of wounds 24 April 1917 at the Battle of Arras. He is buried at Bethune Town Cemetery, France and commemorated on the Evenwood War Memorial. He was 22 years old, born c.1895 at Evenwood to Ralph and Elizabeth Wardle and in 1901 was brother to Elias and Jane. In 1917 the family lived at 8 Evenwood Gate.

14526 Private Ralph Wardle, 14th Battalion, the Durham Light Infantry

The Battle of Arras – 14/DLI

The 14/DLI saw action between 20 – 23 April to the southeast of Loos when they were ordered to take Novel Alley and Nero Trench. On 20 April, the battalion went into the line south east of Loos on the extreme left of the battle line at the northern limit of the Canadian advance of the opening day, occupying Netley Trench. On 21 April the battalion was ordered to complete the capture of Novel Alley and take Nero Trench and the concrete strong point where previously 3 attacks had failed. In the afternoon, British heavy artillery pounded the German positions. B and C Companies were detailed to attack. The objective was captured and 2 counter attacks repulsed. The 14/DLI suffered heavily from enemy shell fire both before and after the fighting to capture these trenches. At 8 am, 22 April, following an artillery barrage, A and D Companies advanced to take Nash Alley and the redoubt called the Dynamite Magazine. A squad of bombers from B Company bombed up the trench and the objectives were taken. A counter attack was repulsed about 9am. The 14/DLI proceeded with the task of consolidating the captured positions. There was little cover from sniper and machine gun fire from houses at Cite St. Laurent. During the afternoon, 2 counter attacks were driven back. The Germans put down a heavy artillery barrage then attacked on the left of the 14/DLI. The troops in this part of Nash Alley were driven back as the German infantry assailed the left and bombed the barricades on the right.

> "The 14th though very weak in numbers maintained the struggle for some time but had to give ground at last. Fighting hard they fell back slowly to Novel Alley leaving only 3 badly wounded men in the hands of the enemy."

In the morning, 23 April, the 14/DLI was relieved and withdrew to les Brebis.

> "Losses in the ranks amounted to 231 and among the killed was 2nd Lieut. L.W. Mansell…Many honours fell to the battalion."

Private Ralph Wardle died of wounds 24 April 1917.

Private Ralph Wardle is buried at Bethune Town Cemetery. Bethune is 22 miles north of Arras in the region of Pas-de-Calais, France. The town was comparatively free from bombardment and remained an important railway and hospital centre, as well as corps and divisional headquarters. The 33rd Casualty Clearing Station was in the town until December 1917. The Bethune Town Cemetery contains 3,004 Commonwealth burials of the First World War.

Pioneer SIDNEY ROE RUTTER 1895-1917

131500 Pioneer Sidney Roe Rutter, "Z" Special Company, Royal Engineers was killed in action 6 May 1917 whilst engaged in special operations near Bullecourt. He is buried at Beaulencourt British Cemetery, Ligny-Thilloy, France and commemorated on the Evenwood War Memorial. He was 22 years old, born c.1895 at Evenwood to Thomas and Sarah Rutter who in 1901 lived in Alpine Terrace with his brother Samuel and his sister Beatrice. By 1917, his parents lived at Allendale House, 15 Shirley Terrace, Evenwood.

Pioneer Sidney Rutter was engaged in special operations which involved loading gas and/or chemical canisters into shells destined for enemy lines. The following is an extract from the Company's War Diary:

> "1 May 1917
> Strength 18 officers, 259 O.R.'s, 42 Infantry.
> Move gas towards Hindenburg Line (for 6th Brigade, 2nd Division ANZAC Corps.)

Corps in front of Norceuil, Lt. Yarwood wounded, O.R.'s gassed.

For the 1st Australian Division wire cutting in Hindenburg Line, some bombs filled with ammonal.

Brigadier White BGGS, 1st ANZAC Corps expressed appreciation of excellent bombing.

Preparations were made for attack on Bullecourt with H.E. Bombs.

6 May 1917

Preparations made for attack on Bullecourt with H.E. Bombs.

At Biefville les Bapaume a concentration of waggons, some had unloaded but others had not at 250 yards from the crest of a ridge from which projectors were to be fired. A chance shell struck a waggon containing propellant charges which exploded. Heavy casualties occurred immediately enemy artillery concentrated on the area. There were 88 casualties. Z Company lost 14 killed including Lt. Oakes and 7 were wounded.

10 May 1917

Lt. General Birdwood Corps Commander ANZAC Corps called on Z Company and expressed his sympathy about heavy casualties among Z and P Companies of the Special Brigade."

Pioneer Sidney Roe Rutter was killed in action 6 May 1917.

Report of the Death

The Parish Magazine reported:

"In regard to personal items of the month, I ought to have mentioned in my July letter that we have had another loss in the person of Sidney Rutter, whose parents live in Shirley Terrace. I regret the omission but did not know of it when I wrote last month. I am told on all hands that this is a lad whose good influence and general excellence will be much missed in the place.

Sidney R. Rutter is buried at Beaulencourt British Cemetery, Liny-Thilloy. The village is located south of Bapaume and about 20 kilometres south of Arras in the region of Pas-de-Calais, France. The cemetery contains over 700 casualties from the 1914-18 war including 427 identified casualties.

131500 Pioneer Sidney Roe Rutter, "Z" Special Company, Royal Engineers Medal Roll

There are 49 deaths for 6 May 1917:
- 20 – Royal Engineers "P" Company,
- 14 – Royal Engineers "Z" Company,
- 8 – Royal Engineers "G" Company,
- 4 – Royal Field Artillery, 58th Division Ammunition Company,
- 1 – Royal Field Artillery, 59th Division Ammunition Company and
- 2 – 4th Battalion Special Company.

Private ERNEST ROBINSON 1895 – 1917

39208 Private Ernest Robinson, 7th battalion, the Yorkshire Regiment, was killed in action 13 May 1917 at the Battle of Arras. He is commemorated on the Arras Memorial, France and on Shildon War Memorial. He was 22 years old, born 1895 at Evenwood to John and Mary Ada Robinson. By 1901 the family lived at 9 Back Garbutt's Buildings, Shildon with his 5 sisters and younger brother Herbert – all of whom were born at Evenwood as was his mother. By 1917, John and Mary, his parents lived at the Club House, Front Street, Shildon.

The 7th (Service) Battalion, Yorkshire Regiment (Green Howards) was formed in September 1914 at Richmond and attached to the 50th Brigade of the 17th (Northern Division). The Division landed in France in July 1915 and initially held the front line in the southern area of the Ypres Salient. It was involved in the first phase of the Battle of the Somme 1916 and then the Battle of Arras 1917.

The service record of 39208 Private Ernest Robinson has not been researched but since he was not awarded the 1914 or 1914-15 Star it is evident that he did not enter France until after 31 December 1915.

The Battle of Arras – 7/Green Howards

At 6.30 am, 12 May, the 4th and 17th Divisions joined an attack along the whole front. The objective of the 17th was to advance to Cupid, Curly and Cash Trenches then onto Charlie Trench. The 50th Brigade operated on the right with 7th Green Howards on the right and the 7th East Yorks. on the left.

> "The attacking companies went forward under a very effective shrapnel barrage in two waves of two companies each "B" Company on the right of the first wave and "A" on the right of the second, each wave being composed of two lines. "A" and "D" Companies detailed a mopping up party, consisting of one officer and 30 men from each, to clear Crook Trench which ran roughly at right angles to their objective. Dust and smoke from the barrage made observation impossible once the attack was launched.
>
> At 7.30am a message was received from Lieut. H.A. Wilkinson that Capt. R.W.S. Croft, "C" Company had been killed and that all objectives had been gained with the exception of the junction of Curly, Cupid and Crook Trenches and that the troops were consolidating the position. Touch was maintained with the 1st Battalion Rifle Brigade on the right but the left had been unable to gain their objective. Further attempts were made to secure this trench junction but by dusk it was unoccupied by either side."

At 10.30pm, 2/Lieut. Fox led a bombing attack and established a block in Curly Trench, north of the junction and, after encountering very heavy opposition eventually succeeded in occupying the junction.

On the 13 May:

> "Incessant fighting continued all next day in the neighbourhood of the "stop" in Curly Trench. The battalion held its own however and was ably assisted by the Stokes mortar battery firing from Crook Trench. At 10.00pm an attempt was made to push forward northwards in Curly Trench in conjunction with an above ground attack by the 7th East Yorks. Regt. This attack failed but Lieut. H.A. Wilkinson seconded 2/Lieut. E.V. Fox by dint of hard fighting made their way yard by yard to 100 yards beyond the "stop". This success was only temporary and the enemy forced us to yield ground eventually leaving us with a net gain of only a quarter of that distance. Wilkinson and Fox were severely wounded and only 3 officers were left with the companies after this operation. The men in the front line were becoming very exhausted and there was a shortage of drinking water."

At 4.00 am, 14 May, the remnants of "A" Company withdrew to the Fampoux-Gavrelle line and were relieved by the Dorsets. The 3 remaining companies stayed with the Dorsets to which they were temporarily attached being heavily shelled. In the early hours, 15 May, "B", "C" & "D" Companies were relieved by a company of the 7th Lincolns of the 51st Brigade. The Battalion had gone into the trenches on 9 May with 18 offices and 436 O.R.'s and came out on 15 May with 5 officers and 228 OR's. Casualties:

- Killed – 4 officers and 23 OR's
- Wounded – 9 officers and 130 non commissioned officers and men
- Missing – 42 men
- Total Casualties – 208

Private E. Robinson has no known grave therefore it is assumed that he was initially recorded as one of the 42 missing men. Between 9 – 20 October 1917, 4 officers and 64 O.R.'s died, of which 1 officer and 26 O.R.'s were killed in action 13 May 1917.

Private Ernest Robinson was killed in action 13 May 1917

Private Ernest Robinson is commemorated on the Arras Memorial.

It was in this action that a V.C. was gained – 242697 Private T. Dresser of "B" Company. On 27 June 1917, the London Gazette reported:

"For most conspicuous bravery and devotion to duty.

Private Dresser, in spite of being twice wounded on the way and suffering great pain, succeeded in conveying an important message from Battalion Headquarters to the front line of the trenches which he eventually reached in an exhausted condition. His fearlessness and determination to deliver this message at any cost proved of the greatest value to his Battalion at a critical period."

Private WILLIAM HEAVISIDE 1886-1917

33027 Private William Heaviside, 2nd Batallion, Durham Light Infantry

33027 Private William Heaviside, 2nd Battalion, Durham Light Infantry was killed in action, 7 June 1917 and is buried at Philosophe British Cemetery, Mazingarbe, France and commemorated on the Roll of Honour, Memorial Hall, West Auckland. He was 31 years old, born c.1886 at Evenwood to Ralph and Hannah Heaviside, brother to Richard, Ralph, George, John, Mary Ann, Hannah, Sarah Jane and Pheobe. He was married to Edith Ellen, lived at 2 Millbank, West Auckland and they had 4 children, Annie Mabel, Wilson, John and Harold.

Ralph and Hannah Heaviside lost a son, William aged 31 years and a grandson, Ralph aged 18 years in the Great War. Both are commemorated on family headstones in Evenwood cemetery.

The 2nd Battalion was part of the 18th Brigade, 6th Division. On the 10 September 1914, the Division landed at St. Nazaire and proceeded to reinforce the BEF on the Aisne before the whole army was moved north to Flanders. Although William Heaviside attested on 9 December 1915, he did not enter France until 11 October 1916, joining the 2/DLI on 26 October 1916.

An account of the 6th Division

Over the winter of 1916 into the spring of 1917, the 6th Division occupied positions at the La Bassee sector and on the Loos Salient. The month of March and the first portion of April 1917 were notable for raids and counter-raids, considerable artillery and trench mortar activity which:

> "gave place to more or less continuous fighting consequent on the withdrawal of the enemy opposite the right of the Division after the successful attack by the Canadians at Vimy."

The Diary at Appendix III informs:

> "June 1st – 1st K.S.L.I. (3 offcers and 130 other ranks under Capt. E. Spink MC) raided enemy near Hendon Alley – 16 Germans killed and machine gun entrenchments blown in.
> 4th – Two officers and 40m other ranks of 1st K.S.L.I. raided same trenches and got in but no prisoners taken.
> 6th – Small raid 2nd D.L.I. (2 officers and 50 other ranks) unsuccessful – enemy barrage too heavy.
> 8th – Enemy small raid on 9th Suffolks at Newport Sap repulsed – 4 enemy dead left on our wire.
> 10th – 9th Suffolks (3 officers and 94 other ranks) raided as far as enemy support trenches but found no-one."

The above text illustrates the nature of warfare in the Loos Salient. The consequence of which was 4,884 casualties between 2 March and 25 July 1917 at Loos as a result of "Raids and attacks, Hill 70."

The following extract also confirms the tactic of the raid.

> "8th April – the 2nd Battalion raided the enemy and their retaliation cost the 14th D.L.I. some casualties."

The 18th Brigade was in the vicinity of Mazingarbe, to the east of Lens and Private William Heaviside is buried at Philosophe British Cemetery, Mazingarbe. This date is some weeks before the next major British offensive in which the 6th Division and the 2/DLI took part – this being in August 1917 with the action at Hill 70 in support of the Battle of Arras. It can be stated with reasonable certainty that he was caught up in this activity. The following extract was written by the late Mike Heaviside of Cockfield and provides an account of the operation in which Private William Heaviside was killed:

"In June 1917 William was serving with the 2nd battalion Durham Light Infantry near the small village of Loos-en-Gohelle between Bethune and Lens in northern France. This lies close to the sites of major battles at Arras, Vimy and the Somme. However in June 1917 little was happening other than nightly shelling of each of the warring parties trenches and sporadic raids upon the opposing trenches.

On the night of 6th / 7th June a raid was launched upon the German lines with the object of bringing back prisoners in order to gather intelligence. The party of about 35 men was lightly armed, some with rifles and machine guns, some with flares and some, including Pte. Heaviside armed with "Knobkerries"*. The enemy barbed wire was shelled to break a gap but the enemy was expecting the raid and retaliated with artillery and machine gun fire. Our party became pinned down in "no mans land" and never got through the wire.

The commanding officer's report finishes:

"The dash of the men was excellent in every way and though the raid was a failure it was a gallant attempt.

Casualties: Killed 7; Reported killed 2 (bodies not yet identified); Wounded 10 other ranks".

On 7 June 1917, 7 O.R.'s were killed in action including 33027 Private William Heaviside and another 3 men died of wounds on 7 and 8 June 1917.

Private William Heaviside was killed in action 7 June 1917

Private William B. Heaviside is buried at Philosophe British Cemetery, Mazingarbe. Mazingarbe lies between Bethune and Lens, in the region of Pas-de-Calais, France. The cemetery was started in August 1915. There are now 1,996 Commonwealth burials of the First World War.

* a trench club

Corporal WILLIAM ROBERTSON STOREY 1896 – 1917

26501 Corporal William Robertson Storey, 1st Battalion, the Loyal North Lancashire Regiment was killed in action 10 July 1917 during the German attacks on Nieuport. He has no known grave. He is commemorated on the Nieuport Memorial, Belgium and Evenwood War Memorial. He was 22 years old, born c.1886 at Evenwood to Ralph and Elizabeth Storey who in 1901 lived at Stones End.

He enlisted 5 June 1915 and served with the Durham Light Infantry (service number 3851 D.L.I.) and was transferred to the 1st Loyal North Lancs 5 September 1916, entering France 20 July 1916. In late July/early August 1917, his parents were informed that he was missing then waited about 11 months before official news came, in July 1918 that he was presumed dead. The 1st Battalion, the Loyal North Lancashire Regiment was a Regular Army unit and in August 1914 was based in Aldershot and as part of the 2nd Brigade, 1st Division was one of the first to move to France as part of the British Expeditionary Force and it remained on the Western Front throughout the war. It took part in most of the major actions.

German Attacks on Nieuport 10 – 11 July 1917

The XV Corps of the Fourth Army, including the 1st and 32nd Divisions moved up to the Dunkirk area from the Somme to take part in Operation Hush. On the 20 June 1917, the 32nd Division took over the Nieuport bridgehead from the French Corps. The 1st Division and the 66th (2nd West Lancashire) Division moved up before the end of June. These formations began intensive training for an amphibious landing in locations along the coast, "Operation Hush". However, the Germans detected the British plans and the Marines Korps Flandern launched a successful pre-emptive attack codenamed "Operation Strandfest" and the British plan was cancelled. The British plan was associated with the Third Battle of the Ypres – the attack out of the Ypres Salient to take the Passchendeale Ridge then to sweep north and cut off the ports of Ostend, Zeebrugge and Bruges which were Germany's important U Boat bases. While the Germans attention was focused on this battle, other British forces would:
- land to the north of Nieuport on the Belgian Coast
- breakout from the bridgehead across the Yser River at Nieuport
- and link up with the amphibious landing

The German operation was preceded by a 3 day artillery bombardment. Fog and low cloud prevented detection of the German build up then at 5.30am on the 10 July 1917, the massed German artillery including 3 no. 24cm. naval guns in shore batteries and 58 artillery batteries opened up the British positions. Mustard gas was used for the first time in the barrage. All but one of the bridges across the Yser was destroyed isolating the 1st Northamptonshire Regiment and the 2nd King's Royal Rifle Corps of the 2nd Brigade, 1st Division on the extreme left flank. The German bombardment continued throughout the first day. At 8.00pm the Germans launched their infantry assault by which time the 2 British battalions had suffered 70-80% casualties. German storm-troopers attacked down the coast outflanking the British. Waves of German Marines supported by flamethrower teams mopped up the dugouts. The British battalions were overwhelmed.

The German attack on the 32nd Division further east was less successful but British casualties amounted to approx. 3,126 of all ranks killed, wounded and missing. Of these 50 officers and 1,253 O.R.'s belonged to the 1/Northants and the 2/KRRC of the 2nd Brigade.

On 4 July, the 1/Loyal North Lancs battalion relieved the 2/KRR Corps at Nieuport Bains and all was relatively quiet until 7 July when heavy German shelling hit the "front system" and Nieuport Bains. There were only 2 casualties. The next 2 days were very quiet. The 1/Northants and the 2/KRR Corps sent out a small raiding party which retired under heavy machine gun fire. The 1/Loyal North Lancs. War Diary provides details:

"10/7/1917 About 6AM the enemy commenced a heavy bombardment of the front system – the river NIEUPORT BAINS and the back areas COXYDE & COXYDE BAINS. This increased during the day & about 7.25PM he successfully attacked, taking our trenches up to the E bank of the river – the two Bns. in the front line were practically annihilated.*(a report of the operations is attached) An advance party totalling 4 officers and 36 OR who went up to the left Bn. in the early morning of the 10th were present during the attack & of these only two OR returned.

* Immediately this was observed 23983 Pte. Higson, one of the Battalion Scouts secured a rope and swam with it across the YSER, closely followed by Capt. H. A. Pallant MC RAMC attached Bn who was largely responsible for the safe crossing of men unable to swim and of others in the last stage of exhaustion. By their joint efforts the whole party was safely brought across."

The Battalion occupied the trenches on the W Bank of the Yser as the front line. A & B Coys being in the front line, C & D Coys. in support.

After the attack, the bombardment slackened slightly but it was not until 5AM the following morning that it really ceased. About 8 o'clock in the evening the enemy's planes dropped bombs on RINCK CAMP which was occupied by details of the Bn. 1 or was killed & 1 officer & 6 OR wounded, the officer & 1 OR being attached. Total casualties for the day – 4 Officers missing, 3 officers wounded, 2 OR killed, 29 OR wounded 34 OR missing.

11/7/1917 After 5AM the bombardment ceased & the rest of the day was very quiet.

Corporal William Robinson Storey was killed in action 10 July 1917

It would seem probable that Corporal William Storey was one of the 34 O.R.'s missing following the action of 10 July – a total of 1 Officer and 11 O.R.'s were killed in action on this date.

News of "Missing"

The Auckland Chronicle on the 9 August 1917 reported:

> "Mr. and Mrs. Wallace Storey, Gordon Lane has been informed that their son Corpl. Wm. Storey is missing. The officer who sent the information from France speaks highly of his character and abilities as a soldier."

News of his Death

The Parish Magazine of August 1918 reported:

> "Then there are Ptes. Arkless, DLI and W.R. Storey (nephew of our good friend and sidesman Mr. J. Brass) both of them once reported missing, now officially notified as dead…I well remember preparing and presenting William Robertson Storey for confirmation."

Corporal William R. Storey is commemorated on the Nieuport Memorial. Nieuport is a town in the province of West Flanders, Belgium on the southwest side of the river Yser, 3km from the sea.

The Memorial commemorates 548 British officers and men who fell in operations of 1914 and 1917 on the Belgian coast and whose graves are not known. Commonwealth forces relieved French troops in June 1917 and the XV Corps saw fierce fighting in July before handing the sector back to the French in November 1917.

The Nieuport Memorial
26501 Corporal William Robertson Storey,
1st Batallion, the Loyal North Lancashire Regiment

The THIRD BATTLE OF YPRES (PASSCHENDAELE)
31 July – 10 November 1917: an overview

January 1917 and the British were still recovering from the Battle of the Somme. In March, the Germans made a tactical withdrawal to the Hindenburg Line to better consolidate their defences. On the 6 April, the French began their Nivelle offensive on the Aisne which ended in failure and in its wake mutinies broke out amongst French units in May 1917. On the 9 April, British and Canadian forces launched what was to become known as the Battle of Arras during which they captured Vimy Ridge then political pressure necessitated another British offensive. At the

end of July 1917, the Third Battle of Ypres began, what is now known as Passchendaele. The offensive had 8 distinctive phases:
- Battle of Pilckem, 31 July – 2 August
- Battle of Langemarck, 16 – 18 August
- Battle of the Menin Road, 20 – 25 September
- Battle of Polygon Wood, 26 September – 3 October
- Battle of Broodseinde, 4 October
- Battle of Poelcapelle, 9 October
- First Battle of Passchendaele, 12 October
- Second Battle of Passchendaele, 26 October – 10 November

Many Divisions visited the Ypres Salient during the 3rd Ypres and on more than one occasion. A total of 54 Divisions were thrown into battle. For example, the 11th saw action at Langemarck, Polygon Wood, Broodseinds and Poelcapelle. On the 6 November, the village of Passchendaele was entered and the whole campaign ended a few days later when more of the ridge was taken. It achieved none of its objectives although the Germans could no longer look down on the Ypres Salient which had been deepened by about 5 miles and they had been prevented from attacking the French when its army was in disarray following the failure of the Nivelle Offensive. The Third Battle of Ypres cost the British nearly 310,000 casualties, the Germans slightly less and had consumed all of the available reserves and it achieved none of its strategic objectives.

Sapper HERBERT WARDLE M.M. 1897-1917

131539 Sapper Herbert Wardle, M.M., 234th Field Company, the Royal Engineers was killed in action 31 July 1917 at the Third Battle of Ypres, the Battle of Pilkem. He is buried at New Irish Farm, Ypres and commemorated on the Evenwood War Memorial. He was 20 years old, born c.1897 at Evenwood to Edward and Mary Wardle and in 1901 was brother to George, Elizabeth, William, John and Fred. The family probably lived at 61 Lands Bank. He worked as a coal miner at Gordon House Colliery Cockfield.

He joined up 12 August 1915, landed in France 8 March 1916 was awarded the Military Medal 23 August 1916 for rescuing 3 wounded men. He was a carpenter.

The Auckland Chronicle of 2 November 1916 reported:

> "Lands Bank with less than 100 houses and Wind Mill with only a few scattered houses are 2 wings of the extensive parish of Evenwood and Barony. The inhabitants are naturally proud of the two heroes who have distinguished themselves for bravery and have been awarded the Military Medal. Pioneer Herbert Wardle formerly resided at Ramshaw and attended the Old Colliery School. On removing to Lands Bank with his grandmother he attended the old Morley School. Corp. Oliver Rushford is a son of Mrs. Rushford and the late Mr. John Rushford. He also attended the old school at Morley."

The war diaries of the 234th Field Company have not been researched but it is assumed that the Military Medal was awarded during the action at Ancre Heights. He was killed in acion at St. Julien, near Ypres.

The Battle of Pilckem 31 July – 2 August 1917

From the outset, it was obvious to the German Fourth Army that a new attack was being prepared and the Germans had spent the previous year strengthening their defences by installing concrete pillboxes for their machine gun emplacements on the higher ground in Flanders. It was obvious to the Germans from their vantage points that an offensive was imminent and the attack at Messines Ridge on the 7 June 1917 was a further indication of the Allied intent. However delays occurred and it was not until the 11 July that the air offensive began followed on the 18 July by a massive artillery bombardment then on the 31 July the attack itself commenced. Nine Divisions of the British Fifth Army attacked north east from the Ypres Salient. Initially good progress was made but after strong counter attacks the advance, no more than 2 miles, stalled. Heavy rain fell on the first night flooding the swampy ground whose drainage system had been totally destroyed by the 10 day bombardment. As a result the whole operation was held up and the next significant attack did not take place until the 16 August – the Battle of Langemarck.

Field engineers were engaged in improving the lines of communication, duck boarding tracks, bridging streams, constructing mule tracks, building advanced field dressing stations, building divisional unit battle headquarters and building cover for field guns, screening roads in exposed places, clearing blocked streams, removing obstacles from paths of tanks, destroying bogged down tanks, hauling guns from the mire and laying tape to guide infantry units forward.

Sapper Herbert Wardle M.M. was killed in action 31 July 1917

Sapper H. Wardle is buried at New Irish Farm Cemetery, near Ypres. The cemetery is located to the north east of Ypres, Belgium near a small country village of Zwaanhofweg. It was initially used from August to November 1917 then again in April and May 1918.

131539 Sapper Herbert Wardle, M.M., 234th Field Company, the Royal Engineers

Private EDGAR EDWARD JULIAN COOKE 1885 – 1917

202043 Private Edgar Edward Julian Cooke, 1st Battalion, the Border Regiment was killed in action 13 August 1917 during the Third Battle of Ypres. He is buried at Artillery Wood Cemetery, Boezinge, Belgium. To date, a British commemoration has not been located. He was 33 years old, born c.1885 at Norton, North Riding of Yorkshire to Arthur and Mary Cooke and in 1901 was brother of Emily, Alfred, Cecil, Lucy and Reginald. He enlisted at Bishop Auckland and was a resident of Evenwood.

The 1st Borders was a regular battalion stationed in Burma at the commencement of the war. It returned to England in January 1915 and was attached to the 87th Brigade, 29th Division. The Division saw action in Gallipoli landing on the 25 April 1915 and withdrawn 2 January 1916. The Division landed at Marseilles 29 March 1916 and proceeded to the Western Front and took part in the Battle of the Somme (the Battle of Albert) then the Arras Offensive of 1917 before moving north into Flanders and the Third Battle of Ypres, the second phase, the Battle of Langemarck.

Private E. E. J. Cooke was killed in action 13 August 1917 – this date is after the conclusion of the Battle of Pilkem and prior to the beginning of the Battle of Langemarck. The War Diary for the 1st Borders confirms that in early August 1917, it was posted at De Wippe Cabaret near Elverdinghe in Belgium. The weather was wet and preparations were being made for next offensive action. The battalion moved up to the Steenbeek Sector 11 August and into trenches at Fouches Farm.

The War Diary contains the following entry:

> "FRONT LINE TRENCHES.
> 13th More shelling at stand to this morning. 2 LT. G.F. HAMLETT killed & a/CAPT. A FULTON (just promoted that day) wounded and about ten casualties to other ranks. Again heavy shelling, principally in the early morning between 2.30 and 3.30 a.m. an absolute barrage was put down on the line.
> FOURCHES FARM. CAPTAINS FARM getting 3 or 4 direct hits on FOURCHES FM. – Bn H.Q. causing about 5 casualties in the Green line & around."

This entry clearly indicates that casualties were suffered by the 1/Borders on the 13 August. There were 16 O.R.'s killed in action on that date. It is reasonable to assume that Private Edgar Cooke was a victim of German shelling either in the front line trenches or at the battalion H.Q. at Fourches Farm.

Batallion War Diary confirms German shelling activity 13 August 1917

Private E. E. J. Cooke was killed in action 13 August 1917

Private E. E. J. Cooke is buried at Artillery Wood Cemetery, Boezinge, to the north of Ypres, Belgium. The cemetery was commenced after the Battle of Pilkem and continued as a front line cemetery until March 1918 and it was greatly enlarged after the Armistice when graves were brought in from small burial grounds around Boezinge.

Lance Corporal JOHN JOSEPH WALTON 1893-1917

19677 Lance Corporal John Joseph Walton, 6th Battalion, the Yorkshire Regiment was killed in action 14 August 1917 at Passchendaele. He has no known grave. He is commemorated on the Tyne Cot Memorial, Zonnebeke, Belgium and the Evenwood War Memorial. He was 25 years old, born c.1893 at Evenwood and in 1901 lived with his grandparents John and M.J. Walton of the Oaks, Evenwood and his uncles Robert, Charles, James, and E.A.H. (?). He enlisted prior to April 1915 and at that time lived in Swan Street.

The 6th (Service) Battalion of the Yorkshire Regiment (Alexandra, Princess of Wales's Own) was formed at Richmond, 25 August 1914. It was attached to 32nd Brigade, 11th (Northern) Division. The Division was formed of volunteers, the recruits were judged to be ready by late spring 1915 and it was ordered to reinforce the beleaguered garrison on Gallipoli. It sailed from Liverpool on the 1 July 1915, docking at Alexandria and Mundros before landing at Sulva Bay, Gallipoli on the 7 August 1915. The 6th Battalion lost nearly every officer and almost 75% of the men from fighting and disease. John J. Walton joined the ranks in January 1915 and it is highly probable that he served in Gallipoli. It must be pointed out that his service records are unavailable therefore it remains unknown whether or not he did serve in this disastrous campaign. If he did, then he survived one of the most severe ordeals of the Great War.

In July 1916, the battalion landed in Marseilles, France and spent the rest of the war on the Western Front. The Division took part in the third Battle of Ypres but first, Messines Ridge which guarded the southern flank of the Ypres Ridge needed to be taken. The battalion was again called upon to assist operations. It then moved on to Passchendaele.

The Third Battle of Ypres (Passchendaele)

The battalion did not take part in the opening action, the Battle of Pilckem. From the 1 – 7 August it was encamped in woodland in close proximity. On 8 August the battalion moved up to the Yser Canal dug outs to take over from the 51st Division and provided working parties for the next 2 days and nights. The German artillery hit the roads with gas shells. On the 11th the Battalion moved up to relieve the 8th Duke of Wellington's Regiment – "A" & "C" Companies were in the line and "B" & "D" were in reserve. On 12 August, it was quiet and patrols went out at night to discover enemy positions. On the 14 August, an attack was planned and the following details are taken from the 6th Battalion War Diary:

> "13th 4 am. – Outposts withdrawn to W. of STEENBEEK to allow heavy Artillery to shell enemy's posts. These posts were re-occupied at "Stand-to" in the enemy.
>
> 14th – at 3 am. Outposts withdrawn to W. Bank of STEENBEEK and formed up preparatory to an advance. "A" Coy attacking on the right with 2 ½ platoons and 1 ½ platoons in support to occupy the old line of posts. 2 platoons of "B" Coy immediately in rear to occupy a prepared position on the W. bank of the STEENBEEK. "C" Coy. On the left with 2 ½ platoons and 1 platoon in support to occupy old line of posts.
>
> At 4 am. The barrage came down and the advance commenced. "C" Coy. gained their objective on the left. "A" Coy held up on the right by hostile M.G. fire from the dug outs untouched by bombardment. Enemy delivered several small attacks during the day on "A" Coy. which were easily repelled by rifle fire. Intense shelling all day by the enemy. At night battn. relieved by 5th Dorset Regt. who took up positions on the W. Bank of the STEENBEEK our posts being withdrawn through them.
>
> Casualties 2nd Lt. C.S.M. WELDON and 2nd Lt. W.F. JELLEY wounded. OR 20 killed. 63 wounded. 26 missing.
>
> 15th – Relief completed at 4.30 am. Battn. moved into dug outs on E. Bank of the Canal. March from E. Bank of Canal at 7.45 am. to Hutments A 30 Central."

L/Corporal John J. Walton was killed in action 14 August 1917

The battalion suffered 27 O.R.'s killed in action on that date, 3 O.R.'s on the 15 August and a further 5 O.R.'s died of wounds during the following days. It is therefore assumed that Lance Corporal John Joseph Walton was one of the 26 O.R.'s missing. His body was never recovered from where he fell. Lance Corporal John Joseph Walton is commemorated on the Tyne Cot Memorial. The Tyne Cot Cemetery is located 9 kilometres north east of Ypres, West-Vlaanderen, Belgium. The Memorial to the Missing if one of 4 memorials to the missing in Belgian Flanders known as the Ypres Salient which stretched from Langermarck in the north to Ploegsteert Wood in the south. The Tyne Cot Memorial to the Missing is in Tyne Cot Cemetery and bears the names of almost 35,000 officers and men whose graves are unknown.

Tyne Cot Memorial

19677 Lance Corporal John Joseph Walton, 6th Battalion, the Yorkshire Regiment. Also 54506 Rifleman Matthew Thomas Raine, 1/7th Battalion, West Yorkshire Regiment was killed in action 9 October 1917

Private WALTER DINSDALE 1884-1917

203309 Private Walter Dinsdale, 22nd Battalion, the Durham Light Infantry died of wounds 13 September, 1917. He is buried at Trois Arbres Cemetery, Steenwerck, Belgium and commemorated on the Roll of Honour in St. Ann's Church, Bishop Auckland. He was 33 years old, born c.1884 at

Evenwood to George and Mary Dinsdale and by 1917 they lived at 10 Boddy Street, Tindale Crescent, Bishop Auckland. He enlisted at Bishop Auckland.

203309 Private Walter Dinsdale, 22nd Battalion, the Durham Light Infantry Attestation Form.

The 22nd (Service) Battalion (3rd County Pioneers) was formed 1 October 1915 by the Durham Recruiting Committee and moved to France 17 June 1916 attached to the 19th Division then 2 July 1916 the battalion was transferred to the 8th Division. It remained on the Western Front throughout the war taking part in many actions. In late August 1917, the 22/DLI moved up to Nieppe to repair communication trenches leading to the front line south of Warneton and west of the river Lys. There had been 2 advances in this sector since 6 June and although little ground had been gained there was much work to do – "D" Company was employed on tramways forward of Ploegsteert wood and "B" Company repaired roads. There was little interference from the enemy and great progress was made. Work at the front continued throughout September and October before the 22/D.L.I. was relieved 12 November by the 3rd Canadian Pioneer Battalion.

"All through these 2 months there was a steady trickle of killed and wounded men, which reduced the amount of effective men available for work."

Private Walter Dinsdale was one of those casualties.

Private Walter Dinsdale died of wounds 13 September 1917

Private Walter Dinsdale is buried at Trois Arbres Cemetery, Steenwerck. The site of the cemetery was chosen for the 2nd Australian Casualty Clearing Station in July 1916 and was used by that hospital until April 1918 when Steenwerck and Trois Arbres passed into German hands. After the Armistice, graves were brought in from Steenwerck, Nieppe, Bailleul and Neuve-Eglise.

Rifleman MATHEW THOMAS RAINE 1885 – 1917

54506 Rifleman Matthew Thomas Raine, 1/7th Battalion, West Yorkshire Regiment was killed in action 9 October 1917 at Passchendaele, the Battle of Poelcapelle. He has no known grave. He is commemorated on the Tyne Cot Memorial, Zonnebeke, Belgium and the Evenwood War Memorial. He was 32 years old, born c.1885 at Eggleston to George and Elizabeth Raine. By 1917 he was married to Jane Ann Raine and lived at 5 Brasses Houses, Lands Bank.

The 1/7th (Leeds Rifles) Battalion was formed in August 1914 as part of the West Riding Brigade, West Riding Division it landed at Boulogne, France 15 April 1915. It became part of the 146th Brigade, 49th Division 15 May 1915 and the Division was involved in action during the Third Battle of Ypres, the Battle of Poelcapelle

The Battle of Poelcapelle 9 October 1917

The 49th Division was part of the Second Army, allied to the 2nd ANZAC Corps along with the 66th Division and was not involved in any action until the 9 October. The Australians made the main assault but the poor state of the ground contributed to the lack of progress. The ridge upon which Passchendaele stood was the objective. The Australian War Memorial, Australian Military Units reports as follows:

> "Like earlier battles in the Ypres offensive, the aim of the Poelcappelle attack was to secure a series of objectives in turn, protected by a heavy artillery barrage, the troops involved would be drawn from the 49th and 66th British and 2nd Australian Divisions. Rain however had begun to deluge an already poorly drained battlefield and adequate numbers of guns were unable to be brought within range. The infantry's advance also wallowed in the mud. The Australians were able to secure some of their objectives for a short time but with little artillery support and both flanks open, they were forced to withdraw. The 2nd Australian Division sustained 1,250 casualties in the battle."

Details of the British casualties have not yet been researched.

Rifleman Mathew T. Raine was killed in action 9 October 1917.

Rifleman Mathew Thomas Raine is commemorated on the Tyne Cot Memorial.

Corporal GEORGE PARMLEY 1890-1917

235587 Corporal George Parmley, 1/4th battalion, the King's Own Yorkshire Light Infantry died of wounds 16 October 1917, received at the Battle of Poelcapelle, part of the offensive more commonly known as "Passchendaele", the Third Battle of Ypres. He is buried in Wimereux Communal Cemetery, France and is commemorated on the Evenwood War Memorial. He previously served with the Northumberland Fusiliers (service number 246683).

He was about 27 years of age and was born in 1890 at Middleton-in-Teesdale to Joseph and Margaret Parmley. The family moved to Gordon Lane, Ramshaw and George was one of 10 surviving children. In 1911,

235587 Corporal George Parmley, 1/4th Battalion, the King's Own Yorkshire Light Infantry

George and his wife, Selina

he married Selina Robinson and they lived at Bill Quay near Gateshead having 3 children – Maud, George and Joseph. At the time of his death, Selina was pregnant with their fourth child – Thomas who was born in March 1918.

The Battle of Poelcapelle 9 October 1917

The King's Own Yorkshire Light Infantry 1st/4th Battalion War Diary reported the action:

9th October 1917

Ypres-Gravenstafel

Orders were received on the 7th October, 1917, from the 148th Infantry Brigade that the 49th Division would resume the Offensive West of Passchendaele on the 9th October 1917 in conjunction with the 66th Division on the right and the 48th Division on the left.

The attack of the 49th Division was carried out with two Brigades. 148th Infantry Brigade on the right. 146th Infantry Brigade on the left. The 147th Infantry Brigade being in reserve. The attached map shows the frontage, Battalion boundaries and objectives allotted to the 4th Y & L Regiment, 5th Y & L Regt., and the 5th Bn. K.O.Y.L.I.

This battalion was in reserve with orders immediately after zero to take up a position in reserve on the South Side of the WIELTJE Road immediately north of the RAVEBEEK.

At 12.15 a.m. the Battalion led by LT. COL. H. MOORHOUSE, D.S.O. moved from the Old German front line, immediately followed the 5th K.O.Y.L.I. The night was intensely dark, the trench grid track was in bad repair and progress was consequently very slow. The head of the battalion reached the support line behind ABRAHAM HEIGHTS at zero. This was at least 800 yards from our position of assembly. Before the battalion had closed up the enemy placed a heavy barrage on the ridge and caused a certain amount of delay and a number of casualties. The Commanding Officer issued orders to the battalion to move forward in attack formation in two waves. Z.Coy. on the right and X, Y & W Coys on the left. In the advance on the forward slope of the ridge many casualties were caused by enemy machine gun fire at each side of and from a strong enemy position of the BELLE VUE SPUR. 2/Lt. P.F. BEAUMONT was killed and Captain J.W. MOREHOUSE. 2/Lt. H. NICHOLIS, 2/Lt. J. BRANALD, and 2/Lt. W.B. GREAVES wounded at this stage of the operation. To take up our position north of the RAVEBEEK companies were forced to close on to the MEETCHEELE-GRAVENSTAFEL road on account of the condition of the ground caused by the overflowing of the RAVEBEEK which was badly damaged by shell fire. On the left, enemy machine gun and rifle fire caused many casualties and on the right many men were temporarily lost owing to the fact that it was impossible to get them through the mud. Requests for reinforcements were received from the 5th Y. & L. Regt., on the left and the 4th Y. & L. Regt. on the right.

Z & Y Coys under LIEUT. G.H. CHADWICK and CAPT. R.W. MOORHOUSE respectively were sent forward on the left and W & X Coys under LIEUT. G.H. BROOK and 2/Lt. G. E. PARSONS (Capt. J.W. MOREHOUSE having being previously wounded) on the right. The advance up the slope was done by sections owing to the heavy machine gun and rifle fire from WOLF COPSE on the left and BELLE VUE on the top of the ridge. During this advance CAPT. R.W. MOORHOUSE was killed whilst gallantly leading his company. Many casualties in the ranks were also suffered. Half an hour afterwards LT.

COL. H. MOORHOUSE, D.S.O. was also killed by a bullet when leaving his headquarters. Owing to the heavy machine gun fire and the fact that the companies averaged not more than from 30 to 40 strong a position was taken up by Z and Y Coys on the slope about 400 yards N.E. of the point where the RAVEBEEK crosses the road, while W & X Coys formed a defensive flank on the right of the 4th Y. & L. Regt. A large gap having occurred between the battalion and the 146th Infantry Brigade on the left a defensive flank was formed by a party of Z Coy.

5.30 p.m. The enemy intensely bombarded the area from the Ravebeek to the top of ABRAHAM HEIGHTS for at least an hour. A party of the enemy who were assembling on the BELLE VUE SPUR were dispersed by rapid fire and no counter attacks developed.

GRAVENSTAFEL-YPRES.

10th

Intense enemy bombardment of our forward area.

7p.m. An attempt was made by a party of S. Company under Capt. T. Chadwick to take two Pill Boxes on the crest of the Ridge. These were found to be so heavily wired that it was impossible to get near them. The battalion under the command of CAPT. T. CHADWICK was relieved by the New Zealand Imperial Force, and bivouacked the night in a field near the Asylum, Ypres.

Total casualties:

Killed: LT.COL. H. MOORHOUSE, D.S.O.

CAPT. R.W. MOORHOUSE, M.C.

2/LT. P.F. BEAUMONT and 17 other ranks.

Wounded: 2/LT J.W. HUNTINGTON, 2/LT. W.B. GREAVES, CAPT. J.W. MOREHOUSE and 2/LT. H. NICHOLLS and 147 other ranks.

Wounded and missing: 2/LT. J. BRAMALD.

Missing: 19 other ranks.

It must be assumed that Corporal George Parmley, was one of the 147 other ranks wounded. It seems that a total of 5 officers and 40 O.R.'s lost their lives as a result of this action.

The fatalities were:
- 9 October – 28 OR's killed in action, 3 OR's died of wounds

- 10 October – 3 O.R.'s killed in action, 4 OR's died of wounds
- 16 October – 1 O.R. died of wounds (235587 Corporal George Parmley)
- 17 October – 1 O.R. died of wounds

It is confirmed that Lt. Col. H. Moorhouse, Capt. R.W. Moorhouse, 2/Lt. P.F. Beaumont and 2/Lt. Bramald were killed in action. Another casualty amongst the officers was 2/Lt. C.W. Uncles killed in action 9 October. It is highly likely that Corporal George Parmley took part in the same offensive as 54506 Rifleman Matthew Thomas Raine who served with the 1/7th Battalion, West Yorkshire Regiment since both battalions were part of the 49th Division. Rifleman Matthew Thomas Raine was killed on the opening day of the Battle of Poelcapelle and it appears highly likely that Corporal George Parmley was wounded in this battle then taken to hospital at Wimereux where he died of his wounds.

Corporal George Parmley died of wounds 16 October 1917

News of his Death

In November 1917, the Parish Magazine reported:

> "We have received the sad news of the loss of another of our local lads. George Parmley has gone down."

Corporal George Parmley is buried at Wimereux Communal Cemetery. Wimereux is a small town about 5km north of Boulogne. Wimereux was the headquarters of the Queen Mary's Auxilliary Corps during the First World War and in 1919 it became the General HQ of the British Army. From October 1914 onwards, Wimereux and Boulogne formed an important hospital centre and until June 1918, the medical units at Wimereux used the communal cemetery for burials. There are 2,847 Commonwealth burials and amongst them is Lt.-Col. John McCrae, author of the poem "In Flanders Fields."

Serjeant GORDON PRIESTLEY 1893-1917

250165 Serjeant Gordon Priestley, 1/6th Battalion, the Durham Light Infantry was killed in action 26 October 1917 at Passchendaele. He has no known grave. He is commemorated on the Tyne Cot Memorial, Zonnebeke, Belgium and the Cockfield War Memorial. He was 24 years old, born c.1893 at Wackerfield to Emmanuel and Mary Ann Pinkney. By 1917, the family lived at Fell Houses, Cockfield.

The 1/6th Battalion was formed in Bishop Auckland in August 1914 as part of the Durham Light Infantry Brigade, Northumbrian Division and in May 1915 became the 151st Brigade of the 50th Division.

250165 Serjeant Gordon Priestley, 1/6th Battalion, the Durham Light Infantry

Second Battle of Passchendaele, 26 October – 10 November

The 50th Division did not enter the fray until the 26 October and took over from the 34th. The 149th Brigade received orders to attack – the principal objectives included Hill 23 and Colbert crossroads. The 6/DLI did not enter the line until the evening of 31 October. The Battalion history refers to the "renewed acquaintance of Belgian mud" and reports on 20 casualties resulting from an attack by a squadron of Gotha bombers but no date is given for this event. The history states:

> "Exceptionally large working parties were demanded on each of the 3 nights and their experiences were perhaps worse than those of the tour in the line which was to follow."

No further clue is provided to explain the experiences of the 6/DLI. However, the following passages are taken from the history of the 50th Division and they describe in graphic detail the horrendous conditions:

"At the period when this story begins, i.e., towards the end of October, the whole Salient was a dreary desolate area, pockmarked with countless shell holes (those in the forward area being inhabited by small garrisons who constituted the "front line"), lines of water-logged, battered shell-torn trenches, evil-smelling and rat–infested cellars beneath a rubble of bricks, which once marked the dwelling place of farmer or villager in pre-war days, and burrowed holes in sodden earth, dignified by the name of dug-outs. Thick, clinging mud covered duck-board tracks and the few remaining roads to the front line; to slip from a former (a common experience) was to be engulfed in a shell hole feet deep in stinking water which often hid the poor remains of man and beast. Away from the trenches and "roads" the Salient presented an almost endless conglomeration of shell holes, stretches of water and morass; a patch of dry ground was a rarity. And this dismal state of the ground extended almost for miles beyond the front line, back west of Ypres and the Yser Canal, to where the guns were in action, "camouflaged" as much as possible, but always under a hail of shell of all calibre which the enemy's artillery poured upon the Salient, covering almost every yard so that none were safe, even miles behind the front line. And our guns were just as persistent (even more so, for we were attacking) in searching out every hole and corner of the desolate area over which were scattered the enemy's troops, eking out an existence not less precarious and vile than that under which we were living.

The 50th Division, it is true entered late into the operations, but early into the full horrors of the battlefield, for by the end of October, anything more terrible than conditions in the front line and the ground over which the 149th Infantry Brigade attacked, cannot be imagined, while the Divisional Artillery, longer (as usual) in the line than any unit of the Division, faced conditions which appalled even the stoutest-hearted gunner."

"Fifty square miles of slime and filth from which every shell that burst threw up ghastly relics and raised stenches too abominable to describe and over all, and dominating all, a never-ceasing ear-shattering artillery fire and the sickly reek of the deadly mustard gas."

The Divisional Artillery had a terrible time: "The enemy's artillery was very active, especially at night when he deluged us with mustard gas. So intense was this gas that everything one touched was infected with it. Nobody had a voice left after the first few days.

The action of the mustard gas was insidious: "We did not at first realize the full danger of this, and just laughed because no one had a voice; but when people began to blister and swell, and two men of my old Battery died horribly from eating bread which had been splashed with this stuff, we got wind up thoroughly. The whole area was tainted: one could touch nothing with safety; even our own doctor, who came to see us, slipped in the mud and was so badly blistered by it that we never saw him again. The gas casualties were bad enough, but oh! The shell casualties were pathetic. I lost many of my greatest friends in the Battery, horribly mutilated in the mud, and towards the end was as near a raving lunatic as possible … Our guns were in the open; the only protection from the gunners the high explosive; and the mud was over everything and tainted with mustard gas."

A letter dated 18 August 1917 from Sgt. H. Henderson was received by Miss Amelia Gooding which stated:

"I last saw him which was on the night of 24th October….A German sniper was picking off our wounded men was observed by Sgt. Priestley who at once engaged him with a duel. It was a brave act to do in the face of the enemy and that was the last time he was seen by any of his men."

Serjeant Gordon Priestley was killed in action 26 October 1917

In total 8 soldiers serving with the 6/DLI were killed in action on the 26 October 1917, 6 of whom including Serjeant G. Priestley have no known grave and are commemorated on the Tyne Cot Memorial.

The BATTLE OF CAMBRAI: 20 November – 7 December 1917: an overview

In popular mythology, the Battle of Cambrai ranks as one of the most thrilling episodes of the whole war – at last, tanks came into their own and the notion that the Hindenburg Line was impregnable was exploded. However, the early success was not capitalised upon and the German counter attack regained much land and even captured areas previously held by the British.

Cambrai was an important railhead which lay at the junction of railways connecting Douai, Valenciennes and Saint-Quentin. It was also located on the Saint-Quentin Canal. Cambrai was an important HQ and billeting town. As a military target, its capture would deny the enemy of a key part of their communication system.

The Battle of Cambrai can be sub-divided into 3 separate engagements:
- 20 – 21 November: the Tank Attack
- 23 – 28 November: Capture of Bourton Wood and
- 30 November – 3 December: the German counter attack

At 6.10am 20 November, an artillery bombardment – 1000 guns and howitzers firing 900,000 rounds of shells opened up but the secret weapon was the 476 Mark IV tanks, the entire strength of the Tank Corps. Initially, good progress was made and the 6th Division crossed the Hindenburg Line and captured Ribecourt. The 5th Cavalry advanced through them but were repulsed at Noyelies. An advance of 3 to 4 miles in a little over 4 hours at a cost of just over 4,000 casualties was astounding but nevertheless the Third Army failed to meet its objectives by the end of the first day. On the 27 November offensive operations were closed down and units were ordered to consolidate. Three days later the German Army struck back. On the right flank, the break into the British positions was swift – the defending 55th (West Lancashire) Division and much of the 12th (Eastern) and 20th (Light) Divisions evaporated. By 9.00am, 30 November, the Germans had penetrated almost 3 miles towards Havrincourt Wood and the Third Army faced disaster. On the 3 December, Haig ordered a retirement. The plan had failed and although some ground had been gained, the small salient at Flesquires remained in an exposed position. Elsewhere ground had been lost to the advancing enemy.

Between 20 November and 8 December, British losses of dead, wounded and missing amounted to 44,207. Of these, approx. 6,000 had been taken prisoner. German losses were estimated at 45,000.

Serjeant JOHN W. SPENCE 1891-1917

4/8777 Serjeant John W. Spence, 2nd battalion, the Durham Light Infantry died of wounds 1 December 1917. He is buried at Ribecourt British Cemetery, France and is commemorated on the Evenwood War Memorial, Butterknowle War Memorial and the Memorial in St. Mary's Church, Staindrop. He was 27 years old, born in 1891 at Staindrop, the son of Joseph and Charlotte Spence and brother to Sarah, Mary, Thomas, Charlotte, Alfred, Louisa and Elizabeth in 1901. He left a wife, Ellen and 2 children Robert and Monica.

The 2/DLI formed part of the 18th Brigade, 6th Division and it landed at St. Nazaire, France 10 September 1914. John W. Spence attested 10 August 1914 and he entered France 10 June 1915. On 13 November 1916, he was paid as Lance Corporal, a Corporal 17 February 1917 and was promoted to a Serjeant 19 June 1917 in "A" Company. He was wounded 18 May 1917.

The Sixth Division history informs:

> "Nov. 15th -19th – Commenced march to Cambrai front
> 20th – Battle of Cambrai – 16th Infantry Brigade on right, 71st Infantry Brigade on left, 18th passed through – broke both systems of Hindenburg Line, capturing Ribecourt and Premy Chapel Ridge – first company into Marcoing – over 1,100 prisoners and 23 guns. All objectives gained with few casualties by 12 noon.
> 21st – Action of 14th D.L.I. supporting cavalry in advance to Cantaing
> 26th – 27th – 18th Infantry Brigade extended front to Cantaing. 1st Buffs cleared and occupied Noyelles.
> 30th – Enemy counter attack in force on the Third Army. 16th Infantry Brigade moved from Divisional Reserve to near Beaucamps and ordered to counter attack on Gouzeaucourt – found guards already in possession. Arranged to attack by night on La Vacquerie-Gonnelieu – attack unsuccessful. Gallant action of the 18th Infantry Brigade

transport under Shea QM, 2nd D.L.I. and Paul, Transport Officer, 1st West Yorks – both died of wounds.
Night Dec. 2/3 – 16th Infantry Brigade relieved part of 29th Division north of St. Quentin Canal"

More detail is provided:

"The 18th Infantry Brigade advanced without tanks…The 18th Infantry Brigade pushed through the 71st Infantry Brigade and secured Premy Chapel Ridge in good time…The West Yorks and the 2nd D.L.I. each charged over the Premy Ridge spur and captured a battery at the point of the bayonet……On the night of the 26/27th November the 18th Infantry Brigade extended its left up to the south east edge of Cantaing….the enemy delivered a heavy counter attack on the morning of 30th November….the Germans reached Gouzeaucourt at about 9am but were stoutly opposed by transport details of the 18th Infantry Brigade…and checked the enemy in a portion of the village until it was retaken by the Guards about midday."

The 2/DLI and the 14/DLI were heavily involved in this battle. On the night of the 2/3 December, the 14/DLI "having stiff fighting" across and astride the canal to the east of Marcoing – an action which inflicted casualties of 15 officers and 262 other ranks, more than half being killed. Capt. Lascelles gained his V.C. here. On the 10 December the Division was withdrawn, after 3 strenuous weeks, to the Basseux area to the south west of Arras. A further report notes:

"The only other incidents of note were the repulse by the 18th Infantry Brigade of a half-hearted enemy attack on Cantaing on the 1st December and D.H.Q. being three times shelled out of its headquarters between 30th November and 9th December."

The 2/DLI War Diary confirms that on 30 November 1917 there was heavy enemy shelling of the line causing a number of casualties. 2/Lt. Adlington was killed and the Germans broke through at Gouzecourt. Captain Shea was mortally wounded and 4 O.R.'s were wounded. On 1 December the enemy landed another attack at Cantaing from Lafoilie Wood and the ridge to the south of it. This was driven back.

In addition to 2/Lt. G.W. Adlington and Capt. J.P.L. Shea M.C., 6 O.R.'s serving with the 2/DLI were killed in action or died of wounds around this date. It is reasonable to assume that Serjeant John W. Spence was one of the four O.R.'s wounded as a result of enemy action on 30 November 1917. He died whilst being treated at 18th Field Ambulance and is buried at Ribecourt British Cemetery. The village was taken 20 November 1917 by the 6th Division and at the conclusion of the Battle of Cambrai, remained practically on the front line. Ribecourt is a village about 10km south west of Cambrai.

4/8777 Serjeant John W Spence, 2nd Battalion, the Durham Light Infantry

Serjeant John W. Spence died of wounds 1 December 1917

He is buried at Ribecourt Cemetery which was begun by the 6th Division in November 1917 and used until March 1918 when it was recaptured during the German spring offensive. Between 20 November and 10 December 1917, the Divisional History confirms that it suffered 1,790 casualties

Private GEORGE WILLIAM BRYANT 1893 – 1917

1182 Private George W. Bryant, 3rd Field Ambulance, the Royal Army Medical Corps was killed in acion 1 December, 1917 during the Battle of Cambrai. He is buried at Metz-en-Couture Communal Cemetery, British Extension in France and is commemorated on the Evenwood War Memorial. He was 24 years old, born c.1893 at Witton Park to Albert and ? Bryant. By 1901 Albert was a widower and father to James and George living at Victoria Cottages, Howden-le-Wear. He lived in the Parish of Evenwood and Barony.

The Royal Army Medical Corps provided non-combatants who handled the evacuation and treatment of casualties. It was supplemented by the Red Cross, St. John's Ambulance, Voluntary Aid Detachments and other groups. The Field Ambulance provided one or more Advanced Dressing Stations in reasonable proximity to the front line. It was under the command of the Division and was attached to an infantry or cavalry Brigade. The Casualty Clearing Station was the next stop on the evacuation chain for casualties. It was not part of the Divisional structure but part of the Lines of Communication unit. The hospitals (general and stationary) were the last stop. There were 61 locations including Amiens, Rouen, Abberville, Etaples, Wimereux throughout France and Belgium.

From August 1914 to August 1915, the 3rd Field Ambulance formed part of the 1st Division then until November 1918 was part of the Guards Division. The Guards Division was regarded as one of the elite units of the British Army and remained on the Western Front throughout the war.

The service details of Private G. W. Bryant and the war diaries of the 3rd Field Ambulance have not been researched but it is assumed that since the 3rd Field Ambulance was attached to the Guards Division then Private G. W. Bryant was involved in the following engagements.

23 – 28 November: Capture of Bourton Wood and
30 November – 3 December: the German counter attack

The Guards Division was part of the IV Corps of the Third Army for the second phase and the III Corps of the Third Army for the last phase. The Guards Division were thrown into battle and advanced into Fontaine. Once the Germans had been driven from Bourton Wood, they switched artillery upon it and those battalions caught in the wood were wiped out. The Guards attacked the village of Fontaine Notre Dame but were beaten back. On the 30 November, the Germans struck back. Many artillery batteries soon came within range of advancing German infantry and the Guards Division, still recuperating from a mauling in Fontaine Notre Dame, headed into a bitter fight to hold onto Gouzeaucourt On the 3 December, Haig ordered a retirement and the audacious plan had failed although some ground had been gained, in places the Germans were now on ground previously occupied by the British. By the 5 December, the line had re-stabilised.

One of the British casualties was Brigadier-General Roland Boyes Bradford V.C., officer commanding the 186th Brigade aged 25 when killed in action, 30 November 1917. He is buried in Hermies British cemetery.

Private George W. Bryant was killed in action 1 December 1917

Private George William Bryant is buried at Metz-en-Coutre communal British cemetery. Metz is located to the south west of Cambrai and was behind British lines between 4 April 1917 and 23 March 1918. It was re-taken on the 6 September 1918. The British section of the cemetery was begun in April 1917 and was used until March 1918.

1182 Private George W. Bryant, 3rd Field Ambulance, the Royal Army Medical Corps

CHAPTER SEVEN

1918 & 1919

Following the peace treaty with Russia, about 1 million German troops were transferred from the Russian Front to the Western Front and an all out attempt was made to win the war before the Americans arrived in vast numbers to sway the balance of power. This offensive was the last throw of the dice for the German High Command. In August 1918, the tide turned with the successful defence of Amiens and the next 96 days saw the Allies force back the Germans. The High Command realised that the war could not be won and sued for peace.

The Armistice was signed 11 November 1918. The fighting had finished but officially the war was not over until the Treaty of Versailles was signed 7 months later in June 1919 and with the end of the war many of the European dynasties collapsed.

January – September	T.E. Lawrence leads Arab guerrillas in successful campaign against Turkish positions in Arabia and Palestine
January 8	US President Woodrow Wilson makes "Fourteen Points" speech to Congress
February 11	US President Woodrow Wilson makes "Four Principles" speech to Congress

March 3	Soviet Russia concludes separate peace negotiations in treaty of Brest-Litovsk
March 21	Germany launches Spring push, eventually mounting five major offensives against Allied forces, starting with the Battle of Picardy against the British
March 26	Doullens Agreement gives General Ferdinand Foch "co-ordinating authority" over the Western Front
April 9	Germany launches second Spring offensive, the Battle of the Lys, in the British sector of Armentieres
April 14	Foch appointed Commander-in-Chief of Allied forces on Western Front
May 25	German U-boats appear in US waters for first time
May 27	Third German Spring offensive, Third Battle of the Aisne, begins in French sector along Chemin des Dames
May 28	US forces (28th Regiment of 1st Division) victorious in first major action, Battle of Cantigny
June 6	US 3rd Division captures Bouresches and southern part of Belleau Wood
June 9	Germans launch fourth Spring offensive, Battle of the Matz, in French sector between Noyan and Montdider
June 15	Italians prevail against Austro-Hungarian forces at Battle of Piave
July 6	US President Woodrow Wilson agrees to US intervention in Siberia
July 15	Final phase of great German Spring push, the Second Battle of Marne, begins
July 16-17	Former Tsar Nicholas II, his wife, and children, are murdered by the Bolsheviks
July 18	Allies counterattack against German forces, seizing initiative
August 8	Haig directs start of successful Amiens offensive, forcing all German troops back to the Hindenburg Line; Ludendorff calls it a "black day" for German army
September 12	US forces clear the St.-Mihiel salient, during which the greatest air assault of the war is launched by the US

September 19	Start of British offensive in Palestine, the Battle of Megiddo
September 26	Battle of the Vardar pits Serb, Czech, Italian, French and British forces against Bulgarian forces
September 26	Meuse-Argonne offensive opens; the final Franco-American offensive of the war
September 27 – October 17	Haig's forces storm the Hindenburg Line, breaking through at several points
September 29	Bulgaria concludes armistice negotiations
September 28 – October 14	Belgian troops attack at Ypres
October 3-4	Germany and Austria send peace notes to US President Woodrow Wilson requesting an armistice
October 17 – November 11	British advance to the Sambre and Schledt rivers, taking many German prisoners
October 21	Germany ceases unrestricted submarine warfare
October 27	Erich Ludendorff resigns
October 30	Turkey concludes an armistice with the Allies
November 3	German fleet mutinies at Kiel
November 3	Trieste falls to the Allies; Austria-Hungary concludes an armistice
November 7-11	Germany negotiates an armistice with the Allies in Ferdinand Foch's railway carriage headquarters at Compiegne
November 9	Kaiser Wilhelm II abdicates
November 10	Kaiser Wilhelm II flees to Holland
November 10	German republic is founded
November 11	**Armistice day; fighting ceases at 11am**

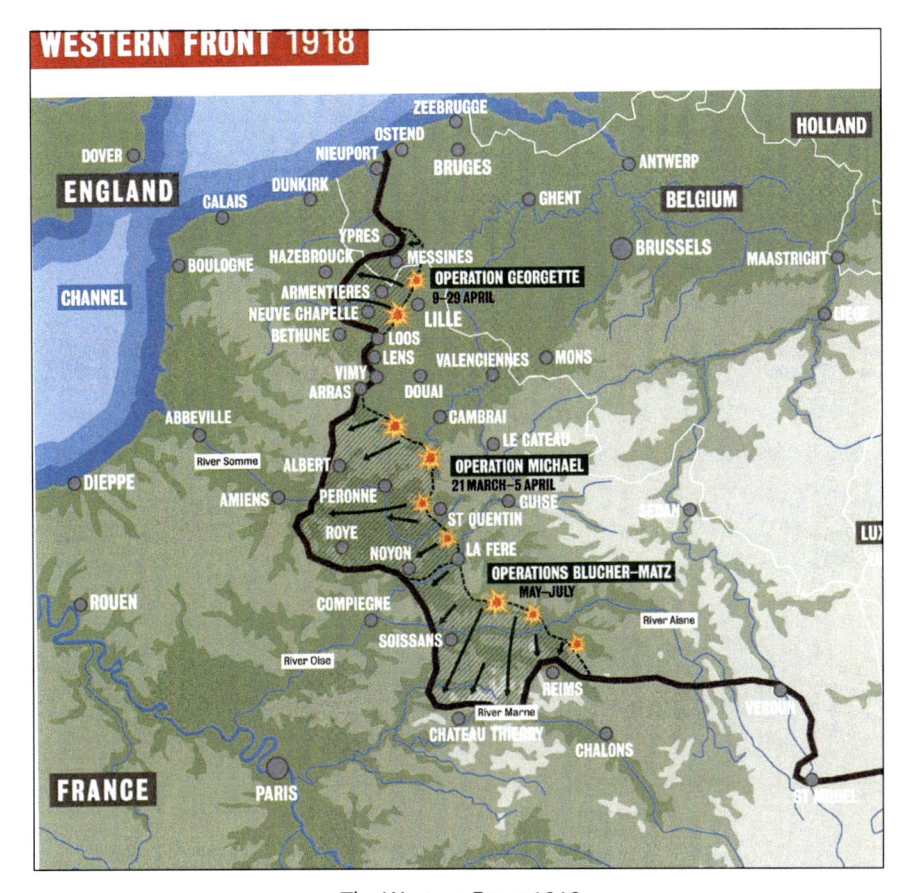

The Western Front 1918
Courtesy of the Thiepval Project Charity Fund

The final year of the war saw the 50th Northumbrian Division all but wiped out as it attempted to hold back German spring offensive. Many men from the north east of England served in this Division including many from Evenwood. In total 23 men with connections to Evenwood lost their lives as the war inflicted severe casualties. The 2 Marquis brothers, born in Hamsterley, who served with the Australian Imperial Force (A.I.F.) are recorded in this work as a tribute to the sacrifices of the Australians. Those researched are:
- Private Jonathan Hewitt
- Lance Corporal George Dowson
- Private Joseph Hutchinson
- Serjeant Thomas W. Simpson

- Private James Skelhorn
- Private John H. Ellerker
- Second Lieutenant Thomas W. Applegarth
- Private William Morley
- Private David Baister
- Private Oliver Rushford
- Private Joseph J. Marquis
- Private William A. Moses
- Gunner William Gray
- Serjeant John J. Richardson
- Corporal Charles H. Lowson
- Private William Snowball
- Private Albert Burrell
- Private Frederick W. Marquis
- Private Ralph Heaviside
- Private J. Wilfred Howlett
- Private Martin Simpson
- Private Mark G. Middlemass
- Private Thomas Davis
- Sapper Arthur K. Atkinson
- Private Fred Purvis

The Marquis brothers are commemorated on the Hamsterley War Memorial, Corporal C. H. Lowson is included on the commemorative plaque on the Memorial Cottages at St. Helen Auckland and Private A. Burrell is commemorated on the Cockfield War Memorial.

Most of these men were killed as the German spring offensive hit the British troops in France. An exception is Private M. G. Middlemass who was killed one week before the cessation of hostilities on the Italian Front. There were 3 further casualties after the Armistice:
- Sapper A.K. Atkinson was killed clearing away ordnance debris
- Private F. Purvis who died as a P.O.W. in Germany and
- Private J.W. Maughan who died of pneumonia in January 1919.

Private JOHNATHAN HEWITT 1886-1918

57075 Private Jonathan Hewitt, 2/6 Battalion, West Yorkshire Regiment was killed in action 28 February 1918 and is buried at Menin Road South Military Cemetery, Ypres, Belgium and commemorated on Evenwood War Memorial. He was 32 years old, born c.1886 at Hamsterley to William and Jane Hewitt. On 28 December 1912, he married Jessie Bannister at St. Paul's Church, Evenwood and they lived in Victoria Terrace, Evenwood. He served with the West Yorkshire Regiment as did Rifleman Mathew Thomas Raine from Lands Bank who lost his life at Passchendaele.

57075 Private Jonathan Hewitt, 2/6 Batallion, West Yorkshire Regiment – Is this Jonathan & Jessie?

Private Jonathan Hewitt attested in December 1915 and was available for service with the 6/DLI but was posted to the West Yorkshires in May 1917. The 2/6th Battalion of the West Yorkshire Regiment was formed at Bradford 12 September 1914 and attached to the 185th Brigade of the 62nd (2nd West Riding) Division. The Division concentrated on the Western Front by 18 January 1917 thereafter it fought with distinction until the Armistice playing a part in major actions, including:

- 14 March – 5 April 1917: the German Retreat to the Hindenburg Line as part of the V Corps Fifth Army
- The Flanking Battles in support of the Battle of Arras, on the Bullecourt Flank, as part of the V Corps, Fifth Army namely:
  - 11 April 1917: the first attack on Bullecourt
  - 15 April 1917: the German attack on Lagnicourt
  - 3 May – 17 May 1919: the Battle of Bullecourt
  - 20 May – 16 June 1917: actions on the Hindenburgh Line
- 20 & 21 November 1917: as part of the IV Corps, Third Army- the Battle of Cambrai, the Tank Attack.

On 5 January 1918, the Division took over the front line in the Arras area between Gavrelle and Oppy.

57075 Private Jonathan Hewitt served 2 years 81 days although the exact date he entered France is undecipherable and was in hospital for 4 days in July 1917 and 33 days in August 1917. It is assumed that he saw action at Cambrai and in the Arras sector. The War Diaries of the 2nd/6th Battalion of the West Yorkshires have not been examined but it is assumed that the battalion was moved northwards from Arras to assume duties in the Ypres sector some time after 5 January 1918 since Private J. Hewitt is buried in Ypres. To date, the circumstances of his death are unknown.

Private Jonathan Hewitt killed in action 28 February 1918

News of his Death

The Parish Magazine of April 1918 reported:

> "I am grieved to say that news has arrived that Pte. J. Hewitt, son of Mr. and Mrs. Hewitt of Alexandra Terrace, has fallen in action. Our deepest sympathies and condolences will go out both to his young wife and to his parents."

Private J. Hewitt is buried at the Menin Road South Cemetery, Ypres. The cemetery was always within Allied lines and used by the Field Ambulances until the summer of 1918. There are 1,657 servicemen of the First World War buried or commemorated in the cemetery.

The GERMAN SPRING OFFENSIVE:
First Phase 21 March – 5 April 1918

The British called this engagement the "March Retreat". To the Germans it was called "the Kaiserschlacht" and this offensive was Germany's last big effort to win the war before the arrival of American troops. The U.S.A had declared war on Germany 6 April 1917 but it took time to build up forces and prepare them for battle. In December 1917, with the Treaty of Brest-Litovsk Russia signed for peace so Germany transferred one million battle hardened troops and 3,000 guns from the Russian Front to the Western Front to attack the Allied forces.

Code-named "Operation Michael", the plan was to punch through the British and French Armies at St. Quentin, pass through the Somme and then wheel north-west to cut the British lines of communication behind the Artois fronts to bottle up the B.E.F. in the narrow neck of Flanders. The British Army would be surrounded with no means of escape and would inevitably surrender. The target of the first phase of the offensive was the British Army who the German High Command believed to be exhausted by the four major efforts of 1917, namely Arras, Messines, Passchendaele and Cambrai.

By mid February 1918, there were 177 German Divisions in France and Flanders out of their world wide total of 241. Of these, 110 were in the front line of which 50 faced the short British front. A further 67 were in reserve with 31 facing the B.E.F. At the same time as the German forces were growing, the British Army was depleted having faced a manpower crisis during the second half of 1917. Lloyd George produced official figures to confirm that there were some 324,000 additional men on the Western Front (i.e. British and Dominion forces) giving a total of 1,850,967 by 1 January 1918 as opposed to 1,526,182 a year earlier but in fact, the effective fighting strength had fallen by as much as 7% in the year. The German attack 21 March 1918 enjoyed a numerical superiority of 56 Divisions against 16. German superiority was overwhelming.

The main weight of the attack was between Arras and St. Quentin. The XIX Corps occupied the line to the east of Peronne and to the north of Vermand facing 9 German Divisions on an eight mile front. The German superiority was about 4.5 to 1 and their success was spectacular:
- In 2 days the Fifth Army was driven back over 12 miles
- Peronne fell 23 March
- Bapaume fell 24 March
- Albert, capital of the old Somme battlefield, fell 26 March

The casualty figures for 21 March have been estimated as:
- British – 38,500
- German – 40,000

However, "only" 2/3rds of the German casualties were wounded so a substantial number would return to the fighting at a later date. By contrast, 28,000 of the British would not return – 7,000 were dead and 21,000 had been taken prisoner.

By 27 March, the Germans were able to cross the Somme at Chipilly which compelled Gough's Fifth Army to retreat to a line running from Bouzencourt to Rosieres. The British held the line throughout the day but to the south, the French were driven out of Lassigny and Montdidier.

Lance Corporal GEORGE DOWSON 18?? -1918

27088 Lance Corporal George Dowson, 7/8th battalion the Royal Inniskilling Fusiliers was killed in action 21 March 1918 during the start of the German spring offensive and is buried at Tyne Cot Cemetery, Zonnebeke, Belgium and commemorated on the Evenwood War Memorial. By 1918, he lived at 22 West View, Evenwood and was recorded as the son of Mr. and Mrs. J. Nicholson.

George Dowson is one of 6 men from the Parish, the others being, Joseph Hutchinson, Thomas W. Simpson, James Skelhorn, John H. Ellerker and Thomas W. Applegarth to be killed during the German spring offensive.

The 7th (Service) and 8th (Service) Battalions of the Royal Inniskilling Fusiliers were part of the 49th Brigade, 16th (Irish) Division. On the 23 August 1917, they amalgamated to become the 7/8th Battalion. The Division served on the Western Front concentrating in the Bethune area taking part in the following actions:
- the Battle of the Somme (fourth and fifth phases), 3 – 9 September 1916,
- the Battle of Messines 7 – 14 June 1917,
- the Battle of Langemarck 16 – 18 August 1917 and
- the Battle of St. Quentin (the First Battles of the Somme, 1918) 21 – 23 March 1918.

The Inniskillings Regimental History confirms that Lance Corporal George Dowson's battalion, the 7/8th Battalion was in action at St. Quentin, France some 50 miles to the south of Zonnebeke, Belgium where he is buried. It is not known why 27088 Lance Corporal George Dowson was in Belgium and detached from his battalion and the circumstances of his death are unknown.

L/Corporal George Dowson was killed in action 21 March 1918

Lance Corporal George Dowson was killed in action during the start of the German spring offensive and his family endured about 20 months of uncertainty. In December 1919, the Parish Magazine reported:

> "We sympathise with the parents and relatives of Pte. G. Dowson, who have received official notice that their son, missing since March 21st, must now be presumed dead."

Lance Corporal George Dowson is buried at Tyne Cot Cemetery which is located 9km east of Ypres, near Zonnebeke, West-Vlaanderen, Belgium. Tyne Cot or "Tyne Cottage" is the name given by the Northumberland Fusiliers to a barn which stood near the level crossing on the Passchendaele to Broodseinde road. The barn which became the centre of several German blockhouses was captured in October 1917 in the advance on Passchendaele. The cemetery was greatly enlarged after the Armistice when remains were brought in from various battlefields.

27088 Lance Corporal George Dowson, 7/8th Battalion the Royal Inniskilling Fusiliers

Private JOSEPH HUTCHINSON 1880-1918

53318 Private Joseph Hutchinson, 9th Battalion, Manchester Regiment was killed in action 23 March 1918 during the start of the German spring offensive. He is buried at Unicorn Cemetery, Vend'huile, France and commemorated on Evenwood War Memorial. He was 38 years old, born c.1880 at Evenwood to Matthew and Margaret Hutchinson and in 1901 was older brother to Ann, Florence,

53318 Private Joseph Hutchinson, 9th Battalion, Manchester Regiment

Charles, Ernest, Fredrick and John. The family lived at the Oaks, Evenwood. By 1918, Joseph lived at Evenwood Gate.

Joseph Hutchinson is the only man from the Parish to be killed whilst serving with the Manchester Regiment. He formerly served with the North Staffordshire Regiment (service number 48308).

The 9/Manchesters formed part of the 126th Brigade, 42nd Division then 19 February 1918, it was transferred to the 198th Brigade of the 66th Division. The 66th Division formed part of the XIX Corps, Fifth Army and was involved in the Battle of St. Quentin 21 -23 March 1918.

The Battle of St. Quentin: 21 – 23 March 1918

The Fifth Army defended the front line to the south of Roisel and north of Vermand. The British Official History quotes a total of 177,739 casualties – men killed, wounded and missing. Of these just under 15,000 died and of the 90,000 missing a very large proportion were taken prisoner as the Germans advanced. A high proportion of those who died have no known grave. The greatest losses were:
- 7,310 – the 36th (Ulster) Division
- 7,149 – the 16th (Irish) Division
- 7,023 – the 66th (East Lancashire) Division

All 3 formations were effectively destroyed and taken out of the order of battle and rebuilt. Six other Divisions each lost more than 5,000 men. For the period up to 30 April including the Battle of Lys, German casualties are estimated at 348,300.

At 04.40, 21 March 1918, heavy German artillery bombardment commenced on the British front held by the First, Third and Fifth Armies. The main weight of the attack was between Arras and a few miles south of St. Quentin. There was thick fog in the morning. Between 7.00am and 9.40am, the German infantry began to attack – it pushed quickly through the Forward Zone but was temporarily checked at Villeret by 2/6 Manchesters. Hargicourt held by the 4/East Lancs was lost by 10.30am. By noon, the Germans had captured the Fifth Army's Forward Zone. Those troops that had been holding this zone were mostly lost, either killed in the bombardment or by the advance of the enemy infantry. Those taken prisoner would have been surrounded as the Germans advanced quickly, unseen in the fog. Severe fighting continued between Grand Priel Wood and Templeux-le-Guerard. The 2/7 Manchesters defend Brosse Wood for several hours and 2/6 Manchesters defended Fervaque Farm near Villeret until a flamethrower attack commenced at 1.30pm. The enemy pushed on but outran its own artillery cover and was halted on the Jeancourt-Hargicourt road. To the north the German attack reached Templeux Quarries which held out until 5pm. The 1st Cavalry Division entered the action and reinforced the XIX Corps.

The German advance continued into the 22 & 23 March and the 66th Division suffered heavy casualties. Between the 21 & 24 March 1918, the 9/Manchesters lost 5 officers and 74 O.R.'s.

Private Joseph Hutchinson was killed in action 23 March 1918

News of "Missing"

The Parish Magazine of June 1918 reported:

"Joseph Hutchinson of Evenwood Gate is also missing and nothing has been heard of him for a considerable time."

Private Joseph Hutchinson is buried at Unicorn Cemetery, Vend'huile. Vend'huile is a village about 19km north of St. Quentin and 24km southeast of Peronne, in the region of Aisne, France. The 50th (Northumbrian) Division laid out the cemetery after the village was taken 30 September 1918. Following the Armistice, graves from other isolated burial sites were brought into the cemetery. There are 1,008 burials and commemorations to servicemen of the First World War.

Serjeant THOMAS WILLIAM SIMPSON M.M. 1891 – 1918

250523 Serjeant Thomas William Simpson M.M., 1/6th Battalion, the Durham Light Infantry was killed in action 27 March 1918 during the German spring offensive. He has no known grave. He is commemorated on the Pozieres Memorial, France and the Evenwood War Memorial. He was 27 years old, born c.1891 to Mary Jane Simpson and in 1901 he lived at Toft Hill with his grandmother Elizabeth Simpson. Thomas had

250523 Serjeant Thomas W. Simpson M.M., 1/6th Battalion, the Durham Light Infantry

1 younger brother, John Luther. His mother Mary later married Charles Welford to whom she had 3 children – Elizabeth Ann, Mary Ethel and James.

The 1/6th Battalion was formed in Bishop Auckland in August 1914 as part of the Northumbrian Division and in May 1915 it formed part of the 151st Brigade of the 50th Division. The Division moved to France 16 April 1915 and served with distinction on the Western Front throughout the war. The 6/DLI was formed with men from the Bishop Auckland, Barnard Castle, Consett, Crook and Spennymoor areas. Thomas Simpson was one of 9 men with associations with Evenwood to lose their lives while serving with the 6/DLI, the others were Alfred Brown, George T. Cox, Jeremiah C. Lee, John H. Pinkney. Gordon Priestley, Oliver Rushford, Walter Snowball and John Walling. As Lance Serjeant he was awarded the Military Medal which was reported in the London Gazette 23 February 1918. To date the details of the citation are unknown.

The German Spring Offensive: 6/DLI

In March 1918, the 6/DLI was in the Fifth Army Reserve near Peronne where it "might have to deliver counter-attacks in the event of a German success." On the 21 March, the German attack began and the 6/DLI travelled from Gouzeaucourt to Brie then marched in the direction of Tincourt and occupied partially dug trenches called "the Green Line." These were behind the Brown Line trench system where the 66th Division had been overwhelmed in the morning. On the morning of the 22 March it was quiet then in the afternoon, enemy shelling became heavier and large massed bodies of the enemy could be seen. Orders were received to hold the line at all costs. By dusk, the first serious casualties occurred and by 9.00 pm orders were received to withdraw to a ridge near Cardigny. At 07.00am, 23 March, orders were received for the Fifth Army to withdraw to the west of the Somme. The Battalion was to cover the retirement of the 5/DLI. German snipers and machine gunners gave considerable trouble. "Y" Company formed the rearguard to the Battalion. The route went through the village of Le Mesnil where there was a light shrapnel barrage and fighting in the village that was in enemy hands. Two officers were lost and about 20 men. The night was quiet. The next morning, orders were received to withdraw to Foucaucourt and by 8.00pm the 6/DLI was in position in reserve, in a line north east of Estres. On the 25th March, the Germans advanced quickly and by 7.00pm the battalion withdrew to old trenches at Pressoire where it had a quiet night with only a few casualties from shellfire. By 09.00am the next morning, the enemy renewed the attack as the 6/DLI passed through the ruins of Lihons and the withdrawal continued almost to Rosieres. They were being heavily shelled. At 9.30am, 27 March, the Labour Battalion withdrew and forced the two forward companies of the Battalion to do the same. A counter attack was delivered and the line was restored by the end of the day. The enemy renewed his attacks on the following morning and the 24th Division on the right retired to Warvillers. "Y" Company then moved to Vrely to cover the withdrawal of the remainder of the Battalion to the line near Caix. On 31 March, the War Diary concludes:

> "During the fighting from 21st-31st March the Battalion suffered the following casualties. Killed: Officers 6 OR 35. Wounded: Officers 5 OR 189. Missing: Officers 2 OR 87. Wounded & Missing: Officers nil OR 3.

Since Serjeant T. W. Simpson has no known grave, it is assumed that he was one of the 87 O.R.'s reported as "Missing".

Serjeant Thomas William Simpson M.M. was killed in action 27 March 1918

Remarkably, given the events of the week only 2 Officers and 6 O.R.'s serving with the 1/6 DLI died on the same date. At Caix, the remnants of the 6/DLI was re-organised and occupied the line before withdrawing to Moreuil, Saleux, Rue then eventually onto Vron. French troops moved up the line to check the German advance. In early April, the 6/DLI was sent to Beuvry near Bethune about 4 miles behind one of the quietest area of the British front. Here a draft of about 400 men arrived and they were being prepared to relieve the 55th Division at La Bassee. However this did not happen and they were sent to Estaires instead. This was to be the location for the Second German Offensive. The account concludes:

> "It may be mentioned that the total casualties in the Battalion during the months of March, April and May had been 60 officers and 1,200 other ranks."

Early in June 1918, the remnants of the 50th Division was broken up.

Serjeant Thomas W. Simpson M.M. is commemorated on the Pozieres Memorial. Pozieres is located some 6km north east of Albert, Somme, France. The Memorial relates to a period of crisis in March and April 1918 when the Allied Fifth Army was driven back across the former Somme battlefields and the months before the Advance to Victory which began 8 August 1918. The memorial commemorates over 14,000 casualties of the UK and 300 South African Forces who have no known graves and who died on the Somme between 21 March and 7 August 1918. The Regiments represented with the most casualties are:
- The Rifle Brigade with over 600 names
- The Durham Light Infantry with approx. 600 names
- The Machine Gun Corps with over 500 names
- The Manchester Regiment with approx. 500 names
- The Royal Horse and Field Artillery with over 400 names.

Private JAMES SKELHORN 1897 – 1918

122510 Private James Skelhorn, 8th Battalion, Machine Gun Corps (Infantry) was killed in action 28 March 1918 during the German spring offensive. He is buried at Heath Cemetery, Harbonnieres and commemorated on the Evenwood War Memorial. He was 21 years old, born c.1897 in Burnley, Lancashire and was the son of James and Elizabeth Skelhorn, who later lived at 48 Murray Street, West Hartlepool. He enlisted at Bishop Auckland into the Durham Light Infantry (service number 73013 DLI). At the time, he lived at Evenwood.

Private James Skelhorn was one of 2 men from the Evenwood area to lose their lives whilst serving with the Machine Gun Corps, the other being Serjeant John Joseph Richardson D.C.M. of the 6th Battalion who lived at Gordon Gill, Ramshaw.

The German spring Offensive

Gough's Fifth Army of 13 Divisions plus 3 cavalry divisions was attacked by 43 Divisions of the German Second and Eighteenth Armies. The 8th Division fought as part of the Fifth Army, XIX Corps in the following engagements:

- 23 March 1918: Battle of St. Quentin
- 24 & 25 March 1918: Actions on the Somme Crossing
- 26 & 27 March 1918: Battle of Rosieres

The village of Rosieres had been located well within the British lines since the German withdrawal to the Hindenburg Line in the spring of 1917 but the swift advance of German storm-troopers soon saw the village under attack. The Fifth Army retreated and was involved in some extremely fierce and sacrificial fighting.

At 8.00am, 27 March, the Germans attacked the Rosieres line. On the left and the centre they were driven off but on the right a Labour Company fell back until a counter attack restored the situation. The 50th Division had practically been reduced to the 149th Brigade which was holding 4000 yards of line between the 66th and 8th Divisions. The retirements north of it had led to a warning order for a withdrawal being issued but this had been misinterpreted by the battalions in the line which began to fall back, abandoning Vauvillers near the junction of the 66th Division. The position at Vauvillers was held until noon at which time they withdrew because the troops on both flanks had retired. At noon an attack developed along the whole of the front line held by the 8th, 50th, 66th and 39th Divisions. At 1.00pm, the 66th retired. At 2.00pm, the 5/N.F. retired (part of the 149th Brigade). The 8th Division which had once formed a defensive flank attacked on the right while on the left the 7/DLI and the 22/Entrenching

122510 Private James Skelhorn, 8th Battalion, Machine Gun Corps (Infantry)

Battalion with some 66th Division Reserves went forward. At 3.00pm, these troops, well supported by artillery were under way and struck the enemy who was advancing in 8 or 10 waves. They drove the foremost waves back and re-established the 50th Division line, recapturing Vauvillers. Brigadier-General Riddell led a counterattack and drove the enemy from Harbonnieres – very heavy losses were inflicted on the enemy. The success was only temporary. The Germans attacked again and when ammunition began to run out, broke in south of the village and caused another retirement. At 7.00pm, the line withdrew to the light railway between Rosieres station and crossroads half a mile to the east. A counter attack was organised and the 50th Division was back on the light railway to the east of Harbonnieres. At 8.00pm, the Germans made another determined attack, advancing in 12 waves but were repulsed again. On the night of the 27th/28th, the Allied line, south of the Somme, ran from Mesnil-St. Georges (west of Montdidier) to Hamel via Boussicourt, Arvillers, Warvillers, Rosieres and Harbonnieres.

On the 28 March, the 8th Division together with the 16th Brigade, the Royal Horse Artillery defended Rosieres. These troops were withdrawn during the night.

Private James Skelhorn was killed in action 28 March 1918

It is assumed that Private James Skelhorn was killed in action at the Battle of Rosieres. He is buried at Heath Cemetery, Harbonnieres. The cemetery is located to the south of the Amiens to St. Quentin road approx 13km from Villers-Bretonneux and to the north of Rosieres. It was made after the Armistice when graves were brought into it from other burial grounds on the battlefields between Bray and Harbonnieres. The majority of casualties died in March or August 1918. There are 1491 burials and memorials.

Private JOHN ELLERKER 1893 -1918

73017 Private John Ellerker, 15th Battalion, the Durham Light Infantry was killed in action 28 March 1918 during the first phase of the German spring offensive. He is buried at Ribemont Communal Cemetery Extension, France and is commemorated on the Evenwood War Memorial. He was 25 years old, born c.1893 at West Hartlepool and in 1901 lived at 43 Sarah Street, West Hartlepool with his widowed mother and sister Ada. Later, he lived at Oaks Bank, Evenwood with his sister Meggie Ellerker.

The 15/D.L.I. formed part of the 64th Brigade, 21st Division which crossed into France 13 September 1915. The 21st Division saw action on the Somme throughout 1916, at Arras, Passchendaele and Cambrai in 1917 then back to the Somme to be caught by the German spring offensive of 1918. 73017 Private John Ellerker did not enter France until 28 November 1917 when the battalion was on the Somme and anticipating the great German Offensive.

The German Spring Offensive: 15/DLI

On the morning of the 21 March under the cover of dense fog, the Germans attacked the whole front held by the British Third and Fifth Armies. No Service Battalions of the Durham Light Infantry actually held the line. The 21st Division occupied the sector around Epehy and the 15th was in reserve at Lieramont. At 5.25am, the 15/DLI moved forward to a position south of Heudicourt and at noon occupied the "brown line" to the south of Heudicourt. The line was fiercely shelled and gas was used. During the afternoon the Germans broke through the left of the Division. The 15/DLI was ordered to counter attack. At 7.15pm, the 15/DLI assembled at Railton crossroads about half a mile east of Heudicourt. The counter attack commenced at 7.45pm in the face of heavy machine gun and rifle fire and there were considerable losses. However, 1 German officer and 60 prisoners were taken. The 15/DLI linked up with the 2/Lincolns but the enemy still held the trench to the left. There was heavy shelling.

At 3.00am, 22 March, the 15/DLI attempted to bomb their way northwards but it was impossible to make headway due to fire from machine gun dug outs. The German bombardment increased at 8.00am followed by an infantry attack. The line held firm but at noon, the 15/DLI was ordered to withdraw and marched to Lieramount. This area then became the target for German gunners. The battalion moved to the Nurlu road. At 6.30pm, the 15/DLI withdrew to a new line on high ground to the north west of Templeux-la-Fosse. German infantry advanced from the south and south east turning the right flank of the Division. The other battalions of the 64th Brigade struggled desperately.

At 8.00am, 23 March, fog again assisted the German infantry advance upon the whole front. The 64th Brigade was ordered to retreat and the 15/DLI withdrew fighting all the way. By noon, the 15/DLI was at Aizecourt-le-Haut. The Germans pressed forward their attack. The 15/DLI retired through Haut Allaines and across the little Tortille river to Feuillacourt. A line was formed with survivors of the 64th Brigade, barely 1,200 left. German batteries were now established at Aizecourt-le-Haut bombarding British positions. Two British field guns replied but they were soon silenced. At 2.00pm, Mont St. Quentin was occupied by the enemy. Further retirement took place under enfilade fire and the survivors assembled at Clery near the river Somme. Here a great deal of transport fell into enemy hands. Fighting continued in the moonlight. The 15/DLI drew back to east of Clery.

At 8.00am, 24 March, a furious bombardment was followed by an infantry attack. The Germans captured Clery. The line fell back to a position north east of Hem. On the afternoon, the 35th Division now began to arrive and a counter attack carried the line forward again. At 5.00pm, another German thrust commenced and the recently gained ground was lost. The 15/DLI rested at Curlu on the Somme. Here the 35th Division took over the line and as darkness fell, the survivors of the 15/DLI withdrew to billets at Suzanne.

25 March, the 15/DLI moved back to Bray where the remnants of the 64th Brigade made a Composite Battalion and the 15/DLI made one weak company under Capt. C.S. Herbert M.C. In this way the Division got a brigade about 1,500 strong which was available as a Reserve. That evening they were in trenches north east of Bray.

26 March, another composite company was formed by the 15/DLI at Chipilly and this detachment numbering about 70 men joined a second composite battalion. Other stragglers were collected at the transport lines at Beaucourt and Bonnay.

Private John Ellerker was killed in action 28 March 1918

30 March, the 15/DLI was at Allonville about 8km north east of Amiens.

In the fighting of the 4 days commencing 21 March, the 15/DLI lost 16 officers and 486 men killed, wounded and missing. The circumstances of the death of 73017 Private John Ellerker are unknown. Fighting was probably continuous throughout the week following the initial onslaught.

73017 Private John Ellerker, 15th Batallion, the Durham Light Infantry. Army Form B. 2090A Field Service

News of his Death

The Parish Magazine of May 1918 reported:

> "I grieve deeply to announce that 2 more of our gallant lads have fallen in action viz.: John Ellerker and John Luther Simpson, both of whose people live in the Oaks."

Private John Ellerker is buried at Ribemont Communal Cemetery Extension. Ribemont is about 8 km south west of Albert, midway between Chipilly and Beaucourt. The first burials took place at the end of March 1918 in the communal cemetery then the extension was begun in May and used until August. The cemetery was enlarged after the Armistice when graves were brought in from other cemeteries and from the 1918 battlefields east of Ribemont. There are 462 identified casualties.

It should be noted that Rev. Collis provided incorrect information and in fact John L. Simpson was not killed and actually survived the war – it was his brother Thomas W. Simpson (see p185–188) who was missing.

Second Lieutenant THOMAS WILLIAM APPLEGARTH 1894-1918

Second Lieutenant Thomas William Applegarth, 11th Battalion, the Durham Light Infantry died of wounds, 8 April 1918 as a Prisoner of War during the German spring offensive. He is buried at Caix British Cemetery, France and commemorated on the Evenwood War Memorial. He was 24 years old, born c.1894 at Piercebridge, County Durham to Thomas and Hannah Applegarth and was brother to Cicily. His father, Thomas senior died in March 1919 leaving his mother Hannah living at 2 Delaware Avenue, Evenwood. He was educated at Emmanuel College Cambridge and was a schoolmaster at Derby.

Thomas Applegarth was one of the few men from Evenwood to serve as an officer. It is understood that 2nd Lieut. Applegarth was a member of "A" company therefore this account refers to that company only.

The German Spring Offensive

21 March 1918: The German forces attacked the whole front. No DLI Service Battalions were in the line. The 20th Division of which the 11/DLI formed part was in reserve located at Golancourt and Voyennes. In the afternoon the battalion left for Villers St. Christophe, north of the Somme canal.

22 March: heavy firing heard to the north east in the direction of Holnon Wood and St. Quentin. The 11/DLI was required to fill a gap between the 61st and 60th Brigades on the line Tugny-Lavesne.

"By 8pm, when A and B companies arrived, the King's had had to evacuate Tugny and the support line thus became the front line. A and B companies, from left to right filled the gap between D company and the Shropshires of the 60th Brigade in position further north. Before 9.00pm Capt. Endean reported that D company and the King's had retired leaving the right flank of A company exposed. A thick fog had gathered and the enemy in Tugny could now be heard shouting in English and making a lot of noise…Soon after midnight B company were rushed from the right rear and there was confused fighting with the Durhams, Shropshires and Germans all mixed together in the fog. On the right Capt. Endean and A company fought stoutly but in withdrawing one party came under machine gun fire at close range and were all killed or wounded.

About 70 men of the 11th with 30 Shropshires and some Machine Gun Corps were collected south-west of Aubigny and withdrew down the Ham road, leaving a rearguard under 2nd Lieut. English to support 2 Vickers guns which were still in action. On the way to Ham, Colonel Hayes received orders to hasten to Offay and hold the bridgehead there.

Meanwhile Capt. Endean and 2nd Lieuts. Galey and Craig and about 40 men of A company had fought a way out in the fog through Dury to Ham. C-S-M T.J. Craggs of Bishop Auckland had done the same with a party of B company and some men of the Rifle Brigade. For his gallantry in the retreat this warrant officer was afterwards awarded the DCM."

23 March early morning:

"Colonel Hayes reached Offay and organised the men who were left with him into one company under the command of Lieut. Bushell, 2nd Lieuts. Martin, Naylor and English were also available and so was C-S-M Craggs who had managed to rejoin."

At dusk German snipers were active and after dark there was German machine gun and trench mortar fire.

4.00 am 24 March: Capt Endean, 2nd Lieut. Galley and over 30 men of A company rejoined.

6.00am: German artillery and mortar attack. Despite a request, there was no reply from the British artillery. Daylight – thick fog, Germans advanced from Canizy village, were fired upon by the British then retreated. B company regained their trench.

> "A German aeroplane flew over their position and Capt. Endean reported that the enemy were coming down the Hams-Nesle road. Other retiring troops of many units now helped to form a defensive flank on the right and a counter attack kept the enemy in check."

5.00pm 25 March: Germans attacked again and the Durhams covered the withdrawal of the French.

26 March: the 11/DLI detailed to dig defences in the neighbourhood of le Quesnel then march off down the Amiens-Arvilles road to dig and repair trenches.

27 March: the 11/DLI began to retire.

28 March: The French were to take over and had already begun to do so when a short fierce bombardment was followed by a German advance. German infantry were seen massing in the woods. A counter attack was organised but it was obvious that the enemy was too strong but the position was maintained until orders were received to retire to Fresnoy later in the day. By the evening, the 11/DLI were in reserve.

29 March morning: the Germans attacked along the Amiens road and entered Mezieres. At 3.15pm, the 11/DLI were called upon to recapture the village though they only had 130 men left.

> "Crossing open ground, a trench mortar barrage was encountered and enfilade machine gun fire smote them. Only here and there could small groups of men get through the barrier of bursting shells and Capt. Pemberton had about 20 Durhams with him when he entered the village. He pushed on until only 2 survived and then

withdrew. On the left 2nd Lieut. R.H. King had also reached Mezieres but all his party were killed and wounded and after working a Lewis gun with great effect he returned alone. Both officers were awarded the Military Cross."

The 11/DLI were now withdrawn to a position between Thennes and Hourges and passed the night in peace.

30 March: The Germans were now in Moreuil Wood and the battalion formed a defensive flank in this direction.

31 March morning: The enemy attacked again. At 4pm came a determined advance but rifle and Lewis gun fire stopped the enemy who retreated leaving many dead and wounded behind. Capt. Endean was wounded during this action. There was some shelling after this but the evening and night passed without further incident.

1 April: no attack. In the evening came relief. Marching to the Amiens road, the battalion now the strength of a strong platoon journeyed by bus to Quevavillers some 12 miles south-west of the city.

"Losses in the ranks during these 10 days totalled 455 and there were 19 casualties to officers. Among the killed or missing were 2nd Lieuts. W.G Craig, R.R. Galley, H. Rutherford, W.T Alexander, W. Banks, V.G. Duckett, F. Arnott, D.E Ellwood, T.W Applegarth and C.A. Morris and Lieut. R. Bushell. 2ndLieuts. P. Naylor, E.W. English, N.F. Gibson, J.H. Dodds, A.E. Wilkinson and H.J. Whitfield and Capts. W.G.L. Sear MC, W.J. Endean were all wounded"

Whether 2nd Lieut. T. W Applegarth was wounded then taken prisoner in the action involving "A" company on 22 March 1918 or some other action remains open to question unless the War Diary of the battalion is examined and can cast some light on the matter.

2nd Lieut. T. W Applegarth died of wounds 8 April 1918

Since on 1 April, he was reported as missing in the War Diary and his date of death is recorded as 8 April it is assumed that he was a P.O.W. and died in German hands.

Report of his Death

May 1918: The Parish Magazine reported:

"Our wounded include Adam Cree (2nd time), T. Braddick, 2nd Lieut. W.C.H. Hobson (in hospital in Newcastle) Rudge Howard (2nd time) Sergt. John Walton MM (3rd time) 2nd Lieut T. Applegarth, BA (and missing) and Jacob Hodgson (in hospital in Devonport)

June 1918:

"2nd Lieut. T. Applegarth is now definitely reported as a prisoner."

August 1918:

"The first we heard of was 2nd Lieut. T. Applegarth BA whose parents live in Delaware Avenue. A short time ago he was reported as missing then we heard of him as a prisoner in Germany, and now as having died of his wounds there."

Second Lieutenant Thomas William Applegarth, 11th Batallion, the Durham Light Infantry

Second Lieutenant T. W Applegarth is buried at Caix British cemetery. Caix is a village located about 20 miles south east of Amiens in the region of the Somme, France. The village was lost to the Germans during the advance of March 1918 and it was recaptured by the Canadian Corps 8 August 1918. The cemetery was made after the Armistice when graves were brought in from the battlefields and small cemeteries in the area. It contains 365 Commonwealth First World War burials.

Private WALTER MORLEY 1882-1918

243094 Private Walter Morley, 4th Battalion, the Yorkshire Regiment was killed in action 15 May 1918 and is buried at the ANZAC Cemetery, Sailly-sur-la-Lys, France and is commemorated on Evenwood War Memorial. He was 35 years old, born in 1882 at Lands to Thomas and Ann Morley and in 1901 was brother to William, David, George, Jane and Thomas. The family lived at Lands. He enlisted at Bishop Auckland.

*243094 Private Walter Morley, 4th Batallion, the Yorkshire Regiment.
Platoon photograph – which soldier is Walter Morley?*

Walter Morley was one of 4 men from the Parish to enlist into the Yorkshire Regiment (more popularly as the Green Howards) and lost their lives for their country. The others were Robert William Wilson, John Joseph Walton and Martin Simpson.

The 1/4th Battalion, the Yorkshire Regiment was a Territorial Force and as part of the York & Durham Brigade, Northumbrian Division landed at Boulogne, 18 April 1915. It became part of the 150th Brigade of the 50th Division, 14 May 1915. The Division served with distinction on the Western Front throughout the war including a most trying time on the Somme and Lys battlefields during the German spring offensive:
- The Battle of St. Quentin 21 – 22 March 1918
- The Actions at the Somme Crossings 24 – 25 March 1918
- The Battle of Rosieres 26 – 27 March 1918

Following the conclusion of this part of the offensive, the battalion's casualties totalled:
- 7 officers and 24 O.R.'s killed
- 11 officers and 147 non-commissioned officers and men wounded
- 1 officer and 10 men wounded and missing
- 3 officers and 168 O.R. missing

In all 22 officers and 349 non-commissioned officers and men were killed, wounded and missing. On 2 April, the battalion moved to Bethune, remaining until the retreat ended being heavily involved in reorganisation after the heavy losses in all ranks since the 23 March. During April no fewer than 22 officers and 802 O.R. joined the 4th Battalion, many of whom had recovered from previous wounds. On the 8 April orders were received to leave Bethune to move to Lavente since the 50th Division was required for the Battle of Lys, just commencing.

The German Spring Offensive

9 April: The 50th Division replaced Portuguese troops. At midday, the battalion was ordered to hold the line at Sailly-sur-Lys and at 2 pm. The work of digging in started. The 4/East Yorkshires were on the right and the 21/Middlesex was on the left. By 4 pm all Allied troops were withdrawn to the western bank of the Lys. An unsuccessful attempt was made to blow up the Sailly bridge however the bridge was held and the Germans were denied passage over it but they passed the Lys to the north and formed a line to right angles to the 4th Battalion.

10 April, about 11 am: the troops occupying the line at right angles to the 4th battalion were driven back so that the left flank was exposed and at the same time, the battalion was being strongly attacked from the front, they were compelled to fall back. The new line was held all night but the next morning, the 11th the Germans attacked in great force and a further withdrawal was forced upon the Green Howards. Units became considerably disorganised. At the cross roads to the west of Doulieu, battalions of the 150th Brigade were ordered to assemble then Vierhouck was named as the place of assembly. Troops were falling back and many rejoined the Brigade at Arrewage. Many casualties were incurred during the 12th as units reached La Motte-de-Bois. These positions were heavily

shelled at daybreak of the 13th and the battalion was ordered to withdraw to Le Parc – another assembly point for the 50th Division. The remnants of the 4th Battalion reached this place during late afternoon of the 15th April. Trenches were dug south of Bois des Vaches by working parties and stragglers came in to rejoin the ranks.

27 April: the battalion proceed by train to Courville for reorganisation. The Green Howards history states:

"Again for the second time within something like a month, had the Battalion lost many of its best

- 2 officers and 21 O.R.'s had been killed or had died of wounds
- 3 officers and 216 non-commissioned officers and men had been wounded
- 1 officer and 115 O.R.'s were missing
- 1 man was wounded and missing."

243094 Private W. Morley was one of those O.R.'s reported as "Missing". The IX Corps which comprised the 8th, 21st, 25th and 50th Divisions had lost 1,600 officers and 35,000 O.R.'s since 21 March 1918.

Private Walter Morley was killed in action 15 May 1918

The Green Howards' Gazette of July & August 1918 reports 243094 Private W. Morley as "Missing" then the January & February 1919 edition records him as "Killed in Action" with a note – "Previously reported Missing, now reported by German Government as Killed or Died of Wounds." There were 5 other soldiers serving in the 4/Yorks. killed in action on the 15 May 1918. Private Walter Morley is buried at the ANZAC Cemetery, Sailly-sur-la-Lys. The village of Sailly-sur-la-Lys is located on the Bethune to Armentieres road in the region of Pas de Calais, France. It contains 320 Commonwealth burials.

Private DAVID BAISTER 1897-1918

36723, Private David Baister, 1/5th battalion, the Durham Light Infantry was killed in action 27 May 1918 during the German spring offensive at the Battle of the Aisne. He has no known grave and is commemorated

36723 Private David Baister, 1/5th Batallion, the Durham Light Infantry

on the Soissons Memorial, France and the Evenwood War Memorial. He was 31 years old, born c.1887 at Toft Hill to Robert and Isabella Baister. He married Florence Margaret Banks 22 April 1916 at Evenwood. They had one son John David born February 1917. By 1918 the family lived at 13 Copeland Row, Evenwood. David Baister left behind Florrie and an infant son, "Jack". Within the period of about 2 years Florrie was a bride, a mother and a widow and in fact, Florrie died in May 1920 leaving her mother to look after Jack.

David Baister attested 28 February 1916 joining the Royal Engineers then was transferred to the DLI then into the Machine Gun Corps then into 5/DLI. He entered France 1 April 1917. The 5/DLI was a Territorial Force and was part of the 150th Brigade, 50th Division and in February 1918 it was transferred to the 151st Brigade, 50th Division. The 151st Brigade was heavily involved in action against the German Offensive in the spring of 1918:

- The Battle of St. Quentin
- The Actions at the Somme Crossing
- The Battle of Rosieres

The following 2 battles are known as the Battle of the Lys.
- The Battle of Estaires
- The Battle of Hazelbrouck

Following a most trying time on the Somme and the Lys battlefields, the Division was withdrawn and sent to IX Corps then on the Aisne, believed to be a much quieter area. Unfortunately this was not the case and the Division was hit hard by another German attack.
- The Battle of the Aisne 27 May – 6 June 1918

After suffering particularly heavy casualties while on the Aisne, the Division was substantially reorganised.

The Third Battle of the Aisne: 27 May – 6 June 1918

The German attack was launched by 4,000 guns across a 40km front against 4 Divisions of the IX Corps. There was a heavy concentration of British troops in the front line trenches and casualties from this bombardment were severe. In fact the IX Corps was virtually wiped out. The bombardment was accompanied by a gas attack after which 17 German infantry divisions advanced through the gaps in the line. Rapid progress was made and the Germans broke though the reserve troops (8 Allied Divisions – 4 British and 4 French) between Soissons and Rheims. By the end of the first day, the Germans had passed the Aisne and reached the river Vesle gaining 15km of territory. By 3 June, they had come within 90km of Paris and captured 50,000 Allied soldiers and 800 guns. French casualties were heavy, with 98,000 losses. The British suffered 29,000 casualties. But by 6 June, the German advance had run out of steam.

The Last Fight: 27 May 1918 – an account of the 5/DLI

"The 5th DLI had played its part in the Second Battle of Ypres in 1915, on the Somme in 1916 and at Arras and again Ypres in 1917. It has fought well with the Fifth Army in the March retreat and had distinguished itself in the bitter fighting on the Lys. It fought one more fight but it was its last as on May 27th, 1918, the whole Northumbrian Division – infantry, artillery, engineers – was overwhelmed by the enemy and destroyed."

5 May 1918: the 5/DLI marched to Glennes, a village 2 miles south of the Aisne canal. The section of the line allotted to the British Divisions included Craonne at the eastern extremity of the Chemin des Dames range of hills across towards Rheims. The 50th Division held the sector from Craonne to La Ville-aux-Bois. On the left were French troops and on the right was the 8th Division. Further to the right was the 21st Division. The 25th Division was held in reserve. The 50th Division was organised on a 3 brigade front, each brigade having 2 battalions in the line and 1 in reserve. The 150th Brigade was on the left, the 151st in the centre and the

149th on the right. The 50th Division HQ was at Beaurieux. It was peaceful for the first 3 weeks.

6 – 13 May: 5/DLI in the front line facing the village of Corbeny, just within the German held territory.

13 – 18 May: in reserve at Chaudres

18 – 24 May: in the front line trenches then on the night of the 24th/25th they were relieved by the 6/DLI

25 May: went to the reserve trenches at Chaudres and Cuiry-les-Chaudres, 2 villages on the north bank of the River Aisne.

26 May: 7.20pm. orders were received to proceed in fighting order to Centre d'Evreux, the reserve position. Intelligence indicated that a massive enemy attack would be launched at 1.00am. "B" "C" & "D" Companies were put into a huge dug-out near Brigade HQ and "A" Company in another 100 yards away. Gas curtains of the dug-outs retreated with chemicals. Ammunition wagons hastened to load the batteries with shells. 9.00pm. British artillery opened up to harass roads and villages behind the lines. 12.00 all likely assembly places were kept under heavy fire.

27 May – 1.00am.

> "The German artillery spoke with a mighty and awful voice. Those of long experience who lived through it say that this bombardment was the fiercest yet known upon the Western Front; observers tell of German lines from Cordeny eastwards bursting into one vast sheet of flame."

The bombardment continued for three hours – gas & high explosive shells poured into the British and French lines. The front line trenches and wire entanglements were swept away. Dug-outs were broken in, gas filtered into and over the area, communication between areas was impossible, runners may have found their destinations but never returned. The French and British batteries kept their guns in action until they were knocked out or overcome by gas.

4.00am – the German infantry advanced, the attack made rapid progress.

6.30am – the right wing of the 8th Division had been forced back to Gernicourt

8.00 am. The enemy had captured Pontavert

Early afternoon – further south, the 21st Division was hard pressed and there was fighting at Cormicy and Cauroy.

On the left, the French were forced back as the Germans broke through and captured Beaurieux in the morning and bridges at Maizy.

What of the 50th Division?

It was on the left of the British front and casualties had been heavy, survivors were bewildered with the shelling, sick with gas and half blinded with their respirators. The 150th Brigade was practically annihilated.

What of the 5/DLI?

By 7.00 am. The Germans were close to the 151st Brigade HQ, the 5/DLI were in reserve in the dug-outs. They were ordered to proceed to the reserve trenches but this instruction came too late and the enemy were already in these trenches. With no time to get into proper battle formation, confusion was great and it was obvious that a disaster had occurred. Officers tried to get the men clear of the surrounding woods and back to the Aisne bridges in order to hold up the enemy. Casualties were heavy – 9 officers were killed and 5 wounded, others were captured, many ranks were leaderless and failed to reach the bridges. Chaudardes was heavily shelled. The bridge at Concevreux had not yet been captured Men of whatever battalion collected at the higher ground at Concevreux and were re-organised into one weak brigade. Its position was heavily shelled and by 5.00pm. German infantry advanced to high ground above Muscourt. The pressure continued – Ventelay and Bouvancourt both fell, the Germans entered Courlandon. The remnants of the Division fell back to Montigny.

The 5/DLI War Diary describes this cataclysmic state of affairs as follows:

> "CHAUDARDES
> 27th 1am – Terrific enemy barrage consisting of every calibre of shells and trench mortars accompanied by gas and tear shells.
> 6.30am – C & D Coys were ordered to proceed to the Intermediate Line.
> 7.am – A & B Coys were ordered to reinforce this position.

The enemy attack had commenced at 4.0am but owing to the heavy barrage all communications were cut and no information had come back from the front line.

28th – On reaching the Intermediate Line it was found that the enemy were already round right and left flanks. The Battn had suffered extremely heavy and only a portion of B Coy was to be found. This detachment withdrew and held a position at a clearing N.W. of PONTEVERT and held up the enemy in their front for a considerable time. Ammunition was very short. The enemy were again found to be round both flanks of the detachment. A withdrawal was made to a line S. of PONTEVERT which was in continuation of a line held by a portion of the 25th Divn.

The enemy by this time had crossed the AISNE higher up and it was therefore plain the position then held was likely to be turned. It was decided to withdraw to CHAUDARDES but a reconnaissance ascertained that the enemy were between this place and CHAUDARDES which rendered this withdrawal impossible. Nearly all this detachment were cut off a few escaping over the AISNE before the bridge was blown. This was the last organized body of the battn. Odd portions and men sent up from the Transport Line continued fighting with the 25th Divn until the 50th Divn was withdrawn on the 29th.

Casualties during this battle amounted to 33 officers and 650 ORs but owing to the wooded country, large extent of ??? and no survivors from the Btn no accurate details of these casualties are available.

30th – Remnant of Btn moved to IGNY; crossing the Marne at PORT a BINSON; where Divn concentrated

31st Moved to VERT la GRAVELLE."

Private David Baister was killed in action 27 May 1918

31 May, the following details were reported:

"The casualties of the Battalion on May 27th were 24 officers and about 650 men. Of the officers 10 were killed, 5 wounded and 9 taken prisoner. Of the men 53 killed, 151 wounded and brought back across the Aisne to safety. 446 were taken prisoner but this number includes a large number of wounded who had to be left. Of the 3 gallant battalions of the 151st Brigade only 103 men of those who were in the line on May 27th answered to their names when the roll was called at Vert la Gravelle on the 31st May."

There were 47 men of the 5/DLI who were killed in action or died of wounds on 27 May 1918. Of these 47 only 14 were born in Durham, about 1/3rd whereas at the beginning of the war, the Durham battalions were exclusively men of Durham. This probably signifies that the Durham battalions had suffered heavily during the war and losses were so great that finding plentiful replacements from the "home" county was impossible. There was a shortage of men from Durham available for conscription as most of those fit and able would be employed on vital war work, notably in the traditional areas of coal mining, coke production and steel production. Thus men from other areas filled the ranks – Manchester, Lincolnshire, Devon, Oldham, Ilford, Hull and Cardiff to name but a few.

It seems that David Baister intended to join the Royal Engineers, probably thinking that his skills as a mason could be utilised but he ended up with the DLI after training with the Machine Gun Corps. He served a total of 2 years and 90 days, 1 year 57 days in France. Like many, he suffered as the full weight of the German onslaught annihilated the British Army – he has no known grave.

Reports of his death

August 1918: The Parish Magazine reported:

"Included in the list of wounded are Ptes. John Friend, J. Baister (son-in-law of Mrs. J. Banks) W. Bowman (hospital in Bradford) A. Metcalfe (son of Mr. and Mrs. Metcalfe, Co-op Stores) T. Braddick (amputation of left hand) W. Studholme (2nd time) Edwin Carrick M.M. (gas poisoning) and Jasper Lauder, Stracona's Horse, who was in a hospital that the Germans have said to have bombed but is now in a Surrey hospital."

Private David Baister is commemorated on the Soissons Memorial. Soissons is in the region of Aisne, France approx. 100 kilometres northeast of Paris. The Soissons Memorial commemorates almost 4,000 officers and men of the United Kingdom who died during the Battles of the Aisne and the Marne in 1918 and who have no known grave.

Private OLIVER RUSHFORD M.M. 1894 -1918

250440 Private Oliver Rushford M.M., 1/6th battalion, the Durham Light Infantry was killed in action 30 May 1918 during the German spring offensive. He has no known grave. He is commemorated on the Soissons Memorial, France and both the Evenwood and Etherley War Memorials. He was 24 years old, born c.1894 at Escomb to John and Annie Rushford and by 1901 the family lived at Wind Mill, in the Parish of Evenwood and Barony. His father was a farmer and butcher. Oliver and his older brother Edgar were "travelling" butchers selling meat from their horse and cart. He enlisted prior to February 1915. By 1918 his father John had died and his mother lived at 59 Albion Street, Witton Park

Private Oliver Rushford survived the Battle of the Somme and the infamously futile and costly attack on the Butte de Warlencourt, 5 November 1916 which saw so many of his comrades lose their lives including Serjeant George T. Cox from Evenwood and Private Alfred Brown from Staindrop. He survived the early storm of the German spring offensive of 1918 through March and April before being killed in late May. He has no known grave and is commemorated on the Soissons Memorial along with Private David Baister of Evenwood (5/DLI).

The Battle of Le Transloy
8th Phase of the Battle of the Somme 1916

Private Oliver Rushford had a very distinguished career signified by the award of a Military Medal during operations associated with the Battle of Le Transloy. This action, part of the Battle of the Somme, commenced 1 October 1916. The village of Eaucourt L'Abbaye was captured and the attack is famous for the action of Lieut.-Col. R. B. Bradford who was awarded the Victoria Cross.

> "The casualties during the 2 days had been very heavy and included amongst the officers, in addition to those already mentioned 2nd Lieut. Peacock killed and 2nd Lieut. Lean, Capt. Peberdy, Lieut. Cotching, 2nd Lieut. Barnett and 2nd Lieut. Appleby wounded. Amongst the

decorations gained were Military Medals awarded to Corporal Dixon and Privates Rushford and Atkinson, all signallers, and Private Turnbull of X Company. Good work was also done by Serjeants Gowland and Winslow.

On the night of the 2nd October Lieut.-Col. Bradford handed over the command of the Battalion to Lieut. Ebsworth, and it was relieved by the 7th Northumberland Fusiliers the night after."

The Auckland Chronicle reported as follows:

"Lands Bank with less than 100 houses and Wind Mill with only a few scattered houses are 2 wings of the extensive parish of Evenwood and Barony. The inhabitants are naturally proud of the two heroes who have distinguished themselves for bravery and have been awarded the Military Medal. Pioneer Herbert Wardle formerly resided at Ramshaw and attended the Old Colliery School. On removing to Lands Bank with his grandmother he attended the old Morley School. Corp. Oliver Rushford is a son of Mrs. Rushford and the late Mr. John Rushford. He also attended the old school at Morley."

The award was reported in the supplement to the London Gazette 9 December 1916.

The Third Battle of the Aisne: 27 May – 6 June 1918

The German attack was launched by 4,000 guns across a 40km front against 4 Divisions of the IX Corps. There was a heavy concentration of British troops in the front line trenches and casualties from this bombardment were severe. In fact the IX Corps was virtually wiped out. The bombardment was accompanied by a gas attack after which 17 German infantry divisions advanced through the gaps in the line. Rapid progress was made and the Germans broke though the reserve troops (8 Allied Divisions – 4 British and 4 French) between Soissons and Reims. By the end of the first day, the Germans had passed the Aisne and reached the river Vesle gaining 15km of territory. By the 3rd June, they had come within 90km of Paris and captured 50,000 Allied soldiers and 800 guns. French casualties were heavy, with 98,000 losses. The British suffered 29,000 casualties. But by 6 June, the German advance had run out of steam.

The first week of April saw the 6/DLI involved in action in what was to become known as the Battle of Lys before it was relieved and sent to join the French troops in the line at Chemin des Dames in the area of Soissons, thought to be a quieter area. In early May, an epidemic of influenza visited the training camp at Arcis before the battalion marched to billets at Glennes, a small village near Aisne. The 6/DLI moved up the line to relieve the 73rd French Infantry in the woods east of the Craonne Plateau. All was quiet until the evening of 26 May when the message was received that an enemy bombardment was to take place the next morning.

27 May 1.00am: heavy barrage, 3,000 yards flooded with high explosives, shrapnel and gas shells.

4.50am: enemy attack had overwhelmed the forward posts. X Company wiped out, enemy advancing rapidly, reserve company (Z) close to HQ had the enemy on top of them. Lieut.-Col. Walton and about 40 men searched for the best place to make a stand, still under a barrage. The 5/DLI came up to the communication trench to find it occupied by the enemy. Battalion practically "annihilated"

Afternoon: Lieut.-Col. Walton, a few men of the 8/DLI and 5/Northumberland Fusiliers Northumberland Fusiliers held the bridge at Concevreux. They were not joined by any men from the front.

For the next 2 days, 2 commanding officers of the 6/DLI and 8/DLI found themselves in command of various men of other battalions.

29 May: the remnants were ordered to move from Villers Argon to Baslieux-sous-Chatillon:

> "before reaching the latter place, every available man was again collected to form part of a company under Major Heslop, representing the remnants of the 151st Brigade in a Battalion to which each Brigade of the Division contributed one Company."

After a night at Quisles Chateau, this battalion moved towards Vile-en-Tardenois to support the 74th Brigade. The 151st Brigade Company were ordered to act as advance guard and to seize the high ground north and east of Romigny. This was done but the enemy attacked in force and the Company was driven out to a position south of the village which they held until reinforcements arrived.

"The remnants of the Division, except the Composite Battalion, were assembled at Vert-la-Gravelle, south of the Marne when a Composite Brigade was formed...After a week spent in reorganisation, moved up to Chaumuzy and the Bois de Courton where it did good work in a counter attack on the Bligny Ridge."

Private Oliver Rushford M.M. was killed in action 30 May 1918

The exact circumstances of 250440 Private Oliver Rushford's death remain unknown. A total of 14 O.R.'s serving with the 1/6 DLI were killed in action 30 May 1918 including Private Oliver Rushford and 76809 Private E. Hindmarch from Bishop Auckland. The War Diary of the 6/DLI for June 1918 provides the following details:

> "VERT la FRAVELLE June 1st – Remnants of Battn (about 35 fighting men) inspected by GOC Divn. About 35 men under Capt. HARE were still in the line and were in action with the French near BOIS de BONVAL.
>
> 2nd Composite Bde formed. Lt Col Walton to command 151 Bde Composite Battn.
>
> Capt. HARE's party moved to BOIS de COURTON."

News came that the 50th Division was to be broken up and early in June the remnants entrained at Sezanne for the Abberville area. They took billets at Caumont where orders were received that the battalions were to be reduced to the strength of Training Cadres (10 officers and 50 other ranks)

> "It may be mentioned that that the total casualties in the battalion during the months of March, April and May had been 60 officers and over 1,200 other ranks."

250440 Private Oliver Rushford M.M., 1/6th Batallion, the Durham Light Infantry. The Soissons Memorial

The Training Cadres of the 5th, 6th and 8th DLI moved to Dieppe then about the middle of August moved onto Rouen.

Private Oliver Rushford M.M. is commemorated on the Soissons Memorial. The town of Soissons is in the region of Aisne, France approx. 100 kilometres north-east of Paris. The Soissons Memorial commemorates almost 4,000 officers and men of the United Kingdom who died during the Battles of the Aisne and the Marne in 1918 and who have no known grave.

Private JOHN JOSEPH MARQUIS 1893 – 1918

3128A Private John Joseph Marquis, 28th Battalion, Australian Infantry, A.I.F. was killed in action 1 June 1918. He is buried at Franvillers Communal Cemetery Extension, France and is commemorated on the Hamsterley War Memorial. He was 25 years old, born c.1893 at Hamsterley, County Durham to Henry and Eleanor Marquis and was brother to James, Thomas, Margaret, Arthur, Mary, Jane, Frederick, Edward and Eleanor. In 1909, the family emigrated to Australia and in 1910 took up land at Datatine in the Shire of Dumbleyung, Western Australia. The farm was known as "Hoppland Park", Katanning East, Western Australia. His brothers Frederick and James also enlisted for service. His younger brother, 5893 Private Fredrick William Marquis, 28th Battalion, Australian Infantry, A.I.F. was another victim of the war, he was killed in action 4 September 1918.

3128A Private John Joseph Marquis, 28th Batallion, Australian Infantry, A.I.F.
Family photograph prior to leaving Britain c.1909.
Back: Mary, Joseph, Arthur, Meg, Jim, Jane, Fred
Front: Eleanor, Nell. Henry, Ned

The 28th Battalion AIF (Western Australia) was raised in April 1915 and took recruits from Western Australia. The Battalion departed Freemantle for service overseas 29 June 1915 and after 2 months spent in Egypt training, landed at Gallipoli 10 September 1915. The 28th had a relatively quiet time at Gallipoli and the battalion departed the peninsula in December, having suffered only light casualties.

After another stint in Egypt, the 7th Brigade proceeded to France and the Western Front, as part of the 2nd Australian Division. The 28th Battalion took part in its first major battle at Pozieres 28 July – 6 August 1916.

Private John Joseph Marquis enlisted 20 July 1916 and left Freemantle 9 November 1917. He entered France 10 October 1917 joining his battalion in the field 14 October 1917. He was sick 8 February 1918 – 17 April 1918 and rejoined his unit 6 May 1918.

In April 1918, the 28th fought to turn back the German spring offensive and from 8 August participated in the joint British and French offensive that marked the beginning of Germany's defeat. The Battalion was prominent in the fighting to secure crossing points over the Somme River around Perrone, and in the advance beyond Mont St. Quentin. The 28th's last actions of the war were fought as part of the effort to break through the Beaurevoir Line in the first week of October1918. The first members of the battalion began returning to Australia in January, and the 28th was disbanded in March 1919.

The 28th Battalion war diaries have not been researched and the circumstances of his death remain unknown. The 2nd Australian Division had been involved in the Battle of the Avre 4 April 1918 and their next action was 4 July with capture of Hamel. Thus at the time of his death, the Division was not involved in any major engagement. Perhaps Private John Joseph Marquis was a victim of the usual violence of warfare and caught up in the German spring offensive which swept over the Somme as the Allies forces defended their positions – shelling, machine gun fire, sniping, bombing, gas attack.

Private John Joseph Marquis was killed in action 1 June 1918

Private John Joseph Marquis is buried at Franvillers Communal Cemetery Extension. Franvillers is a village located between Amiens and Albert and stands on high ground above the river Ancre. The communal cemetery was used between May 1916 and May 1918, the extension was used from April to August 1918 by units and field ambulances engaged in the Amiens District. It contains 248 Commonwealth burials.

Private WILLIAM ALDERSON MOSES 1897 – 1918

220168 Private William Alderson Moses, 7th Battalion, The East Yorkshire Regiment was killed in action 8 June 1918 and is buried in Hawthorn Ridge Cemetery Number 1, Auchonvillers, France and is commemorated on both Evenwood and Etherley War Memorials. He was 21 years old, born c.1897 at Bishop Auckland to Robert and Elizabeth Moses and in 1901 was brother to Emily, Ethel and Beatrice. The family then lived at Etherley Lane near the Bay Horse Inn but later lived at Morley. William Alderson Moses was the only Evenwood man to fall whilst serving with the East Yorkshire Regiment. He enlisted at Bishop Auckland and previously served with the Yorkshire Regiment (service number 204893).

The First Battle of Bapaume
(second phase of the First Battles of the Somme 1918)

Along with the 2nd, 12th, 47th & 63rd Divisions, the 17th Division formed the V Corps, part of the Third Army which were involved in this action on the 24 & 25 March 1918 which signified the commencement of the German Spring Offensive. The next significant action, in which the 17th Division took part was in early August 1918, the Battle of Amiens. The service details of 220168 Private William Alderson Moses and the war diary of the 7/East Yorks have not been researched therefore the circumstances of his death are unknown. Since he is buried near Auchenvilliers, it would normally be assumed that the 7th Battalion, the East Yorkshire Regiment held trenches in the Auchonvillers area and was involved in an engagement, probably an exchange of artillery fire.

Private William Alderson Moses was killed in action 8 June 1918

220168 Private William Alderson Moses, 7th Battalion, The East Yorkshire Regiment. Hawthorn Ridge cemetery

Private William Alderson Moses is buried at Hawthorn Ridge Cemetery No.1 Auchonvillers. This cemetery was made by the V Corps when the Ancre battlefield was cleared in the spring of 1917. There were 13 O.R.'s serving with the 7/East Yorks who were killed in action or died of wounds on that day including 220168 Private W.A. Moses and 30986 Private W. Fenby. They are buried side by side.

Gunner WILLIAM GRAY 1878 – 1918

178943 Gunner William Gray, 52nd battery, 15th Brigade, Royal Field Artillery died of wounds 3 July 1918 during the Lys Offensive, action at La Becque. He was 40 years old and is buried at Terlincthun British Cemetery, Wimille, France and commemorated on Evenwood War Memorial. He was born in 1878 at Normanby, Yorkshire. By 1915, he lived at 20 Evenwood Gate with his wife Mary and 4 children, Sarah, Eva Eliza, John George and Anne. He enlisted at Woolwich, Kent and formerly served in the Royal Army Vetinary Corps.

178943 Gunner William Gray, 52nd Batallion, 15th Brigade, Royal Field Artillery

William Gray was the oldest man from Evenwood to be lost in the First World War. He was obviously a man of high standing in the community, who at the age of 38, enlisted into the Army to "do his bit" for King and country. Until he volunteered for service in December 1915, he was the Secretary of the Soldiers and Sailors Fund, a Parish Councillor and a member of Evenwood Workmen's Club. Whilst on active duty, he was an occasional contributor to the Parish Magazine. Councillor J. Stokeld Robinson succeeded him as Secretary of the Soldiers and Sailors Fund. He was checkweighman at Randolph Colliery, Evenwood.

The Lys Offensive 9 – 29 April 1918

Ludendorff's first and biggest offensive had resulted in the greatest advance since the first months of the war but it had failed to achieve any decisive results. The chief error was that he had concentrated his efforts on the strongest sector held by the British Third Army and the operation was affected by severe transport problems and low morale of undernourished troops. Casualties were enormous – 240,000 Allied losses, slightly more German casualties. Unable to make further progress on the Somme, Ludendorff turned to Flanders and the Lys Offensive.

The Battle of Lys, also known as the Fourth Battle of Ypres and the Battle of Estaires, was planned as Operation Georgette with the objective of capturing Ypres. In one of the greatest failures in the military history of Portugal, the Second Portuguese Division, approx. 20,000 men commanded by General Gomes da Costa lost about 300 officers and 7,000 men killed, wounded and prisoners, resisting the attack of 4 German Divisions with 50,000 men of the Sixth German Army commanded by General Ferdinand von Quast in the first day of the offensive.

The 5th Division saw action at the Battle of Hazelbrouck, (the third phase) on the 12 – 15 April playing a part in the defence of Nieppe Forest. The offensive was abandoned 29 April when attempts to seize the Flanders heights ended in failure. The second German offensive had resulted in an advance of up to 10 miles but none of their strategic objectives had been achieved and the channel ports remained safe in Allied hands. The Germans had lost 350,000 men the Allies about 305,000, the great majority of them British since the beginning of the Spring Offensive.

Action at La Becque: 28 June 1918

The bitter fighting of the Battle of Lys ended with the failure of the German Army to break through to Hazebrouck. The front line in the Vieux Berquin sector was established in front of Aval Wood, on the eastern fringe of the Nieppe Forest. On 20 June the 5th and 31st Divisions received orders to attack on a 6,000 yard front east of Nieppe Forest. The operation was designed:

1. to disrupt any plans the enemy might have for a renewed offensive and
2. to push the British lines away from the edge of the wood where they had made an easy target for hostile artillery.

In a night-time operation aimed at securing a position from which enfilade fire could be used to support the main attack, 2 companies of the 13th York and Lancasters supported by 2 companies of the 18/DLI captured Ankle Farm in the early morning, 27 June. Later in the day the main attack was carried out by the 92nd Brigade, 31st Division in the area of la Papote. The following extracts are from the Accrington Pals website and simply relate to artillery involvement rather than the action as a whole:

> "An intense shrapnel barrage broke over the enemy front line at 6am on the 28th, the first wave of attacking troops left their trenches.... At the moment the shrapnel barrage lifted, British troops swarmed forward giving the enemy little or no chance to reach machine guns or man parapets before being overrun. Behind the lines, gun batteries, road junctions and likely assembly points were being targeted by heavy artillery while the main road through Vieux Berquin was cloaked by a thick smoke screen laid down by Australian artillery.... In circumstances that were repeated along the length of the front, attacking troops pressing too closely to the (creeping) barrage were inevitably hit by their own shrapnel, accounting for many of the (15th/17th West Yorkshires) battalion's 170 casualties...In the operations of the 27th-28th June, 31st Division reported the capture of 278 men from I.R. 102 along with 3 field guns, 10 heavy machine guns, 29 light machine gun, 4 heavy trench mortars, 5 light trench mortars. 223 of the enemy were buried in the area of the advance....More were undoubtedly killed by the barrage of artillery and machine gun fire placed beyond the line of the objective. All objectives were reached

practically on time. To the right of 31st Division, 5th Division was no less successful."

The 5th Division attacked the sector to the south of the 31st. It is assumed that the artillery positions held by the 52nd Battery were some way south of Aval Wood. Following the retreats of March and April, La Becque was one of the first successful operations when the Allied forces went on the offensive. No-one could have foreseen that the war would be over in 5 months!

Gunner William Gray died of wounds 3 July 1918

He is buried at Terlincthun British Cemetery at Wimille on the outskirts of Boulogne, Pas-de-Calais, France. Boulogne and Wimereux housed numerous hospitals and other medical establishments. The reports included in the Parish Magazine indicate that he died as a result of gas poisoning thus it is assumed that enemy shelling in retaliation during or after the operation hit his position. Thus it is assumed that Gunner William Gray was wounded in the action at La Becque, 28 June 1918 and was transported to a military hospital in the vicinity of Boulogne but did not respond to treatment and died as a result of wounds received on the battlefield.

Notification of his Death

The Parish Magazine of August 1918 reported his death:

> "But the death which seems to have thrown all Evenwood into mourning is that of Gnr. William Gray, who died in hospital on July 3rd from the effects of gas poisoning. He was so well-known to us all and was of himself such a part of the life of the place that it is almost too difficult to realise that we shall never see him bustling about our streets in his old cheery business-like way any more in this life. William Gray I firmly believe was a great man. Far greater, I think, than he ever knew or thought himself to be. I will confess here that I was looking forward with great hope to his influence upon the place when he came back amongst us again. God however has other work for him to do, for nobody I am sure will ever think of William Gray as being unemployed."

The minutes of the Evenwood and Barony Parish Council meeting 10 July 1918 provide a formal response:

> "Death of Mr. Wm. Gray
> Unanimously agreed – This Council deeply regret the loss of William Gray an active member of the Council through death whilst on service in France and that a letter of sympathy be sent to his widow and family."
>
> Geo. Parkin Chairman

Memorial Service: 21 July 1918

The September edition of the Evenwood Parish Magazine reported:

> "…there is one thing that stands out in my memory and that is the Memorial Service which we had for the late Gunner William Gray. This was held on Sunday afternoon, July 21st at 3pm. There was a large attendance of relatives and friends."

Serjeant JOHN JOSEPH RICHARDSON D.C.M. 1890 – 1918

20786 Serjeant John Joseph Richardson D.C.M., 6th battalion, the Machine Gun Corps died of wounds 7 July 1918 during action around Ypres as part of the German offensive in Flanders. He is buried at Nine Elms British Cemetery, Poperinge, Belgium and commemorated on Evenwood War Memorial. He was 28 years old, born c.1890 at Lynesack to John Joseph and Sarah Richardson. By 1918 Sarah had died and J.J. senior lived at 3 Gordon Gill, Ramshaw.

The date he enlisted and the date he was transferred from the East Yorks. into the Machine Gun Corps has not been researched. The Medal Roll informs that he entered France 2 September 1915 presumably with the East Yorkshire Regiment.

The 6th Machine Gun Company joined the 2nd Division 4 January 1916 then moved to the 2nd Battalion, Machine Gun Corps 4 March 1918. Until the winter of 1917-18 British machine guns were deployed in companies with a company attached to each infantry brigade but from about the beginning of March 1918 machine guns were re-organised into battalions, one to each infantry division.

Information obtained from the diary of Joseph Harold Swain (1898-1974) who was posted to the 6th Battalion Machine Gun Corps (the machine gun unit of the 6th Infantry Division) until after the Armistice confirms that the 6th Division formed part of the IX Corps, Fourth Army which spearheaded the Allied Advance in the late summer and autumn of 1918. Serjeant John Joseph Richardson died before the advance commenced but up until his reported death 7 July 1918, the 6th Division took part in the following actions, part of the German offensive in Flanders known as the Battle of the Lys:

- The Battle of St. Quentin: 21 – 23 March 1918
- The Battle of Bailleul: 13 – 15 April 1918
- the Second Battle of Kemmel: 25 – 26 April 1918 (the 71st Brigade of the 6th Division).
- The Battle of the Scherpenberg: 29 April 1918.

The German Spring Offensive

On 27 June, the Division passed to the XIX Corps and relieved the 46th French Division (Chasseurs) in the Dickebusch sector.

> "This was in a very unpleasant front, where the dominating position of the enemy on Kemmel Hill made movement, even in the rear lines, impossible by day and practically all work of which there was plenty, had to be done by night.
> July 6th – Enemy's raid on Scottish Wood repulsed."

There were some 4,715 battle casualties in the Ypres sector between 3 April – 24 August 1918 which includes 750 at Neuve Eglise (71st Infantry Brigade) and 250 in attack on Scottish and Ridge Woods.

Serjeant John Joseph Richardson D.C.M. died of wounds 7 July 1918

The War Diaries of the Machine Gun Corps and the service record of Serjeant J.J. Richardson have not been examined therefore it is impossible to state with certainty when he received his fatal injuries. He died of wounds therefore it appears likely that he was wounded as a result of one of the following scenarios:

20786 Serjeant John Joseph Richardson D.C.M., 6th Batallion, the Machine Gun

- during the defence of Scottish Wood
- indiscriminate shelling, mortar attack, sniping or a raid

Serjeant J. J. Richardson was posthumously awarded the Distinguished Conduct Medal. The Distinguished Conduct Medal was instituted in 1854 and was awarded to enlisted men for acts of gallantry. It was replaced in 1993 by the Conspicuous Gallantry Cross. The following announcement appeared in the London Gazette 3 September 1918 but to date the action to which this citation refers remains unknown.

"For conspicuous gallantry and devotion to duty in action in charge of a machine gun.

Three times he drove back a fierce hostile attack with very heavy casualties and when his officer was killed, he continued to fire his gun until practically surrounded. Finally, his gun being knocked out, for five hours he assisted to take up ammunition to a battery across exposed ground until ordered to retire. His gallantry and determination was quite exceptional."

Serjeant John Joseph Richardson D.C.M. is buried at Nine Elms British Cemetery which is located to the west of Poperinge, West-Vlaanderen, Belgium. It as first used from September to December 1917 for burials from the 3rd Australian and 44th Casualty Clearing Stations, which had been moved to Poperinge in preparation for the 1917 Battle of Ypres. The cemetery was used again by fighting units between March and October 1918, the period of the German offensive in Flanders. The cemetery contains 1,556 Commonwealth burials of the First World War and 37 German war graves from the period.

The BATTLE OF AMIENS 8 – 11 August 1918
The 100 Days to Victory: An overview

The great German offensives on the Western Front petered out by July. The Germans had advanced to the River Marne but failed to achieve a decisive breakthrough. British casualties between March and the end of July were about 450,000, between March and the end of June the French suffered 433,000 casualties. The Germans suffered even more, about 1,375,000. Then from June 1918, the mysterious new illness dubbed "Spanish Flu" began to circulate through the warring nations. It is estimated that Britain had 229,000 fatalities, France 166,000 and Germany 225,000 – the Western Front was not immune. For example, the newly arrived American troops appear to have been heavily hit – 51% of her deaths were through disease (57,460) of which 83.6% was pneumonia.

Illness mattered little. There was a war to win. The Allied Supreme Commander, Marshal Ferdinand Foch ordered a counter offensive. The Americans under their commander General John Pershing were now present in France in large numbers and ready for action. The British Army had been reinforced by large numbers returning from Palestine and Italy and replacements previously held back by PM Lloyd George. A proposal by Field Marshal Haig to strike on the Somme to the east of Amiens, south west of the 1916 battlefield was chosen. This area was suitable because it was the defined boundary of the French and British armies so both could take part and the Picardy countryside provided a good surface for tanks. Importantly, the German defences were manned by their Second Army under General von der Marwitz and regarded as relatively weak since they had been subjected to continual raiding by the Australians.

The offensive started at Amiens then action up and down the front saw allied advances and German withdrawal. There were 23 officially recognised battles from Amiens (August) to the Battle of the Sambre (November) and casualties on all sides were as high as ever. The engagements were:
- Battle of Amiens 8 – 11 August
- Actions round Damery 1- 17 August
- Battle of Albert 21- 23 August
- Second Battle of Bapaume 31-3 September
- The Advance into Flanders 18 August – 6 September
- Second Battle of Arras
    - Action at Outtersteene Ridge 18 August
    - Battle of the Scarpe 26 – 30 August

Battle of Drocourt-Queant 2 – 3 September
Battle of Havrincourt 12 September
Battle of Epehy 18 September
Battle of the Canal du Nord 27 September- 1 October
Battle of St. Quentin Canal 29 September – 2 October
Battle of Beaurevoir 3 – 5 October
Battle of Cambrai 8 – 9 October
The Persuit to the Selle 9 – 12 October
The Final Advance in Flanders
- Battle of Ypres 28 September – 2 October
- Battle of Courtrai 14 – 19 October
- Action of Ooteghem 25 October
- Action of Tieghem 31 October

The Final Advance in Artois 2 October – 11 November
Battle of the Selle 17 – 25 October
Battle of Valenciennes 1 – 2 November
Battle of the Sambre 4 November
Passage of the Grande Honelle 5 – 7 November
Capture of Mons 11 November where it all started!

Haig launched a fresh offensive, the Battle of Albert 21 August which pushed the German Second Army back 34 miles (55km). Bapaume fell 29 August. The Australians crossed the Somme, 31 August, breaking the German lines at Mont St. Quentin and Peronne. Thus, the famous battleground towns of Albert, Bapaume and Peronne were captured by the Allies by 1 September.

Other successes were achieved in September to November by the Americans with French support at the St. Miheil Salient near Verdun and the Argonne Forest. In the north the Anglo Belgian group led by Prince Albert of the Belgians launched the Courtrai Offensive. The French under Petain played a vital role with successes on the Meuse River in October and the Argonne Forest offensive reaching the Aisne River after a 30km advance.

The Battle of Amiens 8 – 11 August 1918

The Battle of Amiens was described by First Quartermaster-General Ludendorff as, "The Black Day of the German Army." The material losses and ground lost would not seem to justify such a gloomy summary but he was referring to the mass surrender of German troops to Allied forces. It was the turning point of the war – the beginning of the end.

The Allies attacked with 10 Divisions, Australian, Canadian, British and French forces, aided by more than 500 tanks and achieved complete surprise. By the end of the day a gap 15 miles (24 km) had been punched through the German lines. The Allies took 17,000 prisoners and captured 330 guns. German losses were estimated at 30,000 and the Allies 6,500. Further gains were made during the following days then the Germans began to pull back towards the Hindenburg Line.

Corporal CHARLES HENRY LOWSON 1888-1918

44008 Corporal Charles Henry Lowson, 7th Battalion, the Lincolnshire Regiment died of wounds 15 August 1918 probably during the defence of Amiens. He is buried at Daours Communal Cemetery extension, France and commemorated on the Memorial Cottages at St. Helen Auckland, Co. Durham. He was 30 years old, born c.1888 at Hamsterley, County Durham to Richard and Maria Lowson and in 1901 was the older brother to Lily. The family then lived at Grieveson Place, Woodland. Prior to enlisting, Charles Lowson was employed at St. Helen's Colliery. He joined up at Bishop Auckland, his place of residence was Evenwood. By 1918 his mother lived at 2 Jubilee Terrace, Evenwood. He formerly served with the East Yorkshire Regiment (service number 14557).

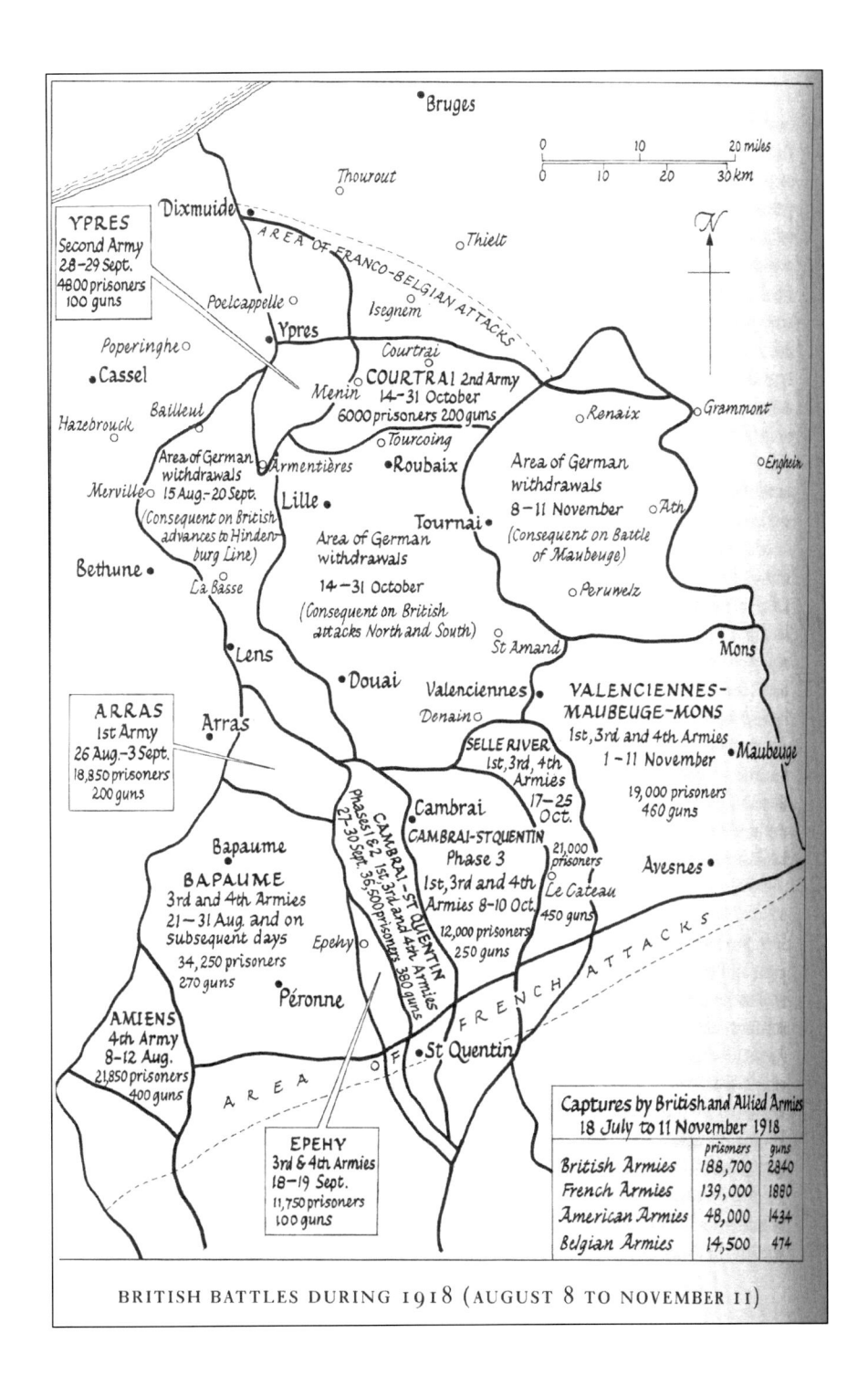

BRITISH BATTLES DURING 1918 (AUGUST 8 TO NOVEMBER 11)

It is possible that he initially served in the 7/East Yorkshire Regiment because this battalion was part of the 17th Northern Division (50th Brigade). The 7/Lincolns also formed part of this Division but were part of the 51st Brigade. It is possible that he was transferred sometime during the German Spring Offensive.

In July 1915, the 17th Division landed in France and spent the early period holding the front lines in the southern sector of the Ypres Salient. The Division saw action at the Bluff, the Battle of the Somme capturing Fricourt after suffering heavy losses, the Arras Offensive, the Third Battle of Ypres (Passchendeale) and in 1918 the Battle of St. Quentin, the First Battle of Bapaume, the Battle of Amiens before Corporal C.H. Lowson met his death and the Battle of Albert following it.

44008 Corporal Charles Henry Lowson, 7th Battalion, the Lincolnshire Regiment

At the Battle of Amiens, the Division operated alongside the Australian Corps as part of the British Fourth Army under Henry Rawlinson

Corporal Charles Henry Lowson died of wounds 15 August 1918

The exact circumstances of his death remain unknown. However, since Corporal C. H. Lowson died 15 August 1918 after the Battle of Amiens (8 – 11 August) and before the next action, the Battle of Albert (21 – 23 August) it is assumed that he was wounded during the defence of Amiens and died in hospital since there were Casualty Clearing Stations in the area. Corporal Charles Henry Lowson is buried at Daours Communal Cemetery Extension. Daours is a village about 10 kilometres east of Amiens. There are 1,231 Commonwealth servicemen buried or commemorated in the cemetery.

Private WALTER SNOWBALL 1897 – 1918

250400 Private Walter Snowball, 6th battalion, the Durham Light Infantry died of illness (kidney disease) 29 August 1918. He is buried in Evenwood Cemetery and commemorated on Evenwood War Memorial. He was 21 years old, born c.1897 the son of Mrs Ellen McConnell (formerly Snowball) and stepson of William McConnell of the 24 The Oaks, Evenwood.

The 1/6th Battalion was formed in Bishop Auckland in August 1914 as part of the Durham Light Infantry Brigade, Northumbrian Division and in May 1915 became the 151st Brigade of the 50th Division. The Division moved to France 16 April 1915 and served with distinction on the Western Front throughout the war, taking part in the following engagements:
- The Second Battle of Ypres (from 24 April – 25 May 1915)
- The Battle of Flers-Courcelette (6th phase of the Battle of the Somme 1916)
- The Battle of Morval (7th phase of the Battle of the Somme 1916)
- The Battle of Le Transloy (8th phase of the Battle of the Somme 1916)

250400 Private Walter Snowball was in France between the 7 July 1916 – 16 January 1917 and it is assumed that he was involved in action on the Somme. The 6/DLI was involved in action at the Battle of Le Transloy which commenced 1 October 1916. The village of Eaucourt L'Abbaye was captured and the attack is famous for the action of Lieut.-Col. R. B. Bradford who was awarded the V.C. Private Oliver Rushford from Morley was awarded the Military Medal. Also, Private Walter Snowball would have survived the attack on the Butte de Warlencourt 5 November 1916 when so many Durham families were affected by the tragic losses.

After 194 days at the Western Front, Private Walter Snowball returned to England and was admitted into the Northumberland War Hospital, Gosforth, Newcastle-upon-Tyne. He was suffering from nephritis (a kidney complaint). He was examined by the Medical Board and on the 28 June 1917 was considered to be "quite unfit for Military Service". The Board concluded that he was physically unfit and the illness, nephritis was not the result of Active Service but aggravated by the cold and exposure whilst on Active Service. The report also stated that "no treatment was required" and it appears that a 50% pension was awarded. Private Walter Snowball was discharged from the Army 19 July 1917.

The entries on this page only require to be made from time to time as they occur.
STATEMENT of the SERVICES of No. 3470 Name Walter Snowball
Showing preliminary training, other special courses of training, Annual Training,† and when mobilized, etc.

Corps	Unit	Promotions, Reductions, Casualties, &c.	Rank	From	To	Signature of Officers certifying correctness of Entries
		Service towards engagement reckons from 27.2.15				
D.L.I.	6	Posted	Pte	27/2/15		
	3/6th	Embodied		27.2.15		
D.L.I.	1/6	Posted				
I F 10 A.B. 68		Attached		16.1.17		
Discharged being no longer physically fit for War Service K.R. Para 392(xvi) (Nephritis)			Pte.	19-7-17		

Total service towards engagement in the Territorial Force to 19-7-17 (date of discharge) 2 years 143 days.

CHARACTER
Very Good.

Discharged in consequence of Being no longer physically fit for War Service K.R. Para 392 xvi

The discharge of the above-named man is hereby approved.

Station .... Signature .... Colonel O. I/c
Date 2 JUL 1917 191 . TERRITORIAL FORCE RECORDS YORK.

250400 Private Walter Snowball, 6th Batallion, the Durham Light Infantry.
Discharge papers

Subsequent reports throughout late 1917 and the summer of 1918 examined this case and revised the level of the award and included the statement "should have medical treatment." However, illness won the day. Aged 18 and standing at 5 ft. 3 ins., there can be no doubt that Walter Snowball was a young man of slight stature but with a big heart who volunteered to serve "King and Country". After service on the Western Front, his health deteriorated and finally he succumbed to illness and died at home at 21 years of age.

Private Walter Snowball died 29 August 1918

Private Walter Snowball is buried in Evenwood Cemetery. The Evenwood Parish Magazine (April 1919) carries a list of burials from July 1918 to February 1919:

"Sept. 2 – Walter Snowball, aged 21 years, the Oaks, Evenwood"

Private ALBERT BURRELL 1884- 1918

339885 Private Albert Burrell, the Labour Corps died 2 September, 1918 and is buried in Cockfield Cemetery and commemorated on Cockfield War Memorial. He was 34 years old, born in 1884 in Evenwood to

*339885 Private Albert Burrell, the Labour Corps.
Despite being discharged as suffering from epilepsy in 1914, Albert Burrell re-inlisted to serve his country*

Jonathan and Tamar Burrell. In 1891, the family lived at Lands Bank and his older brothers were John Joseph, Jonathan and William and Sarah was his older sister. He enlisted at Darlington and lived at Cockfield. To date, the circumstances of his death have not been confirmed but it is known that he enlisted into the 6/DLI in September 1914 only to be discharged after 34 days because of poor health – he suffered from epilepsy. It is possible that due to the dire need for men that he was allowed to re-enlist into the Labour Corps but died whilst on service. His death was registered at St. Giles, Middlesex.

Private Albert Burrell died 2 September 1918

Private FREDERICK WILLIAM MARQUIS 1897 – 1918

5893 Private Fredrick William Marquis, 28th Battalion, Australian Infantry, A.I.F. was killed in action 4 September 1918 during the battle for control of Mont St. Quentin, Second Battle of Bapaume. He is buried at Heath Cemetery, Harbonnieres, France and commemorated on the Hamsterley War Memorial. He was 21 years old, born in 1897 at Hamsterley, County Durham to Henry and Eleanor Marquis and was brother to James, Thomas, Margaret, Arthur, John, Mary, Jane, Edward and Eleanor. In 1909 the family emigrated to Australia and in 1910 took up land at Datatine in the shire of Dumbleyung, Western Australia. Their farm was known as "Hoppland Park", Katanning East, Western Australia. His brothers James and John also enlisted for service. His older brother, 3128A Private John Joseph Marquis, 28th Battalion, Australian Infantry, A.I.F. was another victim of the war. He was killed in action 1 June 1918. (see pages 212–214)

Frederick W Marquis enlisted 20 June 1916 and entered France 29 December 1916. He suffered trench fever and was hospitalized 7 June – 7 July 1916 and also influenza during May 1918.

He suffered gun shot wounds to the face, head and neck in action 2 September 1918 and died of wounds 4 September 1918 in the 5th Casualty Clearing Station.

5893 Private Frederick William Marquis, 28th Battalion, Australian Infantry, A.I.F. Attestation Papers

Second Battle of Bapaume, 21 August – 3 September 1918

The first phase of the battle had seen the British Fourth Army push the Germans back ten miles, from the tip of the Amiens salient back to the front line they held before the first Battle of the Somme (1916). The allied commander-in-chief, Ferdinand Foch, wanted the Fourth Army to launch immediate attack on this line, with the aim of pushing the Germans back to the Somme. Haig believed that the new German position was too strong to attack without careful preparation. The old Somme battlefield had been fought over in 1916, deliberately devastated by the Germans in1917 and then fought over again in 1918 – it was not well suited to tank warfare. It would need heavy artillery bombardment to destroy the wire and it would take time to move the artillery forward. Haig preferred to launch a new offensive further north, using the Third Army (General Byng), supported by 100 tanks, to attack the German Seventeen Army (Marwitz) across more suitable ground. Foch agreed to Haig's plan but he removed the French First Army from British control. The French launched its own offensive on the same day as the British attack.

During the relative lull between 11 and 21 August, Byng's Third Army was reinforced, while the Canadian Corps moved from the Fourth to the First Army (Horne), on the left of the line.

The British attack began on a narrow front on 21 August with an attack by the Third Army. The Germans responded with a counter-attack on 22 August which was quickly beaten off. On 23 August, Haig was able to order a general advance by the Third Army and part of the Fourth, on a 33 mile front. On 26 August the right wing of the First Army joined in, extending the front to 40 miles (this attack is sometimes designated as the second battle of Arras of 1918). At that point the German line ran along the Somme south from Peronne then across open country to Noyon on the Oise. Ludendorff had ordered a retreat from the Lys salient and what was left of the Amiens salient, with the intention of forming a new line on the Somme. This plan was disrupted by the Australians, New Zealanders and Canadians. On 29 August the New Zealanders captured Bapaume (east of Amiens, south of Arras), breaking through the Le Transloy-Loupart trench system. To the south the 2nd Australian Division captured Mont St. Quintin, on the east bank of the Somme, on the night of 30 – 31 August, and on 1 September captured Peronne itself. Further north, on 2 September the Canadians broke through the Drocourt-Queant switch, a strong section of the German line south east of Arras. With two gaps in the proposed new front line, Ludendorff was forced to retreat back to the Hindenburg line, abandoning all the territory won earlier in 1918.

Mont St. Quentin and Peronne

August 30, 1918 – Australian 3rd Division commenced the attack of the "Battle of Mont St Quentin." General Monash's objective was to render the line of the Somme River useless to the Germans as a defensive position and hasten their retreat to the Hindenburg Line. To achieve this called for attack on the key position of the whole line of defence, on a hill called Mont St Quentin. Monash knew that his troops were under strength and badly needed a rest, but by now he considered them "invincible".

The attack was on the key positions in the German line, a dominating hill known as Mont St Quentin, 1.5 kilometres from Peronne. The hill was less than 100 metres high but heavily guarded especially along the northerly and westerly approaches. The Australian 5th Division objectives were the Peronne Bridges and Peronne, while the Australian 2nd Divisions was the bridgehead at Halle the Mont St. Quentin and finally the Australian 3rd Division was to capture the high ground north east of Clery, then Bouchavesnes spur. Facing the Australian Divisions at Mont St. Quentin was the 2nd Prussian Guards, an elite German formation, who had orders to hold the hill "to the death".

The barrage commenced at 5am but much of the Australian's fighting reputation preceded them with the enemy taking panic. The 5th Brigade of the Australian 2nd Division opened the attack, comprising only 70 officers and 1,250 other ranks it was less than one third of its normal strength. The 2nd Division battalions to assault Mont St Quentin were the 17th, 18th, 19th and 20th all from N.S.W. The 17th battalion started along the Clery-Peronne road as the Germans retreated to more defensible ground. Within a short time they had captured their objective, with only 550 men and 220 in support – an objective that British generals considered "impregnable"! However, the 5th Brigade could not hold all of its gains and part of the 2nd Prussian Guards Division drove back scattered troops from the summit of Mont St. Quentin

On the left of the Australian 2nd Division, the Australian 3rd Division attacked Bouchavesnes Spur but had not captured its objectives – this meant that earlier gains were threatened by German flanking moves. General Monash ordered that "Casualties no longer mattered" and "We must get Bouchavesnes Spur and protect Rosenthal's left". The spur was taken and the Mont St. Quentin assault was protected. On September 1, the 6th Australian Brigade, passing through the 5th Brigade seized in a second attempt the summit of Mont St. Quentin while the Australian 14th Brigade (5th Division) captured woods north of Peronne and took the main part of the town. On 2 September, the Australian 7th Brigade (2nd Division) drove beyond the Mont and the Australian 15th Brigade (5th Division) seized the rest of Peronne.

The result was that three weakened Australian Divisions were able to defeat five German Divisions. The action saw its fair share of heroics and losses, eight VC's and 20% casualties. The battle was a true infantry victory achieved without the use of tanks or creeping artillery barrage.

Losses:
Australian 2nd Division 84 Officers, 1,286 others
Australian 3rd Division 43 Officers, 544 others
Australian 5th Division 44 Officers, 1,026 others
Germans 3,500 casualties and 2,600 prisoners

Private Frederick William Marquis died of wounds 4 September 1918

Private Frederick William Marquis is buried at Heath Cemetery, Harbonnieres. Heath Cemetery is situated on the main road from Amiens to St. Quentin some 13 km from Villers-Bretonneux. Harbonnieres was captured by French troops in the summer of 1916. It was retaken by the Germans on 27 April 1918 and regained by the Australian Corps on 8 August 1918. The cemetery was made after the Armistice and graves were brought in from the battlefields between Bray and Harbonnieres. The majority died in March and August 1918. There are 1491 burials.

Private RALPH HEAVISIDE 1900-1918

51585 Private Ralph Heaviside, 22nd (Tyneside Scottish) battalion, Northumberland Fusiliers died of wounds 6 September 1918 and is buried at Pernes British Cemetery, France and commemorated on the Evenwood War Memorial. He was 18 years old, born in 1900 at Evenwood to Richard and Mary Heaviside and in 1901 was the youngest brother to Mary, Margaret, Maud and Susannah. The family lived at Alpine Terrace, Evenwood. Ralph Heaviside was the youngest man from Evenwood to be killed in the Great War.

The 22nd (Service) Battalion (3rd Tyneside Scottish) was formed at Newcastle on the 5th November 1914. In June 1915, it was attached to the 102nd Brigade, 34th Division.

51585 Private Ralph Heaviside, 22nd (Tyneside Scottish) Battalion, Northumberland Fusiliers

On the 10 & 11 April 1918, the 102nd Brigade, was involved in the Battle of Messines after which the Division took part in the Battle of Bailleul on the 13 & 14 April – part of the German offensive in Flanders known as the Battle of the Lys. On 17 May 1918 it was reduced to cadre strength and on 18 June returned to England with the 16th (Irish) Division and absorbed into the new 38th Battalion and then attached to the 48th Brigade, 16th Division. The 34th Division is recorded as taking part in the capture of Beugneux Ridge during the Battle of the Marne, 23 July – 2 August then later in the month, 18 August – 6 September the Advance into Flanders as part of the Second Army, XIX Corps.

Private Ralph Heaviside died of wounds 6 September 1918

To date, the service details of Private Ralph Heaviside and the War Diaries of the 22nd Battalion, the Northumberland Fusiliers have not been researched therefore the exact circumstances of his death remain unknown. Private Ralph Heaviside is buried at Pernes British Cemetery. Pernes-en-Artois is a small town on the main road from Lillers to St. Pol, in the region of Pas-de-Calais, France. There are 1,075 First World War burials. Pernes British Cemetery operated from April 1918 when the 1st and 4th Canadian Casualty Clearing Stations came to town when driven back by the German advance. In May, the 6th and 22nd Clearing Stations arrived then finally in August they were joined by the 13th. Almost all the burials were made by these units but a few graves were brought into the cemetery after the Armistice. It therefore seems reasonable to assume, given the date of death of Private Ralph Heaviside that he was wounded in action and failed to respond to treatment in the clearing station.

Private JOHN WILFRED HOWLETT 1898 – 1918

39146 Private John Wilfred "Wilf" Howlett, 12/13th Battalion, the Northumberland Fusiliers was killed in action 18 September 1918 during the Battle of Epehy. He is buried at Gouzeaucourt New British Cemetery, France and commemorated on Evenwood War Memorial. He was 20 years old, born c.1898 at Shildon to Edward and ? Howlett. By 1901 Edward was a widower looking after his 2 children, Wilf and Eva. The family lived at 24 Cooperative Street, Shildon. By 1915, they lived at Oaks House, Evenwood. He enlisted prior to 1915 at Bishop Auckland.

The 12th and 13th Battalions were Service Battalions formed in Newcastle in September 1914 as part of Kitchener's New Army. They were attached to the 62nd Brigade of the 21st Division. In August 1917 they merged to form the 12/13th Battalion. The 21st Division formed part of the Third Army, V Corps that took part in the Battle of Epehy.

The Battle of Epehy: 18 September 1918

Fought in the wake of successful encounters at St. Mihiel and Havrincourt, the Battle of Epehy was directed against forward outposts of the Hindenburg Line. The British commander-in-chief Sir Douglas Haig authorised an attack 13 September 1918 by all 3 corps of General Rawlinson's Fourth Army, aided by a corps from Sir Julian Byng's Third Army (who had successfully taken Havrincourt village on 12 September). The British assault was greatly assisted by a creeping barrage involving some 1,500 guns with the addition of 300 machine guns. Success was limited on the flanks but the centre of the advance, led by 2 divisions of the Australian Corps under General Monash, quickly gained ground. The 2 Australian Divisions, the 1st and the 4th some 6,800 men in strength, captured 4,243 prisoners, 76 guns, 300 machine guns and 30 trench mortars during the course of the day. They took all their objectives and a distance of 3 miles on a 4 mile front was occupied. The Australian casualties were 1,260 officers and men. The attack closed as a British victory with 9,000 prisoners and 100 guns being taken.

Although Epehy was not a massive success, it signalled an unmistakable message that the Germans were weakening and it encouraged the Allies to take further action with haste before the Germans could consolidate their positions.

Private John Wilfred Howlett was killed in action 18 September 1918

Private John Wilfred Howlett is buried at Gouzeaucourt New British Cemetery. The village is 15km south west of Cambrai. The cemetery was begun in November 1917 and enlarged after the Armistice when graves were brought in from the battlefields of Cambrai area. It contains 1,295 burials and commemorations of the First World War.

39146 Private John Wilfred Howlett, 12/13th Battalion, the Northumberland Fusiliers. Medal Roll

Private MARTIN SIMPSON 1894-1918

60571 Private Martin Simpson, 9th battalion, the Yorkshire Regiment died of wounds 22 October 1918 received during the Allied advance. He is buried at Maurois Communal Cemetery, France and commemorated on the Evenwood War Memorial. He was 24 years old, born c.1894 at Lands to Robinson and Annie Simpson who in 1901 lived at 57 Lands Bank with his sister Mary and his brothers John William, Percy Edgar and Richard Robinson. Private Martin Simpson was one of 4 men from the Parish to enlist into the Yorkshire Regiment (more popularly as the Green Howards) and lose their lives for their country. The others were Walter Morley, Robert W. Wilson and John J. Walton.

The 9th (Service) Battalion was formed at Richmond, North Yorkshire on 22 September 1914 and in October 1914, it was attached to the 69th Brigade of the 23rd Division. The Division saw action at the Battle of the Somme 1916, the Battle of Messines, 1917, the Third Battle of Ypres (Passchendaele) 1917 then in October 1917 it relieved the 70th Italian Division on the front line at Montello. The 9/Green Howards was attached to the 74th Brigade of the 25th Division 17 September 1918.

27 September 1918: Operations by the IX Corps, II American Corps, III Corps and the Australian Corps carried the British Advance from a line stretching from north of St. Quentin, west of Beaurevoir to a position west of Le Catelet. The main Hindenburg Line running north and south through Bellicourt had been the scene of heavy fighting and the village of Beaurevoir, located on high ground needed to be captured to enable artillery to be brought up to support the next advance of the front. The task was allocated to the 25th Division.

3 October: the 74th Brigade was at Moislains, Divisional HQ at Combles. The 9/Green Howards left Moislains at 13.00 hours and marched to the line south of Le Catelet. Orders received to continue (4 October) the attack started by the Australians on the 3rd and to complete the capture of Beaurevoir and the high ground beyond it.

4 October: the 7th Brigade of the 25th Division opened the attack. It was only partially successful and casualties were heavy.

5 October: orders received to continue the attack as very large scale operations were planned for 7 October. At 6.00am. the 74th and 75th Brigades went forward.

> "The attack commenced well, especially on the flanks where good progress was made north of the village of Beaurevoir. The Germans at once launched a counter attack, supported by a large number of machine guns and succeeded in forcing back our troops once more to their original line, except in the centre at Bellevue Farm which was successfully held by man of "A" Company, 9th Green Howards."

By the end of the day the village and the cemetery of Beaurevoir had been captured and some troops of the 74th Brigade made another attempt to reach the high ground at Guisancourt Farm but were unsuccessful.

6 October morning: Guisancourt Farm was taken and made secure by the 9/Green Howards.

7 October: preparations made for a major attack the following day. The 2nd Australian Division and the 50th Division pushed forward encountering little opposition. The artillery moved up to positions east of Guisancourt Farm and Beaurevoir. British positions were heavily shelled during the

2 days. Casualties sustained by the Division were heavy. 508 Germans including 5 officers were taken prisoners.

8 October: the 66th Division passed through the 74th and 75th Brigades to take up the attack with the 7th Brigade. All objectives gained.

9 October, 6.00 am: 75th Brigade advanced between Serain and Premont and gained the first objective. 7.30 am. 74th Brigade came up and joined the 11/Sherwood Foresters, the 9/Green Howards and the 13/DLI in support.

> "Everything went well and the Brigades met with no resistance for about 2½ miles … At about 9.00 am. Resistance was encountered along the railway line running north and south west of Honnechy… The advance was resumed at 2pm … the enemy offered considerable opposition at first but as our troops pressed on his resistance suddenly broke and the line retired rapidly before becoming engaged in close quarters. Honnechy was soon passed …the 9th Green Howards digging in on the east side of the railway … 2.30pm … one party captured Reumont Village …
>
> Intelligence reports indicated that the enemy would probably make a stand on the Selle River to the south and south-east of Le Cateau."

10 October, 5.30 am: The Division moved forward…8.00 am. The leading platoons came under heavy machine gun fire…2.30pm. 74th Brigade launched an attack on St. Benin…the enemy gradually withdrew. The 9/Green Howards dug in."

11 October: 50th Division relieved the 25th Division and the 9/Green Howards found accommodation at Premont.

60571 Private Martin Simpson, 9th Battalion, the Yorkshire Regiment

"The inhabitants of these villages had been for 4 years under German rule and the welcome they accorded those whom they regarded as their deliverers was something to be remembered."

12 – 16 October: the 25th Division remained in the Serain-Premont-Ellincourt area in Corps reserve.

16 October: The Division moved forward but only the 75th Brigade was engaged, fighting under orders of the 50th Division at the crossing of the River Selle. It was not until 23 October that the other brigades were again employed in the front.

Private Martin Simpson died of wounds 22 October 1918

Private M. Simpson is buried at Maurois Communal Cemetery. Maurois is a village located 5 kilometres south west of Le Cateau in the region of Nord, France. It was in German hands from August 1914 until liberated by the South African Brigade on 9 October 1918. There are 78 burials.

Private MARK GOLIATH MIDDLEMASS 1884 – 1918

252054 Private Mark Goliath Middlemass, 12th Battalion, Durham Light Infantry

252054 Private Mark Goliath Middlemass, 12th Battalion, Durham Light Infantry was killed in action 27 October 1918 during the Battle of Vittorio Veneto. He is buried at Tezze British Cemetery, Italy and commemorated on Evenwood War Memorial. He was 35 years old, born c.1884 at Evenwood to John and Alice Middlemass and brother to Mary, Jane, Fred and Robert. Mark married Hannah Wigham 10 June 1905 and their children were Dorothy, Mark, Elizabeth, John and Robert. They lived at 10 Stones Row, Evenwood. Mark worked at Randolph Colliery.

Mark Middlemass originally enlisted at Bishop Auckland prior to February 1916 and served with the 6/DLI being discharged but as the need for men grew, he rejoined the colours April/May 1918.

The Battle of Vittorio Veneto: 23 October – 4 November 1918

The Italians entered the war on the Allied side in May 1915. Commonwealth forces were at the Italian front between November 1917 and November 1918. The village of Tezze was captured by the Austrians in their advance in the autumn of 1917 and remained in their hands until the Allied forces crossed the River Piave at the end of 1918.

21 October: Commonwealth forces comprising XIV Corps (7th and 23rd Divisions) took over the part of the River Piave from Salletuol to Pallazon serving as part of the Italian Tenth Army.

23 October: the main channel of the river was crossed using small boats and the northern half of the island of Grava di Papadopoli was occupied, the occupation being completed two nights later by a combined Commonwealth and Italian force. After the capture of the island, the bridging of the Piave proceeded rapidly, although the strength of the current meant that the two bridges built for the crossing were frequently broken and many men were drowned.

27 October: The Allied attack east of the Piave began early in the morning. Despite stiff resistance and difficulties with bringing forward supporting troops across the river, the Austrians were forced back over the next few days until the Armistice came into effect on 4 November.

Many of those who died on the north-east side of the river during the Passage of the Piave are buried in Tezze British Cemetery. The War Diary of the 12/DLI includes the following details of manoeuvres:

> "27 October:
> At 6.45am, the advance on to the Green Dotted Line commenced. Very deep, swift water was found in the most northerly area of the Piave and whilst wading this, the Battalion suffered heavily from MG fire, the leading Company losing nearly 50% of its strength. Companies reorganised and pressed forward, to be held up by uncut wire close to the objective, which was strongly held. The wire was

cut most gallantly by various parties, amongst whom Capt. Gibbens MC DCM, Sgt O'Hara and Pte Brown were conspicuous. The Battalion pressed on, and C Company captured the first objective. D Company pushed on, overcoming all obstacles and captured the Red Dotted Line (second objective). A Company with B Company (now very weak) pushed steadily on and together captured Blue Dotted Line (the road from C. Padovan to C. Benedetti). Here orders were received as the Italians on the left of the Brigade had failed to cross the Piave, no further advance would be made. The Battalion organised a reserve near C. Borazzuni. Battalion HQ at C. Borazzuni. Major E. Borrow DSO was taken from the Battalion to command the 11th Northumberland Fusiliers, vice Lt-Col St. Hill DSO killed. The Battalion this day captured 3 guns, 2 heavy Trench Mortars, 2 Tank Guns, several hundred prisoners and many machine guns. Our casualties were 2/Lts Hodgson and Fisher, killed; Capt Gibbens MC DCM, 2/Lts Smith and Wade wounded. RSM Burton DCM was killed after the capture of the first objective by a ricochet bullet. 27 other ranks killed, 111 wounded and 11 missing. The night was quiet."

Private Mark G. Middlemass was killed in action 27 October 1918

On the 31 October, the 12/DLI marched to Sacile where they went into billets, the enemy opposition having been overcome

> "During the battle 27th-29th, the total loss of the Battalion was: 2 officers killed, 4 wounded. 39 ORs killed, 153 wounded, 14 missing. During the same period the Battalion captured 1020 prisoners, 18 horses, 7 GS limbers, 4 gun limbers, 46 machine guns, 2 anti tank guns, 2 Anti Aircraft guns, 4 6-inch howitzers, 4 5.9 inch guns and 2 heavy Trench Mortars, vast quantities of ammunition of all calibres."

Private Mark Middlemass is buried at Tezze British cemetery. The cemetery contains 356 Commonwealth burials of the First World War. Mark Middlemass was one of Evenwood's last casualties of the Great War being killed one week before the Armistice came into effect on the Italian Front – 4 November 1918. The Allied forces led by the British heavily defeated the Austrians at Vittorio Veneto and this caused great anxiety within the German High Command and there can be no doubt that this influenced the decision to sign the Armistice on 11 November 1918.

Commerative Plaque

Private THOMAS DAVIS 1898-1918

78830 Private Thomas Davis, 1/4th battalion, the Northumberland Fusiliers was killed in action 4 November 1918 during the Battle of the Sambre, just one week before the Armistice was signed. He is buried at Fontaine-au-Bois Communal Cemetery, France, and is commemorated on Evenwood War Memorial. He was 20 years old, born c.1898 at Evenwood to Charles and Francis Davies and in 1901 was brother to John, Robert and James. The family lived at Alpine Terrace but by 1918 his mother and father lived at 5 Rochdale Street. He enlisted at Newcastle upon Tyne.

Originally, in May 1915 the 1/4th N.F. formed part of the 149th Brigade of the 50th Division but after suffering heavy losses during the German spring offensive by 16 August 1918, the battalion was transferred to the 118th Brigade, 30th Division.

The Battle of the Sambre and the engagement leading to the capture of Le Quesnoy involved the XIII Corps and took place on 4 November 1918. The 50th Division together with 18th and 25th Divisions saw action. The War Diaries of the 1st/4th Battalion of the Northumberland Fusiliers, Vol. 38 1 – 31 October 1918 and Vol.39, 1 – 6 November 1918 state that the Battalion was at Fecamp erecting huts, playing football and several contracted Spanish Flu then in November it was "awaiting demobilization". Clearly, the battalion as a whole was not involved in action at the Battle of the Sambre. However, Vol. 31, 1 – 31 August 1918 contains the following entry:

"Rouxmesnil Aug. 1st – 14th A small number of N.C.Os. & men who were surplus to establishment of cadre Battn. were sent to the Base for disposal."

Elsewhere it is quoted that the battalion joined the 150th Brigade, 50th Division from 15 July 1918 to the end of the war. Thus it must be assumed that remnants of the 1/4th NF including 78830 Private Thomas Davis rejoined the 50th Division. The History of the 50th Division states:

"On the 4th November, the last great battle opened (the Battle of the Sambre) on a front of 30 miles, stretching from the Sambre north of Oisy to Valenciennes. The 50th Division (having been in reserve for a few days) attacked and with the 25th and 18th Divisions of the XIII Corps overran the enemy positions. The 50th Division advanced through the southern portion of the Feret de Mormal. An advance to a depth of 5 miles was made on the 4th and on the 5th a still greater push brought the British Line well to the east of the Foret de Mormal.

Thereafter the enemy was hurrying eastwards in disorder and although during the succeeding days there were stiff encounters up and down the line the German troops never really rallied to the attack, so that by the 11th November incapable of either fighting or offering further resistance, he was forced to seek an Armistice."

Private Thomas Davis was killed in action 4 November 1918

The service records of Private Thomas Davis have not been researched and the exact circumstances of his death remain unknown. 78830 Private Thomas Davis is buried at Fontaine-au-Bois communal cemetery. The village is located some 7 kilometres to the south of Le Quesnoy. The Commonwealth plot in the Fontaine-au-Bois Communal Cemetery was made by the XIII Corps in November 1918 and all the burials date from the October and November period. There are 55 casualties with the recorded date of death as 4 November 1918 some of whom served with the Northumberland Fusiliers. The Northumberland Fusiliers lost 30 men 4 November, 24 of whom are reported to have served in the 2/NF. In view of this evidence Private Thomas Davis must have been involved in this action in the area of Le Quesnoy as Allied forces made for the town of Mons to the north.

78830 Private Thomas Davis, 1/4th Battalion, the Northumberland Fusiliers. Medal Roll

Another to fall that day was Second Lieutenant W.E.S. Owen M.C., 2/Manchesters better known as the poet Wilfred Owen, thought by many to be the greatest of the war. He is buried at the municipal cemetery at Ors only a short distance from Fontaine-au-Bois. "Dulce et Decorum est" is probably the best known poem of the Great War. The final lines, "Dulce et decorum est pro patria mori" – translated, it is sweet and right to die for your country. Three more men from Evenwood were yet to die for their country.

The Advance to Victory is often described as the 100 days – it was actually 96. It was a bloodbath – fierce rear guard fighting by retreating German machine gunners was accompanied by mass surrender of German forces as their morale fell and their capacity to resist reduced.

Between August and the Armistice 11 November, there were about 379,000 British casualties, the French suffered 521,000 casualties between July and November. The Americans lost a total of 50,280 men killed in combat during the war, the majority of whom perished in the final months. The Germans had over 1,140,000 casualties between July and November. But, most disturbing to the German High Command was the number of prisoners taken by the Allies – about 390,000 from 18 July

– 11 November. 6,628 guns were captured. The British took over 174,000 prisoners from Amiens to Mons. However, Ludendorff, Hindenburg and post war German right wing politicians did not recognise the scale of defeat of the German Army and the formulation of their "Stab-in-the- back theory by socialists, communists and Jews" took hold after the war.

THE ARMISTICE CAME INTO FORCE
11.00 A.M. 11 NOVEMBER 1918

11 November 1918 marked the 1,559th day of the war for the British Army. Agreement had been reached at 5.10 am and the Armistice would come into force 6 hours later at 11.00 am. The message was sent out to commanders in the field via radio and telephone. It read:

> "Hostilities will cease on the entire front beginning at 11.00 am. November 11. The Allied troops will not pass the line reached at that date and at that hour without a new order."

Orders for offensive actions had already been issued and plans were in place. These orders were not rescinded. The following action was carried out during the last hours of the conflict:

- The Americans continued their Meuse-Argonne offensive and in crossing the river Meuse on the morning of the 11th, the 2nd, 89th and 90th Divisions suffered 1,130 casualties, 792 seriously wounded and 127 dead. A German unit, the 174th Infantry Regiment went into action that morning with more than 3,000 men. On the last day there were 327 left standing. The last order to cease fire was not received by forward units of the American 2nd Division until 4.15pm. These Americans were returning assumed enemy fire that turned out to be blasting by A.E.F. engineers to remove an obstruction blocking the Meuse.
- Mons, Belgium had been the scene of the first B.E.F. losses and the retaking of this city in the final hours was seen to be a "badge of honour". At 7.00 am the Canadian 2nd and 3rd Divisions entered the city triumphantly but there was still fighting to the north east near St. Denis. The Canadians stood aside to let the cavalrymen, the 5th Royal Irish Lancers (amongst those driven out in 1914) ride onto St. Denis. In that locality, at Lessines, another cavalry unit the 7th Dragoons mounted a charge at 10.50 am to capture a bridge. The horsemen galloped down a tree lined road brandishing their swords, pennants flying, to be met by a hail of machine gun fire! Cavalrymen

fell from their horses and Private G.E. Ellison was killed in this final unnecessary act. He is attributed to be the last British casualty of the war. Private G.L. Price 38th Northwest Infantry Battalion, Canadian 2nd Division* was killed by a German sniper at 10.58 and was the last Canadian to be killed. Both are laid to rest in St. Symphorien Military Cemetery near the grave of Private J. Parr, 4th Battalion, Middlesex Regiment, believed to be the first British fatality of the war – about 700,000 British and 1,000,000 British and Empire lives later!

For the last day of the fighting, basically the 6 hours after the Armistice was signed, the most conservative estimates provide a total of 10,944 casualties of which 2,738 were deaths on the Western Front, on all sides – more than the average daily casualties throughout the war, about 5,000 wounded and 2,250 dead. To draw comparison, the D-Day losses 6 June 1944 when the Allies invaded Normandy 25 years later, were reported to be 10,000 for all sides – nearly 10% lower. When storming the beaches in 1944, the Allied troops were fighting for victory and the Germans were stoutly defending their gains whereas on the 11 November 1918, men were fighting when the outcome had already been decided and still there were about 11,000 casualties!

Such was this a global conflict that in German East Africa, General Paul Emil von Lettow-Vorbeck who had earned the nickname, "the African Hindenburg" did not hear of the Armistice until 23 November. He was the last of the Kaiser's commanders to yield.

Returning to the Western Front, retreating German troops mined the railway station at the Belgian town of Hamont near the Dutch border. At midnight on 12 November, a train filled with German troops arrived from Antwerp, the explosives detonated and hundreds of German soldiers were killed.

The Armistice had come into force 11 November 1918 but it had to be renewed every 30 days. Peace negotiations commenced but the British blockade of the Channel and North Sea ports was still in force and continued to be so until a peace treaty was signed. Thus, thousands of Germans were condemned to starvation and disease. There were still food

* CWGC state his unit and regiment was the 28th Battalion, Canadian Infantry (Saskatchewan Regiment).

shortages and 250,000 Germans died of malnutrition in 1918. There had been food riots and strikes. The turbulent political situation and general unrest continued into 1919 and beyond.

The death toll for Evenwood was not yet finished. Men were still serving in the forces, some were P.O.W.'s. There were 2 more deaths to be reported before the end of the year – 131400 Sapper Arthur Kenneth Atkinson and 340630 Private Fred Purvis.

In Germany and Britain, the casualties of war continued to die and there was another scourge which would account for millions of deaths across the globe – "Spanish Flu". Many residents of Evenwood and the surrounding area would succumb to this epidemic, as would 27 German Prisoners of War held at Harperley P.O.W. Camp to the north of Hamsterley. Another to die of illness after the end of the war was 26952 Private John William Maughan who was Evenwood's last victim. He died in January 1919.

Sapper ARTHUR KENNETH ATKINSON M.M. 1896-1918

131400 Sapper Arthur Kenneth Atkinson, M.M., 206th Field Company, Royal Engineers was killed in action 3 December 1918 "by the explosion of a bomb whist clearing away debris." He is buried at Soumoy Communal Cemetery, Belgium and commemorated on Evenwood War Memorial. He was 22 years old, the son of Mr. and Mrs. Atkinson who lived at Ramshaw. He joined up 17 August 1915 and entered France 21 August 1916, serving a total of 3 years 109 days, 2 years 105 abroad. Sapper A. K. Atkinson was awarded the Military Medal and the announcement appeared in the London Gazette 7 October 1918 but to date details of his citation remain unknown.

News of his Death

The Evenwood Parish Magazine of April 1919 reported as follows:

> "Also for Mr. and Mrs. Atkinson of Ramshaw, whose son Sapper Arthur Kenneth, M.M., R.E., after going through safely four years of fighting, was killed in December 1918, by the explosion of a bomb whist clearing away debris."

131400 Sapper Arthur Kenneth Atkinson, M.M.. 206th Field Company, Royal Engineers

```
                    Royal Engineers Record Office.
                         C H A T H A M .
                             February 1919.
Sir,
        With reference to Army Form B.104-
82 forwarded to you on the 16th.December
last,notifying that your Son, No.131400
Sapper A.K.Atkinson,R.E., was killed
accidentally on the 3rd.December 1918, I have
to inform you that a report has now been
received to the effect that he was killed in
action on the 3rd.December, 1918.
                    I am, Sir,
                        Yours faithfully,

                                Lieut:R.E
                        for Col.i/c R.E.Records.
Mr.J?Atkinson.
   Ramshawron,
   Ramshaw,
   BISHOP AUCKLAND.
```

Sapper Arthur Kenneth Atkinson M.M. is buried at Soumoy Communal Cemetery. Soumoy is located north west of the town of Philippeville, in the region of Namur, Belgium. This cemetery contains the graves of an officer and 5 men of the 206th Field Company, Royal Engineers killed 3 December 1918. The officer is Second Lieutenant William W. Bruce M.C. aged 23 years from Aberdeen and the Other Ranks are:

- Sapper Herbert William Bryant, aged 25 from Cardiff
- Sapper Frank Hackney aged 30 from Cheshire
- Sapper Judah Jacobs aged 25 from Bethnal Green, London
- Sapper William Cuthbert McCarthy M.M. aged 23 from Jarrow, Co. Durham.
- Sapper Arthur Kenneth Atkinson M.M. aged 22.

Sapper Arthur Kenneth Atkinson M.M. was killed in action 3 December 1918

Sapper A.K. Atkinson M.M. was the last Evenwood man to be killed in action overseas whilst on active service some 3 weeks after the Armistice had been signed. 340630 Private Fred Purvis would die as a POW and 14702 Private John William Maughan would die of pneumonia.

Private FRED PURVIS 1893-1918

340630 Private Fred Purvis, 1/5th battalion, the Northumberland Fusiliers died 9 December 1918 as a P.O.W. He is buried at Niederzwhren Cemetery near Kassel, Hessen, Germany and is commemorated on Evenwood War Memorial. He was 25 years old, born c.1894 at Evenwood to George and Mary Purvis. By 1918, he lived at 22 Rochdale Street, Evenwood.

340630 Private Fred Purvis, 1/5th Battalion, the Northumberland Fusiliers

The 1st/5th Northumberland Fusiliers formed part of the 149th Brigade of the 50th Division and was involved in action on the Somme and Lys battlefields when the German Spring Offensive was thrown against the British and Commonwealth Forces. Following a most trying time, the Division was withdrawn and sent to IX Corps then on the Aisne which was believed to be a much quieter sector. This did not prove to be the case. Between 27 May & 6 June 1918, the Germans carried out their offensive in the Champagne region of France – the Battle of the Aisne. This was to be the final large scale German effort to win the war before the arrival of US troops in France.

The Battle of the Aisne: 27 May – 6 June 1918

The focus of the offensive was the Chemin des Dames Ridge and Ludendorff launched a massive surprise attack against the French who held the Ridge. In doing so, he anticipated that the French would divert forces from Flanders to the Aisne and so he could renew his offensive to the north in Flanders, believing the war could be won. At the time of the offensive, the front line at Chemin des Dames was held by 4 Divisions of the British IX Corps including the 50th.

The attack was launched early on 27 May with a ferocious artillery bombardment of 4,000 guns across a 40 km. front, against the four Divisions of the IX Corps. Casualties from the bombardment were severe. It was accompanied by a gas attack after which 17 Divisions of German infantry began their advance through a 40 km. gap in the Allied line. With the element of surprise, rapid progress was made and by the end of the first day, the Germans had gained 15km of territory and reached the river Vesle. By 30 May, the Germans had captured 50,000 Allied soldiers and 800 guns. By 3 June, they were within 90 km of Paris. A German victory seemed possible but problems with supplies and reserves, troop fatigue and prolonged Allied counter attacks halted the German advance at the Marne. By 6 June, the German advance had run out of steam.

French casualties were heavy with 98,000 losses. The British suffered 29,000 casualties and the IX Corps was virtually wiped out. The assumption has been made that Private Fred Purvis was captured during this battle.

Reports of "Missing"

The Parish Magazine of August 1918 reported:

> "Included in the list if missing, believed to be Prisoners of War are Sergt. F. Britton M.M. and bar, Ptes. F. Purvis, Reggie Howard (wounded)."

The April 1919 edition included the following report:

> "Much sympathy will be felt by the parishioners of Evenwood for Mr. and Mrs. G. Purvis. Their son was reported missing in July 1918 and nothing has been heard of since."

Then in June 1919, confirmation of their worst fears was given:

> "We deeply sympathise with the parents and relatives of Frederick Purvis who, after being missing for a long time, is now reported to have died in hospital in Germany."

Private Fred Purvis died 9 December 1918

Private Fred Purvis is buried at Niederzwehren Cemetery, Kassel, Germany. The cemetery was begun by the Germans in 1915 for the burial of prisoners of war who died at the local camp. During the war, almost 3,000 Allied soldiers and civilians including French, Russian and Commonwealth, were buried there. In 1922-23, it was decided that the graves of Commonwealth servicemen who had died all over Germany should be brought together into 4 permanent cemeteries. Niederzwehren was one of those chosen and in the following years more than 1,500 graves were brought into the cemetery from 190 burial grounds in Baden, Bavaria, Hanover, Hessen and Saxony. It is therefore possible that Private Fred Purvis was buried at another P.O.W. Camp cemetery and brought to Niederzwehren at this time. There are now 1,796 First World War servicemen buried or commemorated in the Commonwealth plot at Niederzwehren.

Fred Purvis was reported as missing in July 1918 following the German spring offensive. It appears that his family were not informed that he had died in hospital in Germany until May/June 1919. His date of death is officially recorded as 9 December 1918 so it seems reasonable to assume that he was taken prisoner about June 1918 and was either wounded at that time or became ill during his captivity. The great flu epidemic raged across Europe from the summer of 1918 and into 1919 so perhaps he eventually succumbed to this illness. Regardless of the cause of his death, it seems difficult to accept without good reason that it took about 5 months to inform his family that he had died as a POW in Germany. It can only be concluded that this was not a deliberate act of thoughtlessness by the Red Cross, German or British authorities but there was a reasonable explanation. Possibly, he could not be identified or perhaps he was not in a position to identify himself. This is a tragic story and the Purvis family must have endured great suffering not knowing what had become of Fred for such a long period of time.

SPANISH FLU

The influenza epidemic of 1918-1919, known more commonly as "Spanish Influenza" affected large numbers of soldiers during the summer of 1918 – in one sector of the Western Front over 70,000 American troops were hospitalised and nearly one third of these died. By the end of the summer the virus reached the German Army and this created serious problems for the military leadership as they found it impossible to replace their sick and dying soldiers. The infection had already spread into Germany and over 400,000 civilians died of the disease. The virus killed 228,000 people in Britain, 450,000 in Russia, 225,230 in Germany, 166,000 in France, 450,000 in the USA, an estimated 16,000,000 in India and 70 million people world wide.

During the summer of 1918, the epidemic hit the coal mining areas of Northumberland and Durham. Press reports indicate that Spanish flu reached Evenwood in July 1918, "At one pit 46 boys were employed only 7 were present on Thursday" and "Ramshaw School closed due to influenza epidemic." Then it appears to have returned to the locality during November and December, "Seventeen deaths in Cockfield from influenza in the last week." and "Miss Jane Cox daughter of Mrs. Cox, Oaks Bank died on Saturday of pneumonia following influenza aged 17 years." Jane was the sister of 3471 Corporal George Thomas Cox, 1st/6th D.L.I. who was killed in action 5 November 1916 on the Somme. The Evenwood Parish Magazine provides details of burials throughout the period of the war and usually there were between 2 and 5 burials per month but the winter of 1918 – 1919 brought about a higher than average death rate:

- December 1918 – 13 burials
- January 1919 – 7 burials
- February 1919 -19 burials
- March 1919 – 8 burials

By way of further comparison, in November 1918 there were only 3 burials and in April 1919 there were 4 burials.

The following headline was reported, "Influenza deaths in Evenwood" and then, "Mrs. Gaffney wife of Mr. Cornelius Gaffney, Oaks died of influenza."

Another to succumb was Mrs. Selina Parmley, wife of 235587 Corporal George Parmley, 1/4th battalion, the King's Own Yorkshire Light Infantry who died of wounds 16 October 1917 at Passchendaele. She died 22 February 1919 at Bill Quay on Tyneside from pneumonia leaving her mother to look after her 4 children, all under 10 years of age.

NOVEMBER 1918: PRISONER OF WAR BURIALS

The Prisoner of War camp at Harperley was located to the north of Evenwood, in the Parish of Hamsterley. The local publication, "Evenwood's Heyday" provides the following reference:

> "In Evenwood in one week of November/December 1918 there were 7 deaths of which 5 were from influenza and pneumonia....A few miles away from Evenwood at Hamsterley the mortality was the worst ever recorded and consisted almost wholly of German prisoners of war."

27 German POWs were buried in Hamsterley churchyard. In the 1960's their bodies were re-interred in the German Military Cemetery at Cannock Chase, Staffordshire. The details are as follows:

HAMSTERLEY BURIALS			CANNOCK CHASE GERMAN MILITARY CEMETERY BURIALS		
DATE OF BURIAL	NAME	AGE	DATE OF DEATH	NAME	COMMENTS
12/11/1918	A.Schink	37	08/11/1918	Albert	Gem.
12/11/1918	F. Wolczyk	26	08/11/1918	Felix Wloczyk	Musk.
12/11/1918	E.F.P. Sternberg	47	07/11/1918	Paul Ernst Friedrich	Tambour
14/11/1918	F.Bertholdt	29	11/11/1918	Fritz	Ers. Res.
14/11/1918	E.C.F. Garling	26	11/11/1918	Ernst Karl Friedrich	Gefr.
14/11/1918	J.A.C. Lange	31	11/11/1918	Alfred Karl John	Res.
15/11/1918	R.O. Karl	27	11/11/1918	Otto Karl Rosnick	Husar
15/11/1918	R.P. Lebwarn	27	12/11/1918	Richard Lehmann	Musk.
15/11/1918	E. Kaula	41	11/11/1918	Eduard Hadla	Wehtm.
17/11/1918	W. Schwendler	26	12/11/1918	Willy	Schtz.
17/11/1918	K.W. Fink	35	12/11/1918	Karl Eduard Wilhelm	Wehrm.

HAMSTERLEY BURIALS			CANNOCK CHASE GERMAN MILITARY CEMETERY BURIALS		

DATE OF BURIAL	NAME	AGE	DATE OF DEATH	NAME	COMMENTS
17/11/1918	O. Fischer	29	12/11/1918	Otto	Musk.
19/11/1918	A. Balzke	28	13/11/1918	Alfred Paul Alwin	Tag.
19/11/1918	A. Rudloff	22	13/11/1918	Alfred Paul	Musk.
19/11/1918	E. Merkle	22	13/11/1918	Ernst Heinrich	Schtz.
20/11/1918	F.B. Blankefort	28	14/11/1918	Franz Berhard	Ers. Res.
20/11/1918	A.W.F.E. Grasshoff	25	15/11/1918	Arthur	Tag.
20/11/1918	A.E. Kempe	22	14/11/1918	Ernst	Musk.
22/11/1918	H.G. Kausman	32	17/1/1918	Hermann Gustav Kaussmann	Fus.
22/11/1918	W.C.A. Hoswege	29	15/11/1918	Willy Klaus August Horwege	Res.
22/11/1918	K.G. Schneider	29	15/11/1918	Kurt Gustav	Ers. Res.
23/11/1918	K. Beck	28	17/11/1918	Karl Eduard	Gefr.
23/11/1918	F.W.A. Bedorf	34	16/11/1918	Anton	Offz-Stellvertr.
23/11/1918	A. Walkowiak	28	17/11/1918	Anton	Kriegs. Freiw.
25/11/1918	R.M.H. Meier	22	23/11/1918	Rudolf Max Heinrich	Fus.
25/11/1918	M.H.Krinn	23	18/11/1918	Heinrich Max	Musk.
25/11/1918	K. Braungen	29	23/11/1918	Kurt Braunigen	Erst. Res.
TOTAL 27					

The Hamsterley Parish Magazine of December 1918 carries no further details of the burials however it mentions Rev. and Mrs. C.E.P. Shearman who lost their eldest daughter, "by the epidemic now raging the land" – a clear reference to the influenza epidemic.

The 27 Germans were re-interred at the German Military Cemetery at Cannock Chase, Staffordshire which was established under the terms of an agreement 16 October 1959 concluded between the governments of the U.K. and the Federal Republic of Germany. Most of those who lie here died in POW camps. Others were airmen, killed when their airships and aircrafts were brought down or crashed or sailors who died at sea whose bodies were washed ashore. Of the total of 4,940 war dead, 2,143 died during the First World War and 2,797 during the World War II. In 1962/63 and 1966/67 a total of 4,939 German war dead of both World Wars were moved by the "Volksbund" to the Cannock Chase cemetery.

November 1918: Prisoner of War Burials
27 German POWs were buried in Hamsterley chuchyard. In the 1960's their bodies were re-interred in the German Military Cemetery at Cannock Chse, Staffordshire

1919

Whilst the fighting was over, the end of war was not formalised until 28 June 1919 when the Treaty of Versailles was signed.

January 10-15	Communist revolt in Berlin
January 18	Start of peace negotiations in Paris
January 25	Peace conference accepts principle of a League of Nations
February 6	German National Assembly meets in Weimar
February 14	Draft covenant of League of Nations completed
May 6	Peace conference disposes of German colonies
May 7 – June 28	**Treaty of Versailles drafted and signed**
June 21	German High Seas Fleet scuttled at Scapa Flow
July 19	Cenotaph is unveiled in London

Private JOHN WILLIAM MAUGHAN 1889 – 1919

26952 Private John William Maughan, 12th Battalion, Durham Light Infantry, died of pneumonia 27 January 1919. He is buried in Evenwood Cemetery and commemorated on Evenwood War Memorial. He was 30 years old, born c.1889 at Evenwood to Simpson and Alice Maughan and was brother to Walter, Ruth, Mary, Mabel, Elisa Ann, Isabel, Sarah and Mobray. John married Elizabeth in January 1910 and they had 3 children, Sarah Alice, Elizabeth Ann and Walter. Others buried in Evenwood Cemetery are 250400 Private Walter Snowball and 16202 Private Robert Wilson.

26952 Private John William Maughan, 12th Battalion, Durham Light Infantry.

14702 Private John William Maughan attested 7 September 1914 and initially was posted to the 14/DLI then in September 1915 he was posted to the 15/DLI and at that time it is presumed that his regimental number was changed to 26952. He entered France 7 April 1916 and joined his battalion 20 April 1916. The 15/DLI as part of the 64th Brigade occupied positions at la Neuville then 22 April the battalion moved to Meaulte to work on trenches. It went into the front line opposite Fricourt 2 May. After 10 days in the trenches the battalion withdrew to la Neuville and then to Bois de Tailles. The 15/DLI moved up to support positions in Becordel 1 June. Five days later, 6 June, came another tour in the line and 13 June the 15/DLI was at Buire on the river Ancre.

26952 Private John William Maughan was wounded, 8 June 1916 – a gun shot wound to the left leg and he was admitted to the 65 Field Ambulance. The following day, he was transferred to the 21 Casualty Clearing Station. The wound was serious enough for him to be dispatched to England 14 June via SS Dover Castle for treatment. A medical report dated 23 June confirms that "A fragment of shell was removed" and he spent 86 days at the Scottish General, Glasgow (?) being discharged 9 September 1916. There was no major offensive in the British sector during June so the wound must have been as a consequence of the normal violence of war – sniper fire, machine-gun fire or shrapnel.

He was sent back to France, 23 January 1917 originally being posted to the 19/DLI before joining the 12/DLI. He suffered other ailments in April 1917 such as impetigo and was admitted to hospital in Etaples in June 1917. He rejoined his unit 6 August 1917.

The Italians entered the war on the Allied side in May 1915. The Caporetto disaster in the autumn of 1917 threatened the Italian campaign so several French and 5 British Divisions were sent Italy from the Western Front. Commonwealth forces were at the Italian front between November 1917 and November 1918. The 12/DLI formed part of the 68th Brigade in the 23rd Division and commenced the move 8 November 1917 and spent the remainder of the war in Italy. 26952 Private John William Maughan was with the 12/DLI for the whole tour and served alongside 252054 Private Mark G. Middlemass who was killed in action 27 October 1918 at the Battle of Vittorio Venato in northern Italy. It is assumed that these 2 service men were known to each other. 26952 Private John William Maughan survived the campaign. He was awarded 15 days leave 1 December 1918 but on 5 December he was admitted into the Military Hospital at Catterick Camp suffering from pneumonia. He succumbed to the disease on the 27 January 1919.

Private John William Maughan died 27 January 1919

News of his death

The Evenwood Parish Magazine April 1919 included a list of burials from July 1918 to the end of February 1919 and includes the following reference:

> "1919 Jan. 30 – John Wm. Maughan, aged 30 years, Catterick Camp, Yorks."

There is a discrepancy in the date of death. 26952 Private John William Maughan died 27 January but the date on his headstone is 30 January.

Having attested in September 1914, he was one of the first in Evenwood to enlist. It is ironic that he survived the entire war only to be struck down by pneumonia.

PEACE TERMS

The formal end to the Great War did not occur until the signing of the Treaty of Versailles on 28 June 1919 which incidentally was the fifth anniversary of the assassination of Archduke Franz Ferdinand in Sarajevo. The peace terms imposed by the Allies included the following:

> "Germany was to cede all occupied territory on the Eastern and Western Fronts including Alsace-Lorraine, taken from the French in 1870. The Allies would also occupy Germany west of the Rhine and bridgeheads 30km deep on its eastern bank and Germany was to hand over a vast quantity of military equipment including 10 battleships, 14 cruisers and light cruisers, 160 U-boats, 2,00 aircraft, 5,000 field guns and other artillery pieces and 25,000 machine

guns. In all 5,000 locomotives, 5,000 goods wagons and 150,000 railway carriages were also to be confiscated and Germany would be required to pay reparations for her aggression in cash, coal and other goods...the blockade to remain in force until the signing of the final peace treaty."

Just 5 months after the guns went silent in 1918, the war's most caustic poet, Siegfried Sasoon, asked in "Aftermath":

"Do you remember the rats; and the stench
Of corpses rotting in front of the front-line trench –
And dawn coming, dirty-white and chill with a hopeless rain?
Do you ever stop and ask, "Is it all going to happen again?"

In 1914, H.G. Wells published a pamphlet and described the conflict as "The war to end war." The seeds of the Second World War had been sown and sadly, this prediction was not to be the case. The Greek philosopher Plato is attributed the following quote:

"Only the dead have seen the end of war."

Arthur Henderson was the sitting M.P. for Barnard Castle and after the war, he continued his parliamentary career elsewhere when his Barnard Castle constituency was re-organised. He was a key minister in the first 2 Labour governments, in 1929 he became Foreign Minister and in 1932, he was elected as President of the Disarmament Conference. After the Great War, Arthur Henderson had a deep commitment to the cause of world peace and strongly supported the League of Nations, the forerunner to the United Nations. In 1934 he was awarded the Nobel Peace Prize as acknowledgement for his labours on behalf of disarmament. These efforts were to be in vain as Europe headed for another conflict. The seeds of the Second World War, 1939- 1945 had been sown in the Treaty of Versailles.

CHAPTER EIGHT

CASUALTIES & DEMOBILISATION – CASUALTIES OF THE GREAT WAR

The ribbon of cemeteries that run from the Belgian coastline to the Somme, France and beyond "stand as an idealised memorial" to those millions of men who were extinguished on the battlefields. The patriotic epitaphs – "Fur Sein Vaterland", "Mort pour la Patrie" and "For King and Country, Greater Love Hath No Man Than This" on memorials to those who have no known grave and the headstones of those that do, bear witness to the "lost generation".

There is no agreed definitive set of figures. Neil Hanson suggests a total of 42 million casualties, "9 million soldiers dead or missing, 21 million maimed or wounded and at least 12 million civilians killed". John Keegan puts forward at least 8,360,000 dead – "To the 1,000,000 dead of the British Empire and the 1,700,000 French dead, we must add 1,500,000 soldiers of the Habsburg Empire who did not return, 2,000,000 Germans, 460,000 Italians, 1,700,000 Russians and many hundreds of thousands of Turks, their numbers never counted." One website quotes a "Grand total: 65,038,810 mobilised, 8,538,315 dead, 21,219,432 wounded, 7,750,919 prisoners and missing, total casualties 37,494,186 representing 57.6% of those mobilised." Another suggests, "Grand total: 59,798,500 mobilised,

8,283,250 dead, 19,513,000 wounded, total casualties 27,796,250 representing 46% of those mobilised."

Taking a conservative estimate of the loss to Britain and her Empire, the total was 908,000 killed, 2,302,000 wounded, consisting of:
- Britain = 703,000 killed, 1,663,000 wounded
- Canada = 67,000 killed 173,000 wounded
- Australia = 59,000 killed 152,000 wounded
- India = 43,000 killed 65,000 wounded
- New Zealand = 18,000 killed 55,000 wounded
- British Africa = 10,000 killed unknown wounded
- South Africa = 7,000 killed 12,000 wounded
- British Caribbean = 1,000 killed unknown wounded

Of those killed, about half have no known grave:

> "..at the war's end, the remains of nearly half of those lost remained lost in actuality. Of the British Empire's million dead, most killed in France and Belgium, the bodies of over 500,000 were never found or, if found, not identified."

> "Many of the dead…had been lost without trace, blown apart by artillery fire or buried in collapsing trenches and shell holes. Their bodies – food for the omnipresent rats – simply disappeared into the pulverised earth of the battlefield."

In Britain, the monthly toll of casualties was never lower than 6,500 per month (January 1915) hitting the peak during the disastrous Somme campaign, 196,081 for July 1916. 1918 brought about the greatest yearly number of casualties – the German Spring Offensive wrought havoc with 173,721 casualties for March and 143,168 for April. The Advance to Victory was not without its terrible cost – 122,272 casualties for August, 114,831 for September and 121,046 for October.

In round figures, the general consensus is that in one particular year group, 1 in 3 combatants were killed.

> "As in France and Britain, the figures if calculated for the contingents most immediately liable for duty by reason of age display an even heavier burden of loss. Year groups 1892-1895 men who were between 19 and 22 when war broke out were reduced by 35-37%."

In France, by 1918 there were 630,000 war widows and a very large number of younger women were deprived the chance of marriage. The imbalance of the sexes of those aged 20 – 39 stood in 1921 at 45 males to 55 females. There were 5 million wounded in the war.

In Germany, over 2 million soldiers were killed, in 1918 there were half a million war widows and a million fatherless children in Germany. In all 2,057,000 Germans died in the war or of wounds in its aftermath and some 2.7 million Germans had either been disfigured or suffered amputation of one or more limbs.

In Britain, the Times printed its daily Roll of Honour well into 1919, as men continued to succumb to their wounds. There were almost a quarter of a million British amputees. In 1928, two and a half million British men were still in receipt of war pensions because of wounds, disability or shell shock and in that year alone 6,000 new artificial limbs were issued to war wounded men.

And what of the civilian populations – Germany lost the largest number of counted dead, those of Russia and Turkey remain uncounted with any exactitude! The worst proportional sufferer was Serbia, of whose pre-war population of 5 million, 125,000 were killed or died as soldiers but another 650,000 civilians succumbed to privation or disease, making a total of 15% of the population lost compared with something between 2 and 3 % of the British, French and German populations.

EVENWOOD – THE FALLEN & THOSE LEFT BEHIND

The following notes have been compiled using available service records, the 1901 and 1911 census details and Parish Magazines. For those commemorated on the Evenwood War Memorial there were at least 13 widows and 24 children who lost their father, a minimum of 124 brothers and sisters who lost a brother and at least 56 parents who lost a son. For those who were born in Evenwood but lived elsewhere there were a minimum of 11 widows and 18 children who lost their fathers.

The Marquis brothers left behind parents and 7 brothers and sisters in Australia and Anthony Oates who emigrated to Canada left his wife Daisy and their daughter Frances.

No attempt has been made to provide a comprehensive picture of the casualty list, wounded men who returned home because of the lack of known sources of information.

A list is provided below:

Those on Evenwood War Memorial
- 2/Lt. T. W. Applegarth – mother Hannah sister Cicely Annie and brother Maurice George
- L/C J.W. Arkless – parents & siblings Henry, Thomas, George, Margaret and Mabel
- Sapper A.K. Atkinson – parents
- Pte. D. Baister – wife Florence and son Jack
- AB W. Carrick – parents and 12 siblings
- Cpl. G.T. Cox – parents & 6 siblings
- Pte. T. Davis – parents & 3 siblings
- Cpl. H. Dixon – wife Rose and Tom & Cresswell
- Pte. G. Dowson – parents & 7 siblings
- Pte. T.H. Dunn – parents & 8 siblings
- Pte. J. Ellerker – lived with sister
- Gunner W. Gray – wife Mary & Sarah, Eva, John George & Ann
- Pte. J. Heseltine – wife Amy
- Pte. R. Heaviside – parents & 7 siblings
- Pte. J. Hewitt – wife Jessie
- Pte. W. Howlett – parents & 3 siblings
- Pte J. Hutchinson – parents & 7 siblings
- AB A. Lynas – parents & 2 siblings
- Pte. J. Maughan – parents & 5 siblings
- Pte. J. W. Maughan – wife Alice & Sarah, Elizabeth & Walter
- Pte. M. G. Middlemas – wife & Dorothy, Mark, Elizabeth, John & Robert
- Pte. J. Million – wife & son Harold
- Sgt. G. Parmley – wife Selina & Maude, George, Joseph & Thomas
- Gunner F. Purvis – parents & 5 siblings
- Pte. J.H. Raine – wife & Rachel & Rhoda
- Pnr. S.R. Rutter – parents & 3 siblings
- Sgt. T.W. Simpson – mother & step father, brother & half sisters & brother

- Pte J. Skelhorn – unknown
- Pte. W. Snowball – mother & step father
- Sgt. J.W. Spence – wife & 2 children Robert & Monica
- L/Cpl. W. Storey – parents & 3 siblings
- Sgt. E. Towers – parents & 6 siblings
- Pte. J. Walling – wife Isabelle & Edgar (John named on the 1911 census, further research required)
- L/Cpl. J.J. Walton – lived with grandparents
- Pte. R. Wardle – parents & 3 siblings
- Pte. R. Wilson – parents & 6 siblings
- AB J.W. Wren – parents
- G. Bryant – father & brother
- R.W. Conlon – lived with his cousin
- W.E. Earl – parents & 2 siblings
- J.C. Graves – parents & brother
- W. Morley – parents & 8 siblings
- W. Moses – parents & 4 siblings
- M.T. Raine – wife Jane Anne
- J.J. Richardson – parents & 4 siblings
- O. Rushford – parents & 3 siblings
- M. Simpson – parents & 4 siblings
- H. Wardle – father & brother

Elsewhere
- W. Featherstone – Wind Mill – parents & 5 siblings
- A. Brown – Staindrop – wife Clare & child Eleanor
- A. Burrell – Cockfield – parents & 4 siblings
- J.T. Cant – Kirk Merrington – wife Jane & 3 children Rose, Lily & John Thomas.
- C. Cree – Cockfield – wife & 5 children Patricia, Lydia, Laura, Edna & Ronald
- W. Dinsdale – Bishop Auckland – parents
- W. Heaviside – West Auckland – wife Edith & 4 children Annie, Wilson, John & Harold
- F. Hirst – Hamsteels – parents & 3 siblings
- J.C. Lee – Cockfield – wife Mary Jane

- J. Marshall – wife Ann
- T.R. Metcalfe – Witton Park – wife
- W. Million – lived at Byker – wife, Betsy
- J.J. Oates – Normanton, West Yorkshire – wife
- J.H. Pinkney – Stanley, Crook
- G. Priestley – Cockfield – parents & 3 siblings
- E. Robinson – Shildon – parents & 4 siblings
- W. Smith – not traced
- J. A. Wardle – Aycliffe – wife Martha
- E.J. Cooke – not traced
- C.H. Lowson – St. Helens – parents & sister
- J. Richards – not traced
- J.T. Milburn – Shildon – wife Elizabeth & 5 children Elizabeth, William, Jane, Sidney & Thomas

Hamsterley War Memorial

71. J.J. Marquis – Katanning, Western Australia – parents & 7 siblings
72. F.W. Marquis – ditto
73. A. Oates – Calgary, Alberta, Canada -wife Daisy and 1 daughter Frances

DEMOBILIZATION

And what of the survivors?

Initially, a "last in, first out" policy for demobilization had been adopted with the aim being to ensure the rapid return of "key workers" – those who had been conscripted towards the end of the war because the acute shortage of able-bodied men was so critical that even key workers were urgently needed. This provoked fury amongst long serving soldiers. Perhaps anticipating unrest, ex-policemen were the first to be demobilized! Then farm workers then the miners. Being a pit village, it is assumed that the men of Evenwood would have been among the first to be demobilized. Unfortunately, the Evenwood Parish Magazine was not published between September and March 1919 which would have been a critical time to for details of demobilization. The following provides some information for those demobilized:

April 1919

Men not employed at the Mines who have been demobilized:
- Pte. L. Maughan DLI
- Sgl. J.G. Handley DLI
- Pte F. Prudhoe
- L/C H. Foster RGA
- Pte J. Clarke DLI
- Sergt. Nutter
- 2nd Lieut. P.M. Layton
- Maughan RoxboroughDLI
- Pte. J. G. Robinson DLI
- Corpl. J. Lackey RFA
- Pte. T. Dowson RFA
- Pte. N. Dowson DLI (returned POW)
- Sergt. J. Smith RFC
- Pte. Thos. Firby DLI
- Pte. Jos. Smith DLI
- Pte. R. Robinson RGA
- Cadet R. Sunter who has taken up his duties again as a Weslyan Minister in the south
- **17 in total**

On leave:
- Pte. Fred Steel Air-M

May 1919
Demobilised:
- Sergt. R. Simpson DLI Egyptia E Force
- Sergt. W. Dent RAMC
- Sergt. H. Mathews Military Transport
- Cpl. F. Neasham MM Dragoon Guards
- Pte. Wade Emereson ASC
- Pte. G. Stonebamks DLI
- Pte C. Jopling RE
- **7 in total**

On leave:
- Cpl. A. Morland RAF
- Pte. F. Prudhoe DLI
- Pte. J. Robinson DLI
- S. Alderson DLI
- Pte. T. Clarke RAMC
- Pte A. Daniels ASC
- Capt. Campbell MC RAMC
- Lieut. H. Hobson
- 2nd Lieut. J. Sunter
- Pte A. Blenkinsop
- Asst. Paymaster W. Turnbull RN
- G. Wright Mercantile Mariners

On hospital leave:
- Signaller Aarol Howe D.L.I from hospital and recovering
- Pte J. Hull DLI from hospital and recovering
- Pte. W. Bowman ASC from hospital and recovering

June 1919
Demobilized:
- Dr. Campbell home after his 4 years War Service and to hear of the great honour he received in being invested with the Military Cross by His Majesty King George.
- Signaller H. Howe (after recovering from wounds)
- Pte. W. Barnes
- Pte. Jos. Priestley HLI
- Pte. T. Garrett RE
- Pte. Watson Welsh DLI
- **6 in total**

On Leave:
- Cpl. N. Dunn DLI
- Cpl. W. Bowman ASC (recovering from wounds)
- Pte. J. Friend ASC
- Pte. W. Cook DLI

July 1919
Demobilised:
- Ass Paymaster W. Turnbull RN
- Cpl. J. Friend ASC
- Cpl. F. Dunn MM DLI
- Cpl. W. Garrett DLI
- Pte. J. Lowson ASC
- Pte. Watson Welsh RGA
- Pte. T. Firby DLI
- **7 in total**

On leave:
- Cpl. T. Gibson North Staffs
- Pte F. Bussey DLI
- Pte. G. Clennell DLI
- Pte. J.M. Wilkinson DLI
- Pte. J. Shaw DLI
- Pte A. Nicholson DLI

Hospital leave:
- J.W. Horden home for a week from Manchester Hospital

In hospital
- Pte C. Jobling CSG
- F. Robinson returned to hospital suffering from old wounds
- T. H. Rutter ditto
- J. Hull ditto

Army of Occupation:
- Pte J. Cree
- Pte. C. Davis

September 1919
Demobilised:
- Lieut. H.B. Hobson
- Signaller J. Richmond
- Pte. H. Hull
- Pte F. Robinson
- Pte. D. Shipp

- Pte A. Elders RND
- Pte B. Arkless
- W. Kipling RN
- 8 in total

On leave:
- Pte. A. Wilkinson
- Pte. H. Horseman
- Pte. J.W. Hordon
- Pte. G. Towers
- Pte. W. Watson
- Pte G. Raine
- Pte Joe Roe

Hospital leave
- N. Dunn
- W. Bowman

In hospital
- Cpl. C. Jobling
- G. Featherstone – returned for further treatment

October 1919
Demobilised:
- Sergt. W. Rutter RGA
- Cpl. T. Gibson E. Staffs LI
- Sig.Cpl. W. Cook DLI
- Pte. H. Horsman HLI
- Pte Walter Bowman ASC
- L/C N. Dunn DLI
- Pte. M. Wilkinson DLI
- Pte G. Clennell DLI
- Pte. W. Watson DLI
- Pte Jos. Dixon DLI
- **10 in total**

On leave:
- Pte Geo. Flowers

December 1919
Demobilised:
- Sergt. W. Rutter RGA
- Cpl. Thomas Gibson North Staffs LI
- Cpl H. Horseman HLI
- Pte. G. Raine ASC
- Pte. A. Wilkinson DLI
- Pte A. Nicholson DLI
- Pte J. Bussey DLI
- Pte J.W. Hordon DLI
- Pte J. Shaw DLI
- Pte Joseph Dixon DLI
- Pte J. Bland HLI
- Bombardier W. Cook DLI
- **9 in total** (3 repeated, mentioned in October)

Still in the Army:
- Lieut. P. Brass RAF
- Lieut. J. Sunter DLI
- Pte. W. Garthwaite DLI.
- Pte. S. Hutchinson DLI
- Pte. J. Cree DLI
- Pte. C. Davis DLI.
- Pte. S. Allen DLI
- Pte. J. Hull Wearmouth DLI
- Pte. G. Towers DLI
- Pte. N. Dunn DLI
- Pte. G. Rawe ASC
- Pte. R. Priestley RGA

The Parish Magazine reported that between April and November 1919, 64 servicemen had been demobilised and there were still 12 men in the Army. Two men definitely in the Army of Occupation were Pte J. Cree and Pte. C. Davis.

The Parish Magazine reported on a number of important village events associated with the War and provides a social commentary of the times:

14 Feb 1919: The Evenwood & Ramshaw Hero Fund Committee presented the following with Gold Wrist Watches:
- Sergt. Fred Britton MM and Bar DLI
- Sergt. J. Nutter MM RAMC
- Pte W. Hutchinson MM DLI
- Corpl. Fred Dunn MM DLI
- Pte. J. Jackson MM Coldstream Guards
- Pte J.J. Bolton has been awarded DCM for holding up the enemy for 48 hours. Pte. Bolton was employed at Randolph Colliery. This is one of seven of the HLI who made that great stand.

19 July 1919: The National Peace Celebration was held. Evenwood held its own Peace Festival:

"No praise can be too great for all who organised and carried out a display that would have done credit to any town in England. Few places are so favoured as Evenwood in the delightful stretch of country which surrounds it on all sides and in the glorious sunshine that prevailed the whole scene was inspiring. Then with our most creditable Village Band, magnificent Colliery Banners, interesting competitions and school procession we had a picture that will never fade from our memories. Probably 2,000 children and adults took part, reverently and heartily in the Service by which we expressed our gratitude to Almighty God for His great mercy in giving us the Victory."

The vicar also reported that:

"As a nation we are £8,000,000,000 in debt through the war."

14 September 1919: a Church Service at St. Paul's, Evenwood:

"Few more inspiring services can have been held than that of the evening of September 14th when our demobilised soldiers came to church to return thanks for a safe return. Every seat was packed and all the extra ones we could secure were filled with a vast congregation which admirably accompanied by our Evenwood Band gave a hearty rendering of five favourite hymns. All stood whilst Mr. Bird played the Dead March for the brave comrades who did not return."

7 October 1919: The Comrades of the Great War held their meeting in Evenwood School attended by Capt. Appleby and Mr. & Mrs. Wilson:

"some 50 ex-servicemen belonging our Parish have joined and we trust that Evenwood will do its bit in fostering that spirit of comradeship which helped so much to beat our enemies and which can enable the British Empire to realise its possibilities and live up to its privileges."

The identity of "the Wilsons" has not been researched but it is assumed that they were officials of the organisation.

11 November 1919: Of the anniversary of the Armistice, the vicar wrote:

"One of the chief things we should be looking forward to is the Anniversary of the Signing of the Armistice – Nov. 11th – that day when the joy bells rang to tell us that the long drawn out horror of the Great War was over for God had given us victory. The countless thousands whose dearest were swaying in deadly conflict on so many battle fronts constantly exposed to hardship, suffering and agonising death, will never forget the relief which that day and surely they will wish to thank and praise the Giver of all good things. We hope (D.V.) to preach Nov. 9th on the League of Nations that carefully planned scheme which we have so often prayed may abolish war and bloodshed."

There was a short lived economic boom in 1919 but the reality was that Britain's economy was in a terrible plight:

- Russia's repudiation of All Tsarist debt and its nationalisation of all foreign investments (in both cases the vast majority were British)
- The impact of reparations imposed on Germany resulted in so many German ships and liners being transferred to British, French and American flags that domestic and export demand for new ships from Britain no longer existed. Similarly export markets for British coal shrunk by millions of tons as German coal headed for France as a result of reparations.
- Rival nations had benefited from British industry being pre-occupied with the war effort and their manufacturing industries found markets previously dominated by Britain – ferocious competition was led by America and Japan and British engineering and textile firms suffered.

In September 1920, the vicar reported:

> "..we are threatened with much suffering this winter through shortage of work but if we are visited with the calamity of a great strike there is no telling to what this suffering may attain…"

27 October 1920: The Evenwood Comrades Hut was opened amid concern that there was to be a miners' strike.

11 November 1920: The Cenotaph in London was unveiled by King George V and the funeral of the Unknown Warrior took place. He was buried in Westminster Abbey.

8 December 1920: The official opening of the Comrades Hall occurred. Mr. J.R. Lowson acting on behalf of his uncle Mr. H. Lowson performed the opening, Mr. G.S. Robinson D.C. presided and the speakers were Capt. Appleby and Mr. G.B. Wilson.

The economic situation continued to be bleak. In November 1920, total unemployment stood at 500,000 but within 3 months the figure had doubled and by June 1921 it had doubled again to 2,000,000. Two thirds of the male unemployed were ex-servicemen and "ex-gratia" payments of twenty nine shillings a week to unemployed ex-soldiers came to an end in March 1921. For many of those returning home to a land fit for heroes:

> "the greatest indignity was having to watch their children line up at soup kitchens."

The Evenwood area suffered the same as elsewhere. The pits were closed from October to November 1920 due to industrial action and from April to July 1921 as a result of a lockout. In Evenwood, the Salvation Army's Commander Moyle and his wife played a major part in organising the Soup Kitchen in the Comrades Hall which offered some measure of relief by providing meals to the destitute. Rev. R.E. Ragg wrote in the Parish Magazine:

> "The unhappy deadlock in the mining world is disturbing us all and causing much anxiety. Already there are close upon 2 million men out of work and in very many of their cases, families are suffering for want of food and fuel. An aged invalid told me that she prays that this trouble may speedily end every time she awakes in the night. Your

vicar constantly does the same and prayed for weeks beforehand that the deadlock might be averted."
May 1921.

"The mining deadlock continues and the want and suffering entailed, increases daily. In our own parish sacrifice and much downright hard work is being performed to lesson hardship and privation. It has been decided to put in operation, "the Feeding of the School Children Act" probably beginning Sat. 4th June when both breakfast and dinner will have to be prepared and provided. We hope that all those who have worked so nobly hitherto will continue at their post and that numbers of other workers will offer their services. This Act only meets the needs of children from 5 to 14 yrs. But efforts are being put forth to help others also who are really in need."
June 1921

20 June 1921: Amidst this social turmoil, the Memorial to the Men of Evenwood, Ramshaw and Lands was unveiled in Evenwood Cemetery. There was a vast crowd. Mr. T. Heslop, (formerly the Randolph Colliery manager then Chief Agent to the North Bitchburn Coal Company Ltd. and former District and Parish Councillor) was the chairman of the fund raising committee and addressed the gathering. Colonel Dowling who had 27 years knowledge of the Evenwood Volunteers performed the unveilment and spoke of the sacrifice of these brave men. Evenwood Band played "Dead March in Saul" and "The Last Post". The Comrades of the Great War, the Boy Scouts and Girl Guides were well represented. Those who returned must have wondered, "What was it all for?"

Rev. R.E. Ragg wrote more of the struggles:

"The great industrial struggle still goes on…feeding of the children continues."
July 1921

Commander Moyles and his wife received the vicars' thanks on behalf of a grateful community.

"We have seen Mr. & Mrs. Moyles strenuous and self denying labours in feeding children during the mining deadlock and

I feel that we cannot sufficiently thank them for their efforts. The preparation and serving of the meals entailed a very large amount of hard work on a considerable number of people who have served well our parishioners....It was with a great feeling of relief that the meeting on 27th June...had resulted in a settlement of the deadlock... our 2 collieries have been quicker to make a start than most in the county...8000 Durham miners permanently unemployed through the definite closing of pits."
August 1921.

*4 July 1921: Soup Kitchen staff Evenwood
Commander and Mrs Moyles seated in the centre*

The economic situation fluctuated from bad to worse to bad over the next decade and it affected all aspects of community life, even sport as the headline of 20 June 1925 illustrates:

"Wear Valley League suspends activities – the result of trade depression"

Resignations were received from teams at Butterknowle and Evenwood Town. Locally, in 1925 colliery closures occurred such as Marsfield (Butterknowle) Colliery and New Copley Colliery, to the west of Cockfield which closed after 57 years in operation. Then from May to November 1926 the National Stoppage in the coal industry repeated the worst effects of 1921.

Rev. W. Richardson wrote in the Evenwood Parish Magazine:

> "Our village, being in the centre of the mining industry is particularly affected and we shall rejoice when a final settlement is arrived at. A settlement which we hope will be just and lasting." May 1926.

> "At the time of writing things are still the same and there seems little hope. But surely this cannot last, a way out of this deadlock must be found unless disaster on a large scale overtakes us."
> June 1926.

> "Another month and no settlement, surely things cannot go on like this much longer, the tangle must be unravelled some time. If only we could get a just and lasting agreement then we could begin to rebuild the ruins and get back to progress, prosperity and happiness for which we most earnestly hope and pray."
> July 1926.

> "The events of 1926 were tragic and ruinous and we turn eagerly to something better, may 1927 bring improvements and happiness to all."
> December 1926.

In 1926 St. Helens Colliery closed. In 1927, there were more local closures – Quarry Drift (Butterknowle) Collieries, Carterthorne and West Carterthorne Collieries, once owned and managed by Mr. G. Bradford, father of the "Fighting Bradfords". From May 1927 to December 1928, Randolph Colliery was closed. Further extracts from the Parish Magazine read:

> "Our sympathy goes out to the men who are out of employment and to mothers who have such a struggle to make ends meet and bring up their children and feed and clothe their families."
> June 1927

> "Several of our members are leaving the district for other fields of work and we are left the poorer. We wish them happiness, success and prosperity."
> August 1927

"I am thankful to be able to record progress and continued interest in our church life despite the depression that lies over the whole district."
June 1928

The hardship of the post Great War era must have been almost unbearable for many families. Those women who had to raise their children without their husbands must have relied on strong family support to survive.

One such story is that of the family of 235587 Corporal George Parmley, 1/4th battalion, the King's Own Yorkshire Light Infantry who died of wounds 16 October 1917 received at Passchendaele. Up until 1911, George lived locally at Ramshaw then at Rochdale Terrace, Evenwood. He worked as a miner. George married Selina Robinson 11 November 1911. Selina lived at the nearby village of Witton Park. By 1914 and the outbreak of war they had moved north to Bill Quay on Tyneside, presumably in search of regular employment. When George was killed in 1917, Selina had 3 children, Maud aged 7, George aged 5 and Joseph aged 4 and she was pregnant with their fourth child. Thomas was born in March 1918. Further tragedy was to hit the family when almost a year later 22 February 1919, Selina died as a result of contracting influenza – it is assumed that she was a victim of "Spanish Flu".

The 4 children, all under 10 years of age, were brought up by their grandmother, Selina's mother Mary. She had outlived her first husband John Robinson and later married William Mossop thus was known as "Grandma Mossop". Then George junior died in 1926.

In 1927, the oldest child, Maud then aged 16 married John "Jack" Atkinson at Gateshead Registry Office (9 July). In February 1928 their first child George was born. In 1929, no doubt because of the hardships of living in the North East, Maud, Jack and their year old son George decided go "down south" like many others from the region, as Rev. Richardson commented. Maud was only 18 or 19 at the time. The situation on Tyneside was probably no better than the pit villages of south west Durham (described elsewhere) from where the family originated. Many young women from the North East needed to leave home to find work and earn money in order to send some home to support their families – usually this work was as domestics for rich families. In reality, many chose to leave home to try to "better themselves". For Maud to make this decision at such a young age nevertheless must have been "a monumental decision".

The Atkinson's resettled at Edmonton, Greater London. "Grandma Mossop" and her grandsons Joseph and Thomas soon followed. Maud and Jack Atkinson had 3 children, John born February 1928, James born February 1930 and Audrey born September 1932.

There was to be yet another family tragedy – Maud's brother Joseph was killed at work, electrocuted at Enfield Rolling Mills, 7 July 1937 aged 23. His wife Ellen returned back to the North East with their daughter Joan. Eight months later, Mary Mossop died 4 February 1938.

To complete the immediate family picture, Selina's youngest son Thomas who was born 5 months after George was killed, married Connie from the East End. They had 2 children, Tanis and Lynn, both of whom emigrated to New Zealand.

"Grandma Mossop" looked after the children until they were old enough to look after themselves. Maud at a relatively young age and her husband Jack appear to have had the ambition to "move on" in search of a better life and the family followed their lead.

Looking at 235587 Corporal George Parmley's brothers and sisters, the tragedy of the War struck elsewhere.

George's older sister Lily married Robert Close and her brother-in-law was 32627 Private John "Jack" James Close, 14/D.L.I. who was killed in action 11 December 1916. He is buried at Cambrin churchyard, east of Bethune, France and commemorated on Cockfield War Memorial.

George's oldest sister Elizabeth "Lizzie Ann" married Jack Pearson and they had 4 children, one of whom Joe married Dolly Lamb. A relative was 250400 Private Walter Snowball, 6/D.L.I. who died 29 August 1918 as a result of illness contracted whilst on active service. He is buried in Evenwood Cemetery.

In researching the Evenwood men, it is evident that many family members have not forgotten the sacrifice of their grandfather, great grandfather or great uncles. The above account is but one of many stories of that remarkable generation who fought a War and the survivors having contributed to winning War, suffered unemployment and poverty then if they were lucky enough lived through a Second World War. The sacrifices of that generation should not be forgotten and certainly those associated with those mentioned above namely, 235587 Corporal George Parmley, 1/4th King's Own Yorkshire Light Infantry, 250400 Private Walter Snowball, 6/D.L.I. and 32627 Private John "Jack" James Close, 14/D.L.I. notably Jim "Chicka" Atkinson, Lynn Biggs, Lily Bainbridge, John "Jocka" James Close, Melvyn and Edith McConnell have not forgotten.

IN FLANDERS FIELDS

Corporal George Parmley is buried at Wimereux Communal Cemetery. Wimereux is a small town about 5km north of Boulogne. Wimereux was the headquarters of the Queen Mary's Auxilliary Corps during the First World War and in 1919 it became the General HQ of the British Army. From October 1914 onwards, Wimereux and Boulogne formed an important hospital centre and until June 1918, the medical units at Wimereux used the communal cemetery for burials. There are 2,847 Commonwealth burials and amongst them is Lt.-Col. John McCrae, author of the poem "In Flanders Fields."

Lest we Forget

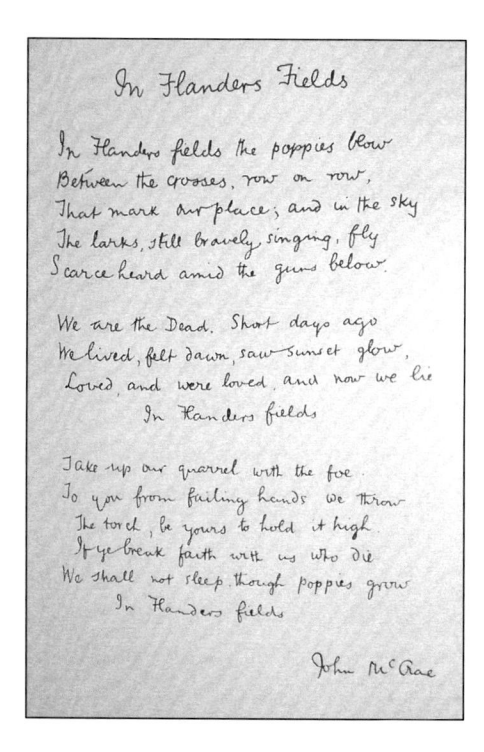

In Flanders Fields

In Flanders fields the poppies blow
Between the crosses, row on row,
That mark our place; and in the sky
The larks, still bravely, singing, fly
Scarce heard amid the guns below.

We are the Dead. Short days ago
We lived, felt dawn, saw sunset glow,
Loved, and were loved, and now we lie
    In Flanders fields

Take up our quarrel with the foe.
To you from failing hands we throw
The torch, be yours to hold it high.
If ye break faith with us who die
We shall not sleep though poppies grow
    In Flanders fields

John McCrae

CHAPTER NINE

REMEMBRANCE

In Britain, until the Great War, there had been little national will to commemorate the war dead other than the national heroes such as Nelson. He was afforded a State Funeral and a monument, Nelson's column in Trafalgar Square in the centre of our capital city whereas "his dead sailors were simply wrapped, weighted and thrown over the side." There are some casualties, few in number, who were brought to Gibraltar for treatment but died of their wounds and were afforded a burial on land rather than at sea. These are probably the earliest British war graves for the "not so famous." The dead from battlefields were simply thrown into mass graves.

Headstone for Lieutenant William Forster, Gibraltar

The first monument to dead soldiers was erected in Lucerne to commemorate the members of the

The Memorial to the Swiss Guard, Lucerne, Switzerland

Swiss Guard killed in the Tuileries on 10 August 1792. In 1916, the first commemoration of the war dead appeared in Liverpool Anglican Cathedral where a marble cenotaph was placed in the north east transept as a memorial to the war dead of the city.

The word "cenotaph" is derived from the Greek words *kenos* and *taphos* meaning "empty tomb" and first came to prominence at the turn of the century when Lutyens designed a garden seat for Gertrude Jekyll that was known as "The Cenotaph of Sigsmunda".

In Britain, a Victory Parade was planned for Peace Day 19 July 1919 and public opinion fuelled by the popular press felt that some form of national shrine or monument was required to which the public at large could pay tribute – a temporary monument was erected in Whitehall for members of the armed forces, ex-servicemen and public to march past. Such was the popularity that the public demanded a permanent memorial.

The Cenotaph, Whitehall, London

The Cenotaph was erected on the same spot, designed by Lutyens and was unveiled by King George V on 11 November 1920, Armistice Day. The funeral of the Unknown Warrior took place the same day and he was buried in Westminster Abbey.

"The Great Silence" lasting 2 minutes – the first minute to commemorate those who fought and came home, the second to remember those who did not – was a tradition imported from South Africa. This mark of respect was also instituted on Armistice Day 1920.

> "More than any eloquence of tongue was this eloquence of silence."

Poppies were not to be adopted as a symbol of remembrance for another 12 months, Armistice Day 1921 – they first became intimately associated with the war dead in the devastated battlefields of the Somme as so eloquently described in John McRae's poem, "In Flanders Fields."

The essential symbols of remembrance were in place – the cenotaph, the tomb of the unknown warrior, poppies and the silence. However, the public also demanded the creation of purely local memorials, recognising the sacrifice of every community from the great industrial cities to the smallest villages and hamlets. Initially, roadside shrines were erected the first being in Hackney in the spring or summer of 1916 and by the end of October of that year 250 had been established in the London area alone. Local committees were formed to raise money for local war memorials and fifty to sixty thousand were erected in Great Britain alone.

The people of the Evenwood area formed such an organising committee and Mr. Thomas Heslop, the Managing Director of the North Bitchburn Coal Company was the chairman. On Monday evening 20 June 1921 the memorial to the 48 men of Evenwood, Ramshaw and Lands was unveiled by Colonel Dowling. It was reported that the Evenwood Band performed for the "vast crowd." The following report appeared in the Northern Echo:

> **Memorial obelisk unveiled on Monday evening at Evenwood.**
> Designed, executed and erected by William Allison & Sons sculptors, Bishop Auckland. Proceedings commenced with a procession which was formed at the top end of Evenwood village consisting of

ex soldiers and sailors, Girl Guides and Boy Scouts headed by the Village Band. The Last Post was sounded."

Memorials took different forms. For instance:

- St. Helen Auckland – the mining company Pease & Partners together with the workmen built 2 pairs of Memorial Cottages for colleagues. These were officially opened 12 November 1921. Memorial plaques on each block commemorate a total of 37 fallen comrades.
- West Auckland – a Memorial Hall was built. A Roll of Honour commemorating 53 men is located within the hall.
- Cockfield – a War Memorial is located on the village green and commemorates 45 men of the village.
- Butterknowle – a War Memorial commemorates 23 men from the village
- Copley – a plaque on the village hall commemorates 8 men
- Woodland – a stone column commemorates 8 men of the village and it includes a record of those who served in the armed forces.
- Etherley – an obelisk in St. Cuthbert's churchyard commemorates the 26 men from Etherley, Toft Hill, Morley and Windmill.
- Staindrop – a highly decorated plaque in St. Mary's church commemorates 40 men from the village.
- Hamsterley – a War Memorial located on the village green commemorates 8 men of the village.

The War Memorial, Evenwood Cemetery

In total 349 men from the wider area are commemorated on these memorials.

CHAPTER TEN

Reverend George J. Collis MA 1871 – 1918

Rev. G. J. Collis

Rev G.J. Collis died 15 September 1918. The Evenwood Parish Magazine ceased publication and with it reports of local news associated with the war. The magazine did not appear regularly until March 1919 when Rev. Ragg was appointed to the parish. The following section looks at Rev. G.J. Collis whose invaluable notes on the Great War have been heavily used in this work. Those who were associated with him are also mentioned here.

G.J. Collis was the sixth vicar of St. Paul's, Evenwood following Rev. H. J. H. Faulkener in 1908. He was to remain vicar for ten years until his sudden death in September 1918, at 47 years old. His previous appointments were as curate at Berwick-on-Tweed 1894-97, Embleton 1897-1905 and Morpeth 1905-08. He was educated at Clare College, Cambridge gaining a B.A. in 1892 and he then went on to attain an M.A. in 1902.

Evenwood National Schools, Shirley Terrace

The Parish was formed in 1866 and St. Paul's Church was built at that time. It was restored 1890-01 but destroyed by fire in December 1907. The church was re-opened on Tuesday 23 March 1909 when the lesson was read by Mr. W. R. Innes Hopkins, managing director of the North Bitchburn Coal Company and father of W. Hustler Hopkins, chairman of the building committee. A public tea followed in the schoolroom.

At this time Rev. G. J. Collis was still the relatively new vicar and no doubt relished the challenge of building up his congregation in his newly built church. Perhaps the Evenwood Parish Magazine would be a valuable tool in "spreading the word". His curate until July 1911 was Rev. A. Armitage who resided at Victoria House and his choirmaster was Mr. J. R. Bouch. Mr. Bouch was the schoolmaster at Evenwood National School and the honourable secretary of the Evenwood Crusaders football team – clearly, he

Mr J. R. Bouch

was an active member of the village community but he departed on being appointed Headmaster at Eaglescliffe National School in the Spring of 1912.

Rev. W. T. Taylor was the replacement curate who came into the village in March 1912. Rev. Taylor appears to have been instrumental in forming the Boy Scouts movement and by September 1913, there were 20 boys in the Evenwood troop. Messrs. J. H. Nutter and J. W. Hordern were Assistant and Deputy Assistant Scoutmasters respectively. In October 1913, it was reported that Rev. Taylor had left the Parish to take up an appointment at Heighington.

The Parish Magazine was well established by this time and communicated local information throughout the district. Details of births, marriages, burials, church services and secular matters were provided but also many other topics were brought to the attention of readers such as local events, presentations, meetings, sporting occasions, educational achievements, schooling matters – even the sinking of the Titanic in 1912!

It was instrumental in passing on information throughout the locality and good news was especially welcome such as the Evenwood Silver Band winning the Boothroyd Challenge Vase at Bishop Auckland in 1910. Rev. Collis is included in the 1908 photograph of the prize winning band

1908: Collis with the Evenwood Silver Prize band Winners of the Hunwick Cup

1910–11: Evenwood Crusaders

Winners of the Shildon Nursing Cup

Back: J. Rutter, Dr. R. A. Milne, J. R. Bouch (Hon. Sec.) Rev. G. J. Collis, T. Stokoe, A. Shipp

Standing: J. Bussey, J. Dunn, J. Bussey (Capt.) C. Simpson, F. W. Neasham, R. Bussey, G. Proud, W. Stringer (Trainer)

Seated: W. Blenkinsop, W. Clennell, J. Coates, E. Bayles, A. Blenkinsop

Front: J. Lowson (Linesman), H. Walker, J. Walker, G. Atkinson, A. Bowman

assembled outside the new vicarage at Shirley Terrace. Also the exploits of the village football teams enjoyed good publicity in the magazine. For instance the league winning Evenwood Crusaders and junior teams are mentioned in May 1909, June 1910 and November 1911. Again Rev. Collis takes pride of place alongside his friend Mr. J.R. Bouch, the village school headmaster, in team photographs. Clearly, Rev. Collis involved himself in various aspects of village life and reported many cheerful events in the magazine.

The Parish Magazine probably was as effective as any other broadsheet or newspaper during the years of the Great War. Rev. Collis gave his opinion as to the progress of the war, trying as would be expected, to paint a "rosy picture" in times of crisis and being as patriotic as the occasion demanded. The magazine also provided an outlet for letters from men on active service away from home. It was passed around, home and abroad and voluntary subscriptions were forthcoming and acknowledged. There can be little doubt that its readers valued the publication.

Rev. Collis offered himself for the war effort but was denied service as the following extract from the Parish Magazine (July 1918) confirms:

> "I have three times offered myself at various times during the war for any National Service to which the Diocesan authorities might care to appoint me and have been three times informed that they considered that the best form of service I could render was in my own parish among my own people."

Perhaps the manner in which Rev. Collis kept his parishioners informed about these events is one of his best achievements. It is evident that matters of life and death, tragedy and sorrow are reported with great sympathy and tact. Perhaps the diocesan authorities were correct in their belief that Rev. Collis should stay in Evenwood.

Sadly, as the war raged on in September 1918, Rev. Collis died aged just 47. The collection of Parish Magazines thus comes to an abrupt end with the September edition.

Mr. Spencer Wade provided the October 1918 which announced the death of Rev. Collis and his contribution contained a warm tribute to him. Apparently he had almost lost his sense of hearing and in August 1918 had enjoyed a month's holiday returning in September "refreshed and re-invigorated". His appearance of good health was obviously masking serious health problems.

To quote Spencer Wade:

> "In the sudden death of the Rev. George J. Collis, Evenwood has suffered a great loss. He was in every sense of the word a good man and good men in this sin stained world are few and far between…I was greatly struck while at Evenwood with the love of the young people for their vicar…Mr. Collis' influence in Evenwood has been such that few men will be able to follow him."

Rev. Collis was buried 18 September 1918. He was succeeded by Robert Edward Ragg in January 1919 and it was not until March 1919 that regular copies of the Parish Magazine recommenced.

There follows some notes referring to 3 serving soldiers who were mentioned at length by Rev. Collis:

Rev. R. E. Ragg

J. H. Nutter – The Scout Master
- September 1915 – enlisted J.H. Nutter – RAMC
- September 1916 – Sergt. J.H. Nutter RAMC – visit then to France
- December 1916 – letter from the front
- January 1917 – awarded MM
- March 1917 – letter from France
- April 1917 – letter from France tells of 2 brothers killed by the same shell
- April 1919 – 14 February 1919 Evenwood & Ramshaw Hero Fund Committee presented the following with Gold Wrist Watches – Sergt. J. Nutter MM RAMC – Demobilised

Date unknown – Evenwood Scouts – could the scoutmaster be J. H. Nutter or J. W. Hordern?

J. W. Hordern – Assistant Scoutmaster
- July 1917 – J.W. Hordon (scoutmaster) joined up
- August 1917 – letter NE Coast station
- July 1919 – home for a week from Manchester Hospital
- November 1919 – Demobilised

F. W. Neasham
1910-11 season Evenwood Crusaders FC – Goalkeeper
- November 1914 – enlisted – Fred Neasham – cavalry barracks
- April 1915 – Swan Street, 2nd Dragoon Guards
- November 1915 – Serbia
- July 1917 – Royal Dragoons – on leave
- May 1918 – letter from France
- May 1919 – Cpl. F. Neasham MM Dragoon Guards – demobilised

F. W. Neasham

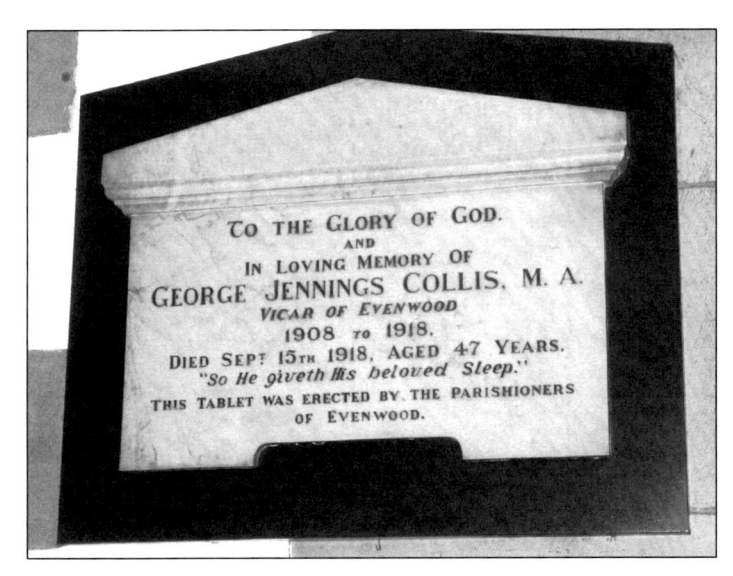

Within St. Paul's Church, a memorial plaque to Rev. G. J. Collis

APPENDIX ONE

The Toll – a chronological list of the Fallen

1915

11/06/1915
4/9455 Private J.T. Cant, 2nd Bn., (C" Coy.) Durham Light Infantry, 18th Brigade, 6th Division, V Corps, Second Army
Ypres Salient – Killed in action
Potijze Cemetery, Belgium
Kirk Merrington War Memorial

09/08/1915
11905 Private Wilson Million, 2nd Bn, the Durham Light Infantry
Hooge – Killed in action
Ypres (Menin Gate) Memorial, Belgium
Etherley War Memorial.

18/09/1915
54973 Acting Bombadier J. Richards, 44th Coy., Royal Garrison Artillery
Home
Pembroke Dock Military Cemetery
Etherley War Memorial

25/09/1915
14525 Serjeant E. Towers, 15th Bn., Durham Light Infantry, 64th Brigade, 21st Division, XI Corps, First Army
Battle of Loos – Killed in action
Loos Memorial, Pas de Calais, France – No known grave
Evenwood War Memorial, St Paul's Plaque

04/10/1915
2130 Corporal H. Dixon, 5th Bn., Border Regiment, 149th Brigade, 50th Division, V Corps, Second Army
Trench warfare (sniper fire) Armentieres sector – Died of wounds
Houplines Communal Cemetery, Nord, France
Evenwood War Memorial, St. Paul's Plaque

1916

02/02/1916
21/1568 Private C. Cree, 21st (Tyneside Scottish) Bn., Northumberland Fusiliers, 102nd Brigade, 34th Division, III Corps, Fourth Army
Trench warfare, Armentieres sector – Died of wounds
Sailly sur la Lys, Canadian Cemetery, Pas de Calais, France
Cockfield War Memorial

31/03/1916
102256 Sapper J.T. Milburn, 177th Tunnelling Company, Royal Engineers, 20th Division, XIV Corps, Second Army
Mt. Sorrel – died of illness
Etaples Military Cemetery
Shildon War Memorial

31/03/1916
17190 Private J. Marshall, 8th Bn., East Yorks. Regt., 8th Brigade, 3rd Division, V Corps, Second Army
Ypres Salient, Belgium – Killed in action, no known grave
Menin Gate Memorial, Ypres

24/05/1916
24781 Private J.H. Raine, 13th Bn., Durham Light Infantry, 68th Brigade, 23rd Division, III Corps, Fourth Army
Trench warfare Souchez sector – Killed in action (details unknown)
Bois de Noulette British cemetery, Aix Noulette, Pas de Calais, France
Evenwood War Memorial, St. Paul's Plaque, WMC Memorial

31/05/1916
Able Seaman J.W. Wren
HMS "Black Prince"
Battle of Jutland
Chatham Naval Memorial
Evenwood War Memorial, St. Paul's Plaque

01/06/1916
Ordinary Seaman W. Carrick
HMS "Ardent"
Battle of Jutland
Farsund Cemetery, Norway
Evenwood War Memorial, St. Paul's Plaque, WMC Memorial

01/06/1916
Ordinary Seaman A. Lynas
HMS "Ardent"
Battle of Jutland
Portsmouth Naval Memorial
Evenwood War Memorial, St. Paul's Plaque, WMC Memorial

02/07/1916
14704 Private T.R. Metcalfe, 15th Bn., Durham Light Infantry, 64th Brigade, 21st Division, XV Corps, Fourth Army
Battle of the Somme, Battle of Albert – Died of wounds
Mericourt-L'Abbe Communal Cemetery Extn., Somme, France
Witton Park War Memorial

13/09/1916
31058 Private R. W. Conlon, 2nd Bn., York & Lancaster Regiment, 16th Brigade, 6th Division, XIV Corps, Fourth Army
Battle of the Somme – Died of wounds
Peronne Road Cemetery, Maricourt, Somme, France
Evenwood War Memorial

15/09/1916
446121 Private A. Oates, 31st Bn., (Alberta Regt.) Canadian Infantry, 6th Canadian Brigade, 2nd Canadian Division, Canadian Corps, Reserve Army
Battle of the Somme, Battle of Flers-Courcelette – Killed in action
Vimy Memorial, France
Hamsterley War Memorial

16/09/1916
32120 Private J.C. Graves, 10th Bn., Durham Light Infantry, 43rd Brigade, 14th Division, XV Corps, Fourth Army
Battle of the Somme, Battle of Flers-Courcelette – Killed in action
Thiepval Memorial, Somme, France – No known grave
Evenwood War Memorial

17/09/1916
24048 Private W. Smith, 9th Bn., Lancashire Fusiliers, 31st Brigade, 11th Division, II Corps, Reserve Army (formerly 5th Reserve Cavalry)
Battle of the Somme, Battle of Flers-Courcelette – Killed in action
Thiepval Memorial, Somme, France – No known grave

29/09/1916
18/1628 Private W.E. Earl, 14th Bn., Durham Light Infantry, 18th Brigade, 6th Division, XIV Corps, Fourth Army
Battle of the Somme, Battle of Morval -Killed in action
Thiepval Memorial, Somme, France – No known grave
Evenwood War Memorial

01/10/1916
30240 Private F. Hirst, 20th Bn., Durham Light Infantry, 123rd Brogade, 41st Division, XV Corps, Fourth Army
Battle of the Somme, Battle of Le Transloy – Died of wounds
Heilly Station Cemetery, Mericourt-L'Abbe, Somme, France
Hamsteels Memorial

01/10/1916
3666 Private J.C. Lee, 6th Bn., Durham Light Infantry, 151st Brigade, 50th Division, III Corps, Fourth Army
Battle of the Somme, Battle of Le Transloy – Killed in action
Warlencourt British Cemetery, nr Bapaume, Somme, France
Cockfield War Memorial

01/10/1916
3914 Private J.A. Wardle, 1st/6th Bn., Durham Light Infantry, 151st Brigade, 50th Division, III Corps, Fourth Army
Battle of the Somme, Battle of Le Transloy – Killed in action
Thiepval Memorial, Somme, France – No known grave

03/10/1916
16202 Private R. Wilson, 6th Bn., Yorkshire Regiment, 32nd Brigade, 11th Division, II Corps, Reserve Army
Battle of the Somme, Battle of Flers-Courcelette – Died of wounds (?)
Evenwood Cemetery
Evenwood War Memorial, St. Paul's Plaque

16/10/1916
14633 Private J. Maughan, 14th Bn., Durham Light Infantry, 18th Brigade, 6th Division, XIV Corps, Fourth Army
Battle of the Somme, Battle of Le Transloy – Died of wounds
Grove Town Cemetery, Meaulte, Somme, France
Evenwood War Memorial, St. Paul's Plaque, WMC Memorial

05/11/1916
3472 Corporal G.T. Cox, 1st/6th Bn., Durham Light Infantry, 151st Brigade, 50th Division, III Corps, Fourth Army
Battle of the Somme, Butte de Warlencourt – Killed in action
Thiepval Memorial, Somme, France – No known grave
Evenwood War Memorial, St. Paul's Plaque

05/11/1916
1672 Private A. Brown, 1st/6th Bn., Durham Light Infantry, 151st Brigade, 50th Division, III Corps, Fourth Army
Battle of the Somme, Butte de Warlencourt – Killed in action
Warlencourt British Cemetery, nr Bapaume, Somme, France
St. Mary's Parish Church, Staindrop War Memorial

24/11/1916
40797 Private J.J. Oates, 18th Bn., West Yorks. Regt., 93rd Brigade, 31st Division, XIII Corps, Fifth Army
Battle of the Somme, Battle of the Ancre – Died of wounds
Etaples Military Cemetery
Normanton War Memorial, West Yorkshire

26/12/1916
36618 Private T. H. Dunn, 11th Bn., Durham Light Infantry, 61st Brigade, 20th (Light) Division, XIV Corps, Fourth Army.
Trench warfare Guillemont area – Died of wounds
St. Sever Cemetery, Rouen, France
Evenwood War Memorial, St. Paul's Plaque, WMC Memorial

1917

01/03/1917
18/65 Private W. Featherstone, 18th Bn., Durham Light Infantry, 93rd Brigade, 31st Division, XIII Corps, Fifth Army
Trench warfare Hebuterne sector – Killed in action
Gommecourt British Cemetery No. 2, Hebuterne, Pas de Calais, France
Etherley War Memorial, Evenwood WMC Memorial

08/03/1917
250188 Private J. Walling, 1st/6th Bn., Durham Light Infantry, 151st Brigade, 50th Division, III Corps, Fourth Army
Trench warfare Berny area – Died of wounds
St. Sever Cemetery, Rouen, France
Evenwood War Memorial, St. Paul's Plaque

17/03/1917
36621 Private J. Million, 18th Bn., Durham Light Infantry, 93rd Brigade, 31st Division, XIII Corps, Fifth Army
Albert area – died of pneumonia
Varennes Military Cemetery, Somme, France
Evenwood War Memorial, St. Paul's Plaque

11/04/ 1917
241784 Lance Corporal J.W. Arkless, 2nd/5th Bn., Lincolnshire Regiment, 177th Brigade, 59th Division, III Corps, Fourth Army
German Retreat to the Hindenburg Line – Killed in action
Thiepval Memorial, Somme, France – No known grave
Evenwood War Memorial, St. Paul's Plaque

14/04/1917
202546 Private J.H. Pinkney, 1st/6th Bn., Durham Light Infantry, 151st Brigade, 50th Division, VII Corps, Third Army
Battle of Arras – Killed in action – No known grave
Arras Memorial, France
Stanley War Memorial, Crook

22/04/1917
31149 Private J. Heseltine, 2nd Bn., York & Lancaster Regiment, 16th Brigade, 6th Division, I Corps, First Army
Loos and Hulloch sector – details unknown
St. Patrick's Cemetery, Loos, Pas de Calais, France
Evenwood War Memorial, St. Paul's Plaque, WMC Memorial

24/04/1917
14526 Private R. Wardle, 14th Bn., Durham Light Infantry, 64th Brigade, 21st Division, VII Corps, Third Army
Battle of Arras – Died of wounds
Bethune Town Cemetery, Pas de Calais, France
Evenwood War Memorial, St. Paul's Plaque

06/05/1917
131500 Pioneer S.R. Rutter, "Z" Special Company, Royal Engineers
Battle of Arras – Killed in action
Beaulencourt British Cemetery, Ligny-Thilloy, Pas de Calais, France
Evenwood War Memorial, St. Paul's Plaque

13/05/1917
39208 Private E. Robinson, 7th Bn., Yorkshire Regt., 50th Brigade, 17th Division, XVII Corps, Third Army
Battle of Arras – Killed in action – No known grave
Arras Memorial, France
Shildon War Memorial

07/06/1917
33027 Private W. Heaviside, 2nd Bn., Durham Light Infantry, 18th Brigade, 6th Division, I Corps, First Army
Trench warfare, Loos sector, raiding party – Killed in action
Philosophe British Cemetery, Mazingarbe, Pas de Calais, France
West Auckland Memorial Hall memorial, Family headstone Evenwood cemetery

10/07/1917
26501 Corporal W.R. Storey, 1st Bn., The Loyal North Lancashire Regiment, 2nd Brigade, 1st Division, III Corps, Fourth Army
Attack on Nieuport – Killed in action
Nieuport Memorial, West Vlaanderen, Belgium – No known grave
Evenwood War Memorial, St. Paul's Plaque

31/07/1917
131539 Sapper H. Wardle M.M., 234th Field Company, Royal Engineers
Third Battle of Ypres (Pilckem) – Killed in action
New Irish Farm Cemetery, Ypres, West Vlaanderen, Belgium
Evenwood War Memorial, St. Paul's Plaque

13/08/1917
202943 Private E.E.J. Cooke, 1st Bn., Border Regt. 87th Brigade, 29th Division, XIV Corps, Fifth Army
Third Battle of Ypres – Killed in action
Artillery Wood Cemetery, Ypres, Belgium

14/08/1917
19677 Lance Corporal J.J. Walton, 6th Bn., Yorkshire Regiment, 32nd Brigade, 11th (Northern) Division, IX Corps, Second Army
Third Battle of Ypres (details unknown) – Killed in action
Tyne Cot Memorial, Zonnebeke, Belgium – No known grave
Evenwood War Memorial, St. Paul's Plaque

13/09/1917
203309 Private W. Dinsdale, 22nd Bn., Durham Light Infantry. Brigade, 8th Division, II Corps, Fifth Army
Third Battle of Ypres – Died of wounds
Tois Arbes Cemetery, Steenwerck, France
St. Anne's Church, Bishop Auckland Roll of Honour

09/10/1917
54506 Rifleman M.T. Raine, 1st/7th Bn., West Yorkshire Regiment, 146th Brigade, 49th Division
Third Battle of Ypres (Poelcappelle) – Killed in action
Tyne Cot Memorial, Zonnebeke, Belgium – No known grave
Evenwood War Memorial

16/10/1917
235587 Corporal G. Parmley, 1st/4th Bn., King's Own Yorkshire Light Infantry, 148th Brigade, 49th Division, 2nd ANZAC, Second Army
Third Battle of Ypres (Poelcappelle) – Died of wounds
Wimereux Communal Cemetery, Pas de Calais, France
Evenwood War Memorial, St. Paul's Plaque

26/10/1917
250165 Sgt. G. Priestley, 1st/6th Bn., Durham Light Infantry, 151st Brigade, 50th Division, VII Corps, Third Army
Third Battle of Ypres (Second Battle of Passchendaele) – Killed in action
Tyne Cot Memorial, Zonnebeke, Belgium – No known grave
Cockfield War Memorial

01/12/1917
4/8777 Serjeant J.W. Spence, 2nd Bn., Durham Light Infantry, 18th Brigade, 6th Division, III Corps, Third Army
Battle of Cambrai – Died of wounds
Ribecourt British Cemetery, Nord, France
Evenwood War Memorial, St. Paul's Plaque

01/12/1917
11182 Private G.W. Bryant, 3rd Field Ambulance, Royal Army Medical Corps, Guards Division, III Corps, Third Army
Battle of Cambrai – Killed in action
Metz-en-Couture Cemetery, British Extn., Pas de Calais, France
Evenwood War Memorial

1918

28/02/1918
57075 Private J. Hewitt, 2nd/6th Bn., West Yorkshire Regiment, 185th Brigade, 62nd (2nd West Riding) Division, IV Corps, Third Army
Flanders – Killed in action (details unknown)
Menin Road South Military Cemetery, Ypres, Belgium
Evenwood War Memorial, St. Paul's Plaque

21/03/1918
27088 Lance Corporal G. Dowson 7th/8th Bn., Royal Inniskilling Fusiliers, 49th Brigade, 16th (Irish) Division, VII Corps, Fifth Army
German Spring Offensive – Battle of St. Quentin – Killed in action
Tyne Cot Cemetery, Zonnebeke, Belgium
Evenwood War Memorial, St. Paul's Plaque

23/03/1918
53318 Private J. Hutchinson, 9th Bn., Manchester Regiment 198th Brigade, 66th Division, XIX Corps, Fifth Army
German Spring Offensive – Battle of St. Quentin – Killed in action
Unicorn Cemetery, Vend'huile, Aisne, France
Evenwood War Memorial, St. Paul's Plaque

27/03/1918
250523 Serjeant T.W. Simpson M.M. 1st/6th Bn., Durham Light Infantry, 151st Brigade, 50th (Northumbrian) Division, XIX Corps, Fifth Army
German Spring Offensive – Battle of Rosieres – Killed in action
Pozieres Memorial, Somme, France – No known grave
Evenwood War Memorial, St. Paul's Plaque

28/03/1918
122510 Private J. Skelhorn, 8th Bn., Machine Gun Corps, XIX Corps, Fifth Army
German Spring Offensive – Battle of Rosieres
Heath Cemetery, Harbonnieres, France
Evenwood War Memorial, St. Paul's Plaque

28/03/1918
73017 Private J.H. Ellerker, 15th Bn., Durham Light Infantry, 64th Brigade, 21st Division, VII Corps, Fifth Army
German Spring Offensive – Killed in action
Ribemont Communal Cemetery Extn., Somme, France
Evenwood War Memorial, St. Paul's Plaque

08/04/1918
Second Lieutenant T.W. Applegarth, 11th Bn., Durham Light Infantry, 61st Brigade, 20th (Light) Division, XVIII Corps, Fifth Army
German Spring Offensive – Died of wounds as POW
Caix British Cemetery, Somme, France
Evenwood War Memorial, St. Paul's Plaque

15/05/1918
243094 Private W. Morley, 4th Bn., Yorkshire Regiment, 150th Brigade, 50th (Northumbrian) Division, VI Corps, First Army?
German Spring Offensive
ANZAC Cemetery, Sailly-sur-la-Lys, Pas-de-Calais, France
Evenwood War Memorial

27/05/1918
36723 Private D. Baister 1st/5th Bn., Durham Light Infantry, 150th Brigade, 50th (Northumbrian) Division, VI Corps, First Army or 9th British Corps?
German Spring Offensive – Battle of the Aisne – Killed in action
Soissons Memorial, Aisne, France – No known grave
Evenwood War Memorial, St. Paul's Plaque, WMC Memorial

30/05/1918
250440 Private O. Rushford M.M., 1st/6th Bn., Durham Light Infantry, 151st Brigade, 50th (Northumbrian) Division, XIX Corps, Fifth Army
German Spring Offensive, following the Third Battle of the Aisne – Killed in action
Soissons Memorial, Aisne, France – No known grave
Evenwood War Memorial

01/06/1918
3128A Private J.J. Marquis, 28th Bn., Australian Infantry, 7th Brigade, 2nd Division, A.I.F.
German Spring Offensive
Franvillers Coimmunal Cemetery Extn., Somme, France
Hamsterley War Memorial

08.06/1918
220168 Private W.A. Moses, 7th Bn., East Yorkshire Regiment 50th Brigade, 17th (Northern) Division, V Corps, Third Army (formerly 204893 Yorks. Regt.)
German Spring Offensive, the First Battle of Bapaume– Killed in action
Hawthorn Ridge Cemetery No.1, Auchonvillers, France
Evenwood War Memorial

03/07/1918
178943 Gunner W. Gray, 52nd Battery, Royal Field Artillery, 15th Brigade, 5th Division, IV Corps, Third Army (formerly RAVC)
German Spring Offensive, Action at La Becque – Died of wounds
Terlincthun British Cemetery, Wimille, Pas de Calais, France
Evenwood War Memorial, St. Paul's Plaque, WMC Memorial

07/07/1918
20786 Serjeant J.J. Richardson D.C.M., 6th Bn., Machine Gun Corps, XXII Corps, Second Army (formerly 14018 E. Yorks. Regt.)
German Spring Offensive, sometime after the Battle of Scherpenburg – Died of wounds
Nine Elms British Cemetery, Poperinge, Belgium
Evenwood War Memorial

15/08/1918
44008 Corporal C.H. Lowson, 7th Bn., Lincolnshire Regiment, 51st Brigade, 17th (Northern) Division, V Corps, Third Army (formerly 14557 East Yorks. Regt.)
German Spring Offensive, Battle of Amiens – Died of wounds
Daours Communal Cemetery, Somme, France
St. Helen Auckland Memorial Cottages Memorial, West Auckland Memorial Hall plaque

29/08/1918
250400 Private W. Snowball, 6th Bn., Durham Light Infantry, 151st Brigade, 50th (Northumbrian) Division, XIX Corps, Fifth Army
Evenwood Cemetery
Evenwood War Memorial, St. Paul's Plaque

03/09/1918
339885 Private A. Burrell, Labour Corps
Cockfield Cemetery
Cockfield War Memorial

04/09/1918
593 Private F.W. Marquis, 28th Bn., Australian Infantry, 7th Brigade, 2nd Division, A.I.F.
Allied Offensive, Second Battle of Bapaume
Heath Cemetery, Harbonniers, Somme, France
Hamsterley War Memorial

06/09/1918
51585 Private R. Heaviside, 22nd (Tyneside Scottish) Bn., Northumberland Fusiliers, 102nd Brigade, 34th Division, XIX Corps, Second Army (?)
Advance into Flanders – Died of wounds
Pernes British Cemetery, Pas de Calais, France
Evenwood War Memorial, St. Paul's Plaque, Family headstone

18/09/1918
39146 Private J.W. Howlett, 12th/13th Bn., Northumberland Fusiliers, 62nd Brigade, 21st Division, V Corps, Third Army
Allied Advance – Battle of Epehy – Killed in action
Gouzeaucourt New British Cemetery, Somme, France
Evenwood War Memorial, St. Paul's Plaque,

22/10/1918
60571 Private M. Simpson, 9th Bn., Yorkshire Regiment, 74th Brigade, 25th Division, XIII Corps, Fourth Army
Allied Advance – Battle of Selle – Died of wounds
Maurois Communal Cemetery, Nord, France
Evenwood War Memorial

27/10/1918
252054 Private M.G. Middlemass, 12th Bn., Durham Light Infantry, 68th Brigade, 23rd Division
Italian campaign, Battle of Vittorio Veneto – Killed in action
Tezze British Cemetery, Treviso, Italy
Evenwood War Memorial, St. Paul's Plaque, WMC Memorial

04/11/1918
78830 Private T. Davis, 1st/4th Bn., Northumberland Fusiliers, 147th Brigade, 50th (Northumbrian) Division, XIII Corps, Fourth Army
Allied Advance, Battle of Sambre – Killed in action
Fontaine au Bois Communal Cemetery, Nord, France
Evenwood War Memorial, St. Paul's Plaque

03/12/1918
131400 Sapper A. K. Atkinson M.M., 206th Field Company, Royal Engineers
Killed when salvaged German ammunition exploded
Soumoy Communal Cemetery, Namur, Belgium
Evenwood War Memorial, St. Paul's Plaque

09/12/1918
340630 Private F. Purvis, 1st/5th Bn., Northumberland Fusiliers, 149th Brigade, 50th Division, XIII Corps, Fourth Army
POW Niederzwehren, Kassel, Hessen, Germany
Evenwood War Memorial, St. Paul's Plaque, Family Headstone

1919

29/01/1919 Private J.W. Maughan
26952 Durham Light Infantry 12th Battalion, 68th Brigade, 23rd Division
Died of pneumonia
Evenwood Cemetery
Evenwood War Memorial, St. Paul's Plaque

APPENDIX 2

THE TOLL – BY REGIMENT

DURHAM LIGHT INFANTRY
1. Cant T. 2nd
2. Million W. 2nd
3. Heaviside W. 2nd
4. Spence J. W. 2nd
5. Baister D. 1/5th
6. Brown A. 1/6th
7. Cox G. T. 1/6th
8. Lee J.C. 6th
9. Pinkney J.H. 1/6th
10. Priestley G. 1/6th
11. Rushford O. 1/6th
12. Simpson T. W. 1/6th
13. Snowball W. 6th
14. Walling J. 1/6th
15. Wardle J.A. 6th
16. Graves J. C. 10th
17. Dunn T. H. 11th
18. Applegarth T. W. 11th
19. Maughan J.W. 12th
20. Middlemas M. G. 12th

21. Raine J. H. 13th
22. Wardle R. 14th
23. Maughan J. 14th
24. Earl W. E. 14th
25. Metcalfe R.T. 15th
26. Towers E. 15th
27. Ellerker J.H. 15th
28. Featherstone W. 18th
29. Million J. 18th
30. Hirst F. 20th
31. Dinsdale W. 22nd

THE NORTHUMBERLAND FUSILIERS
32. Davis T. 1/4th
33. Purvis F. 1/5th
34. Howlett J.W. 12th/13th.
35. Cree C 21st (Tyneside Scottish)
36. Heaviside R. 22nd (Tyneside Scottish)

THE YORKSHIRE REGIMENT (THE GREEN HOWARDS)
37. Morley W. 4th
38. Walton J. J. 6th
39. Wilson R. 6th
40. Robinson E. 7th
41. Simpson M. 9th

WEST YORKSHIRE REGIMENT
42. Hewitt J. 2/6th
43. Oates J.J. 18th
44. Raine M. T. 1/7th

LINCOLNSHIRE REGIMENT
45. Arkless J. W. 2/5th
46. Lowson C. H. 7th

ROYAL ENGINEERS
47. Atkinson A. K. – 206th Field Co.
48. Milburn J.T. – 177th Tunnelling Company
49. Rutter S. R. – "Z" Special Coy.
50. Wardle H. – 234th Field Coy.

MACHINE GUN CORPS
51. Richardson J. J. – 6th
52. Skelhorn J. – 8th

BORDER REGIMENT
53. Cooke E.J. 4th
54. Dixon H. 5th

YORK & LANCASTER REGIMENT
55. Conlon R.W. 2nd
56. Heseltine J. 2nd

EAST YORKSHIRE REGIMENT
57. Marshall J. 8th
58. Moses W.A. 7th

AUSTRALIAN IMPERIAL FORCE
59. Marquis J.J. 28th
60. Marquis F.W. 28th

MISCELLANEOUS REGIMENTS
61. Bryant G.W. Royal Army Medical Corps
62. Burrell A. Labour Corps
63. Dowson G. 7/8th Royal Inniskilling Fusiliers
64. Gray W. Royal Field Artillery 52nd Battery 15th Brigade
65. Hutchinson J. 9th Manchester Regiment
66. Oates A. 31st Batt. Canadian Expeditionary Force, Canadian Infantry
67. Parmley G. 1/4th King's Own Yorkshire Light Infantry
68. Richards J. Royal Garrison Artillery (Pembroke Dock)
69. Storey W.R. 1st The Loyal North Lancashire Regiment
70. Smith W. 9th Bn., Lancashire Fusiliers

ROYAL NAVY
71. Carrick W. RN HMS Ardent
72. Lynas A. RN HMS Ardent
73. Wren J. W. RN HMS Black Prince

APPENDIX THREE

HOME ADDRESSES

The addresses below are the places where those killed lived at the time of their death (to the best of my knowledge).

Ramshaw
Sapper A.K. Atkinson – Ramshaw
L/C J.W. Arkless – Bowes Hill
Sgt. J.W. Spence – Bowes Close Farm
L/Cpl. W. Storey – Gordon Lane
Sgt. G. Parmley – Gordon Lane (when he enlisted he lived at Bill Quay near Felling)
Richardson J. J. – 3 Gordon Gill, Ramshaw

Evenwood
Pte. W. Howlett – Oaks House
Pte. W. Snowball – 4 the Oaks
Pte. J. Walling – the Oaks
Pte. J. Ellerker – the Oaks
Cpl. G.T. Cox – the Oaks
Pte. J. Heseltine – the Oaks
2/Lt. T. W. Applegarth – 2 Delaware Street
Pte. T. Davis – 5 Rochdale Street

Sgt. E. Towers – 19 Rochdale Street
Gunner F. Purvis – 22 Rochdale Street
Pte. J.H. Raine – Osborne Terrace
L/Cpl. J.W. Walton – Swan Street
Pte. M. G. Middlemas – 10 Stones End
Sgt. T.W. Simpson – Stones End
Cpl. H. Dixon – 13 Shirley Terrace
Pnr. S.R. Rutter – Allendale House, 15 Shirley Terrace
AB A. Lynas – 18 Chapel Street
Pte. R. Wilson – Chapel Street
AB W. Carrick – 13 South View
Pte. J. Million – South View
Pte. J. W. Maughan – South View
Pte. J. Hewitt – Victoria Terrace
Pte. G. Dowson – 22 West View
Pte. T.H. Dunn – 4 Randolph Terrace
AB J.W. Wren – Copeland Row
Pte. D. Baister – 13 Copeland Row
Pte. R. Heaviside – Thrushwood
J.C. Lee – his wife lived at 13 Jubilee Terrace
C.H. Lowson – his mother lived at 2 Jubilee Terrace

Evenwood Addresses unknown
- Pte J. Skelhorn

Evenwood Gate
Pte. J. Maughan – 9 Clyde Terrace, Evenwood Gate
Pte. R. Wardle – 8 Clyde Terrace, Evenwood Gate
Gunner W. Gray – 20 Evenwood Gate
Pte J. Hutchinson – Evenwood Gate

The Barony
Earl W.E. – his parents lived at Buckhead Farm

Lands area
Conlon R.W. – 44 Lands Bank
Graves J. C. – Low Butterknowle Farm, Low Lands
Morley W. – 44 Lands Bank
Simpson M. – 53 Lands Bank

Wardle H. – 61 Lands Bank
Raine M. T. – 5 Brasses Houses, High Lands

Morley area
Moses W.
Rushford O.
Bryant G.
J. Richards
W. Featherstone – Cox House Farm, Wind Mill

Not traced
- Cooke E.E.J.

Elsewhere
A. Brown – Ivy House, Staindrop
A. Burrell – Peth Row Farm, Cockfield
J.T. Cant – 21 Front Street, Kirk Merrington
C. Cree – Esperley Lane, Cockfield
W. Dinsdale – 10 Boddy Street, Tindale Crescent, Bishop Auckland
W. Heaviside – 2 Mill Bank, West Auckland
F. Hirst – 3 Church Street, Quebec
J. Marshall – 45 Castle Street, Fatfield
T.R. Metcalfe – 4 Jackson's Row, Witton Park
J.T. Milburn – 6 Robson Street, Shildon
W. Million – 1 Thorne Terrace, Walker Estate, Newcastle upon Tyne
J.J. Oates – 48 Castleford Road, Normanton, West Yorkshire
J.H. Pinkney – 8 Chapel Row, Stanley, Crook
G. Priestley – Fell Houses, Cockfield
E. Robinson – Club House, Main Street, Shildon
W. Smith – Forest Hall
J. A. Wardle – Aycliffe

Overseas
- J.J. Marquis & F.W. Marquis – Hoppland Park, Katanning East, Western Australia
- A. Oates – Calgary, Alberta. Canada

The numbers of casualties are horrific, every number is a person who once had a mother and father, brothers and sisters or a wife, sons and daughter. One particular area of Evenwood which is an easily identifiable "sub-area" is the Oaks. The following passage puts together some known details of this area and provides an insight into the way the war affected the lives of the 1901 Oaks community.

The 1901 census has been used which is quite appropriate since many of those within the census aged 20 and younger would, during the course of the war, be of a suitable age for military service, either as a volunteer or conscript. There were actually 89 boys aged between 1 and 20.

The Oaks consisted of 2 larger terraced streets – Front Row and Back Row running east to west along the contour of the hillside and 2 smaller streets running at down bank, north to south at right angles, called Cross Row. A smaller terrace, called Stable Row led off to Oaks Farm and Oaks House to the west. In all there were 63 houses. The larger terraces were built in the 1840's and Cross Row was built in the early 1850's, all to house miners working at Evenwood and Norwood Collieries. Houses were also built along Oaks Bank leading from Evenwood down to the bridge over the river Gaunless and Ramshaw beyond. Ramshaw School was built on Oaks Bank and opened in 1910.

The Oaks, Evenwood

At the time of the 1901 census, there were 63 households living at the Oaks. Virtually all the men and boys worked as coal miners or cokemen, 101 in total. There were 8 exceptions – Patrick Sheedy, the doctor, George Etherington and John Walton retired coal miners, John Watson a Council roadman, Joseph Teasdale a mason, Thomas William Anderson a general errand boy, Thomas Anderson a farm labourer and Charles Welford a tailor. In their adulthood, many of the children of the Oaks would serve their country and the following passage is a brief examination of those living there in 1901.

The imposing Oaks House, probably originally built for the colliery manager appears to have been sub-divided into 3 dwellings. It was occupied in part by the Irishman Dr. Patrick Sheedy, his wife Isabel and their housemaid Isabella Taylor. By 1914, it appears that Dr. Sheedy had left the area and the 2 doctors were Dr. Milne and Dr. Campbell.

The Cree family lived in the remainder of the house – John and Elizabeth and their 2 sons, 19 year old Adam and 11 year old Towers lived in one dwelling and their older son, 23 year old Christopher Cree, his wife Elizabeth and their infant daughter Patricia lived in the other. All 3 brothers served in the Great War. Adam served in the 4/DLI and was wounded on 2 occasions and returned home safe. It was erroneously reported in January 1918, that Towers Cree and John Luther Simpson had "fallen in action". Towers survived the war as did John Luther. By 1914, their older brother Christopher Cree and his family had moved to Esperley Lane near Cockfield. He worked at Gordon House Colliery, Cockfield. Christopher enlisted with the 21/Northumberland Fusiliers, 2/Tyneside Scottish and within 3 weeks of landing in France died of wounds in February 1916. He was the first fatality for the 2/Tyneside Scottish.

Near neighbours were Thomas and Elizabeth Adams and their 8 and 6 year old sons Alfred and Arthur, both served in the Army and both returned home safe. Alfred served with the West Yorks and suffered wounds to the leg in June 1916. Arthur served with the Royal Engineers.

Sarah Taylor was a 39 year old widow taking care of her 4 children including 6 year old John. He served in the 14/DLI and came home. Mathew and Margaret Hutchinson weren't so fortunate. Their sons Joseph, William and John were called up. Joseph served with Manchester Regt. and was killed in action in March 1918. John was with the 1/DLI and William the 11/DLI and he was awarded the Military Medal.

William and Margaret Gibson's 3 year old son Thomas served with the 1/6 North Staffs. He was demobilized by October 1919 and welcomed back into civilian life. John Friend son of Jacob and Elizabeth served with the

Dragoons and the 1/1 Berkshire Yeomanry. He was wounded in August 1918 and "demobed" by July 1919.

Francis and Margaret lost their son John Henry Raine in May 1916, killed in action in France but their youngest son Siddle, a gunner in the Royal Field Artillery survived. 18 year old Thomas Cant was the son of John and Hannah, and in 1902 he joined the DLI Territorials. By 1914, he was married, had a family and lived at Kirk Merrington. At the outbreak of war he was one of the first to re-enlisted and served with the 2/DLI. He was killed in action in June 1915 at Ypres.

Their neighbours were George and Hannah Towers and their son Thomas served as a gunner in the Royal Garrison Artillery. He returned home.

Edward and Elizabeth Gaffney's youngest son, Ambrose then 5 years old served in the Yorkshire Regiment and returned home.

David Wharton was with the 2/Hussars and survived.

Cecil Jobling was in the Royal Engineers and was "demobed" by May 1919.

William and Sarah Walling's son John was then 11 year old. He served with the 1/6DLI and died of wounds in March 1917.

The 2 sons of John and Annie Cox both served with the DLI – George "Doad" Cox was killed in action at the Butte de Warlencourt in November 1916 and is commemorated on the Thiepval Memorial to the Missing of the Somme. John Wanless Cox, DLI Labour Battalion returned home.

Ernest Hope, son of Christopher and Elizabeth Hope served in the Royal Navy and survived.

As expected, many of the young men worked in the local pits and drifts and were not conscripted but by 1918, the shortage of men was such that coal miners were now required. Locally drafts were organised and those picked out of the hat were enlisted – Robert and Jane Welford's 2 sons William and Henry were both drawn out in the Randolph draw of May 1918. It is not known whether or not they saw active service.

Their neighbours were John and M.J. Walton whose 8 year old grandson John Joseph lived with them. In August 1917, whilst serving with the 6/Yorkshire Regiment he was killed in action at Passchendaele. He has no known grave and is commemorated on the Tyne Cot Memorial.

The 6 year old son of George and Mary Kirkup, Thomas enlisted into the Royal Inniskilling Fusiliers and after being seriously wounded was discharged in the summer of 1918.

Thomas and Margaret Wren's 2 sons 5 year old Thomas Arthur Wilson and Edward Wren served in the East Yorks. Regt. and 4/DLI respectively and both returned home.

George and Mary Metcalfe's 4 year old son James served in the ASC Remounts and survived.

John Hope Anderson was then 6 year old and enlisted into the 17/DLI and returned home safe.

Near neighbours Robert and Sarah Towers 7 year old son Edgar joined the 15/DLI and lost his life at the Battle of Loos in September 1915. He has no known grave and is commemorated on the Loos Memorial.

John and Annie Etherington's son Joseph William Teasdale then 5 year old served with the ASC Remounts as a driver and survived.

John and Mary Priestley's 3 year old son Joseph William served in the Highland Light Infantry and returned.

John Luther Simpson then the 8 year old son of Mary Welford served with the Machine Gun Corps and survived although in January 1918, the Parish Magazine erroneously reported that John Luther Simpson and Towers Cree had "fallen in action". His brother Thomas W. Simpson M.M. 6/DLI was killed in action in 1918.

The 1901 community of the Oaks saw many of its sons serve their country and 7 paid the ultimate price. This can only be a "snapshot" based on evidence provided by the Parish Magazine and 1901 census. It cannot tell the whole picture since the complete list of those who enlisted or wounded is unknown. In total, 6 "children" of the Oaks were killed Joseph Hutchinson, John Walling, George T. Cox, Edgar Towers, John J. Walton and John H. Raine. This excludes Christopher Cree who was much older and had moved to Esperley Lane.

By the time war started, there were another 4 "new" residents of the Oaks who lost their lives – Wilf Howlett, Walter Snowball, John Ellerker and James Heseltine.

APPENDIX FOUR

EVENWOOD PARISH MAGAZINE: THE ROLL

1915: the February edition of the Evenwood Parish Magazine reported that 50 men from the locality had joined the colours.

From Evenwood
1. Adams A J
2. Braddick Thos
3. Brass Percival
4. Cox H.
5. Cree Adam
6. Dent W
7. Featherstone George
8. Gaffney A
9. Gaffney W
10. Heaviside George
11. Hewitt John T
12. Mason M
13. Metcalfe A.
14. Neasham F
15. Patton George
16. Raine John H
17. Rutter Thos. H.

18. Shaw Thos
19. Simpson Robert
20. Smith J
21. Towers Edgar
22. Waling John
23. Walton Jas. H.
24. Walton J.W.
25. Wilkinson W

Evenwood Gate
26. Carling J.
27. Cook
28. Maughan J.
29. Maughan W.
30. Smith G.
31. Walton J. W.
32. Wardle Ralph jun.
33. Young W.

The Mill
34. Baird John
35. Maires George

Ramshaw
36. Carrick Edmund
37. Jobling
38. Kay Chris
39. Layton

Evenwood National School
40. Layton P. M.
41. Rowe H

Ramshaw School
42. Welldon R

Randolph men from West Auckland
43. Britton N L.
44. Hope T
45. Redfern B

46. Vickers D
47. Walker Ernest

Randolph man from Toft Hill
48. Wilson R. W.

Morley
49. E. Rushford and
50. his brother (Oliver Rushford?)

1915 April:
William Gray of Evenwood Gate, the Hon. Secretary of the Soldiers' and Sailors' Fund provided Rev. G. J. Collis, vicar of St. Paul's Church, Evenwood with a complete classified list of those who had enlisted in His Majesty's Forces – 87 men had joined up, followed in the subsequent months up to January 1916, by a further 22 men.

MARRIED MEN
1. **Atkinson William, Evenwood Gate – 14thDLI
2. Baird John, the Mill – Remounts – now serving in France
3. Bell Harry, Glamis Tce, Coldstream Guards
4. Carling John Wm., Oaks – 13th batt DLI
5. Cree Adam, Stones End, – 4th batt DLI
6. Dobson William, Oaks – Remounts
7. Featherstone George, Centre – DLI
8. *Heaviside George, Swan St – 6th DLI
9. Heseltine James, Oaks – 2nd Reserve Batt 6th DLI
10. Hewitt John George, the Centre – 4th batt DLI
11. *Howe George, West Tce – 4th Batt DLI
12. Jackson John, Brookside – Coldstream Guards
13. Kay C., Gordon Lane – Yorks Regt.
14. Maughan William, Evenwood Gate – 4th Batt DLI
15. Patton George, Swan Street – 4th batt DLI
16. Raine John Henry, the Centre – 13th DLI
17. Rutter Thomas H., Victoria St – 14th Batt DLI
18. Shaw Thomas – the Centre – 6th DLI

* now permanently discharged as physically unfit
** temp. discharged owing to sickness

19. Shipp Arthur Wm. – Evenwood Gate – RAMC
20. Taylor James E. Oaks – Remounts
21. Walling John, Oaks – 6th DLI
22. Walton James H., Rochdale St, – 14th DLI
23. Walton John Wm, Oaks – 13th batt DLI
24. Wardle Elias, Centre – RFA Wearside Batt
25. Wilson George, Oaks – 17th DLI

UNMARRIED MEN
1. Adams Alfred, Oaks – Yorkshire Regt
2. Adams Peter, Oaks – NER Batt Pioneers
3. Anderson John Hope, Oaks – 17th DLI
4. Ballantyne James, Farncombe Tce., Northumberland Fusiliers
5. Birnie William, Oaks Bank – no information yet
6. Braddick Thomas, Shirley Tce, – DLI
7. Brass Percy, Victoria House, DLI
8. Brown Arthur, Gordon Bank – 10TH Batt Yorkshire Regt.
9. Carrick Edmund, Delaware Ave – 4th DLI
10. Cook George S., Oaks – Cumberland Borderers
11. Cox Geo. Thomas, Oaks, 2ND Reserve Batt. DLI
12. Cox Harry, South View, – DLI
13. Cutts Percy, Princess of Wales Own
14. Daniel Arthur L. Shirley Tce – Wearside Batt RFA
15. Dent W. Evenwood Gate – RAMC
16. Dixon Robert, the Mill – 13th DLI
17. Dunn Arthur J., South View – Royal Navy – ships carpenter
18. Firby John, Lands Bank – ASC Remounts
19. Gaffney Ambrose, Oaks – Yorkshire Regt
20. Gaffney C. W. Oaks – Yorkshire Regt.
21. Green George, Evenwood Railway Station – NER Batt.
22. Haddock Eric M., Ramshaw House – Officers Training Corps
23. Hodgson John E., Lands Bank – 3rd East Yorks regt
24. Hollis Milburn, Swan St – Wearside Batt RFA
25. Howlett Wilfred, Oaks House – ASC Remounts
26. Hutchinson Arthur G. Oaks, – 17th DLI
27. Layton Alfred, Gordon Gill – 2nd Reserve Batt 6th DLI

28. Layton Percy M., Evenwood National School – 9th Gloucester Regt
29. Maires George, the Mill – 4th batt DLI
30. Mason Mathew, Chapel St – 14th DLI
31. Maughan George, Evenwood Gate – 3rdDragoon Guards
32. Maughan John, Evenwood Gate – 14thDLI
33. Maughan Lawrence, Farncombe Tce – 12th Batt DLI
34. **Metcalfe Alfred, Randolph Tce – 12th DLI
35. Metcalfe James R., Oaks – ASC Remounts
36. Metcalfe John George, the Mill – 17th DLI
37. Miller George W., Royal Scottish Fusiliers
38. Neasham Fred, Swan St – 2nd Dragoon Guards
39. Priestley Robert, Chapel St. – Royal Engineers
40. Proud A., Rochdale St., – Wearside Batt RFA
41. Richmond Fred., Railwayside – NER Batt
42. Rowe H. Evenwood National School, DLI
43. Simpson Robert, Randolph Tce – 2nd Devonshire Regt.
44. Shipp Daniel, Evenwood Gate – RAMC
45. Smith George, Evenwood Gate – 17th DLI
46. Smith Ralph, Gordon Lane – no information yet
47. Smith William, Oaks – 13th DLI
48. Snowball Walter, Oaks – 2nd Reserve Batt DLI
49. Snowdon John, Buckheads – OTC
50. Spence J.W. Bowes Close – 4th Batt DLI
51. Taylor J.J. Raby St – 14thDLI
52. Teasdale Jos. W, Oaks – ASC Remounts
53. Towers Edgar, Rochdale St – DLI
54. Walker Holmes, Alexandra Tce., Wearside Batt RFA
55. Walton John Jos, Swan St – Yorkshire Regt.
56. Wardle Ralph, Evenwood Gate – 14th Batt DLI
57. Welldon R., Ramshaw Council School – DLI
58. Wilkinson Wilfred, Rochdale St – Yorkshire Regt
59. Wilson Francis A. Rochdale St – RAMC
60. Wright Jonathan Oaks – 2nd Reserve Batt 6th DLI
61. Wright Wilfred, Oaks – ASC Remounts

** temp. discharged owing to sickness

62.   Young William, Evenwood Gate – RAMC – now serving in France.

May 1915 edition
1.   Bowman, Thomas, Brookside – Royal Engineers
2.   Britton Fred, Farncombe Tce – 6th Batt DLI
3.   Hird Fred, West View – ASC Remounts

July 1915
1.   Dr. Campbell

August 1915
1.   Barron James, Lands Bank – 6TH DLI
2.   Middlemass Robert
3.   Storey William R. Gordon Lane – 6th DLI
4.   Wilson Josiah, Oaks – 6th DLI
5.   Wren John, Copeland Row – Royal Navy

September 1915
1.   Lowson J. – Drivers in the Army
2.   Nutter J. H., National School – RAMC
3.   Oates P., – Drivers in the Army

October 1915
1.   Carrick W., South View – Royal Navy
2.   Clarke C.T. – RAMC
3.   Lynas G., Chapel St., – Royal Navy
4.   Purdy W. West View – Royal Navy

December 1915
1.   Blenkinsop Joseph – Black Watch
2.   Elders Albert – Army
3.   Gibson Thomas A. – Copeland Row – Royal Navy
4.   Morland Adolphus – Air Service

January 1916
1.   Gray W., Evenwood Gate – RAVC
2.   Metcalfe J. G. the Mill – 6th DLI

APPENDIX FIVE

1918: ABSENT VOTERS LIST: EVENWOOD POLLING DISTRICT L. PARISH OF EVENWOOD AND BARONY

Ref	NAME	ADDRESS	SERVICE etc.
2814	ADAMS Alfred James	12 Oaks	107868 Cpl. 51st W. Yorks. Regt.
2815	ADAMS Arthur	12 Oaks	112, Railway Co.
2816	ALDERSON John Stanley	Rochdale St.	4503 Pte. 1st West Yorks
2817	ALLISON Isaac	2 Provident Tce.	216758 Gnr. R.G.A.
2818	APPLEGARTH William	2 Delaware Tce	2nd Lieut. "A" Co. D.L.I.
2819	ATKINSON Albert	1 Alpine	283622 Gnr. R.F.A.
2820	BAIRD John	1 the Mill	87655 Pte. Middx. Regt.
2821	BAISTER David	13 Copeland	784075 Pte. 5th D.L.I.
2822	BARNES William	Swan St.	121118 Spr. Base Signal Depot, N.E.E.
2823	BARRON Edward	7 Oaks Bank	18700 Pte. 6th Yorks. Regt.
2824	BELL Harry	Swan St.	15688 Coldstream Guards
2825	BELL Robert	12 Alpine	283630 Gnr. No.1 Depot R.F.A.

2826	BENNETT Frederick Henry		14 Alpine 34928 Pte. 4th Res. Batt. R.E.
2827	BLENKINSOP George	26 Oaks	313786 Pte. 774th Area Employment Co.
2828	BOLTON John	3 Accrington Tce.	217175 Gnr. R.G.A.
2829	BOWERS George	16 Glamis Tce.	217157 Gnr. R.G.A.
2830	BOWMAN Walter	10 Brookside	35650 A.O.Co.
2831	BRADDICK William	7 Shirley Tce.	20695 D.L.I.
2832	BRADWELL Henderson Cecil	Raby Street	216754 Gnr. R.G.A
.2833	BROWNBRIDGE Joseph Henry	1 Jubilee Tce.	Gunner 3rd S.A.R.B., R.G.A.
2834	BRASS Percy	Victoria Street	Lieut. R.F.C.
2835	BUSSEY John	14 Jubilee Terrace	217160 Gnr. R.G.A.
2836	BRITTON Frederick Maxwell	Farncombe Tce.	250249 Sgt. 6th D.L.I.
2837	BROWN Joseph Edwin	Osborne Terrace	1053 D.L.I.
2838	BUSSEY Fred D.L.I.	12 Copeland	73943 Pte 4th Batt.
2839	CAMPBELL Angus	33 Swan St.	171st Tunl. Co. R.E.
2840	CARRICK Edmund	8 Delaware	151485 Spr. R.E.
2841	CLARKE Charles Thomas	44 Swan St.	68254 Pte. 107th Field Amb. R.A.M.C.
2842	CLAY John Heseltine	5 Farncombe Tce.	214168 Gnr. S.A.R.B., R.G.A.
2843	CLENNELL George Edward	7 West View	447794 Pte. 204th Employ. Co.
2844	COOK George Sykes	Evenwood Gate	14075 Pte. 9th Border Regt.
2845	COOKE George	6 Oaks Bank	217174 Gnr. R.G.A.
2846	COOKE George William	14 Raby Street	123731 Pte. R.F.A.
2847	CREASOR Ernest	70 Oaks	187401 Pte. 345th H.S Works

2848	CREE Dam	19 Stones End	9566 Pte. D.L.I.
2849	CRISP Robert	Park House Farm	30103 Pte. Lab. Centre Co.
2850	DALIEL Arthur Llewellyan	10 Shirley Terrace	249598 Spr. 34th Divnl. Sig.
2851	DAVIS James	5 Rochdale Terrace	82711 Pte. 2nd Res. Cav.
2852	DICKINSON Arthur	6 South View	271711 Gnr. Royal Regt. Art.
2853	DOBSON William	Oaks	35808 Pte. 1/4thBatt. Duke Cornwall's L.I.
2854	DOWSON George	22 West View	Royal Inniskilling Fus.
2855	DOWSON Norman	11 Jubilee Terrace	1/5th 58952 West Yorks.
2856	DOWSON Thomas	11 Jubilee Terrace	204341 Pte. R.F.A.
2857	DUNN Arthur James	1 South View	M12237 Carp. Crew, Birkenhead
2858	DUNN Frederick	4 Randolph Terrace	R.F.A.
2859	DUNN Nelson	4 Randolph Terrace	40500 L-Cpl. 1st Worcester
2860	ETHERINGTON Thomas	Rochdale Terrace	L/10869 Pte. 21st Lancers.
2861	EMMERSON Wade	Brookside	2/156273 Pte. 977th CO. M.T.A.S.C.
2862	FOSTER Herbert	29 Swan Street	366189 Nth Scottish R.G.A.
2863	FRIEND John Richard	Oaks	X162837 Pte. 1/1st Berkshire Yeomanry
2864	GAFFANY Charles Wilfred		15 Stonesend 421350 Pte. 193rd Lab. Co
2865	GARTHWAITE Herbert	4 West Terrace	142952 Driv. Group 2. R.F.A.
2866	GIBSON Thomas Alfred		Copeland 241938 Pte. 1/6th N. Staffs.
2867	GRAY William	20 Evenwood Gate	178943 Gnr. 52nd Batt. R.F.A.
2868	HALL Charles	26 Oaks	18618 Bdr. 1104th Batty. R.F.A.

2869	HANDLEY John George	The Poplars	11754 R.G.A.
2870	HEWITSON Wilfred	11 South View	535868 Pte. 487th Agric. Co. Labour Corps.
2871	HOBSON Charles Harold	Swan Street	2nd Lieut. Loyal North Lancs. Regt. Inf.
2872	HODGSON Jacob	Alexandra Terrace	18751 6th Batt Queen's Royal West Surrey
2873	HODGSON John George	14 Alexandra Terrace	216768 Gnr. R.G.A.
2874	HOLLIS William Hunter	45 Swan Street	11490 Driv. 48th Div. R.F.A.
2875	HORDON George Septimus	8 Copeland	Pte 4th D.L.I.
2876	HORDON John William	8 Copeland	54401 West Yorks.
2877	HORSMAN Henry	12 Chapel Street	41248 Pte. 2nd R.S. Fus.
2878	HOWE Arol	11 Accrington Terrace	186864 Signaller R.F.A.
2879	HULL John George	Evenwood Gate	"D" Co. 1st Batt. Royal Fus.
2880	HUTCHINSON Ernest William	32 Evenwood Gate	205120
2881	HUTCHINSON John	Evenwood Gate	32453 1st Durhams
2882	HUTCHINSON Joseph	Evenwood Gate	53318 Manchester Regt.
2883	KIRKUP Thomas	Chapel Street	27089 Royal Inniskilling Fus.
2884	LACKEY John Jackson	9 Jubilee Terrace	39193 Cpl. 11th D.L.I.
2885	LAVERICK Charles Ernest	21 Farncombe Terrace	216763 Gnr. R.G.A.
2886	LAYTON Percy Maurice	18 South View	9th Glosters
2887	LOWSON Edmund	11 Victoria Street	82762 Pte. Hussars 2nd Res. Cav.
2888	LOWSON George	12 Chapel Street	O.S. H.M.S. "Zaria" R.N.

2889	McCONNELL Robert Graham	Copeland	M21435 "Conqueror" R.N
2890	McCONNELL Samuel	Copeland	J48325 A.B. H.M.S."Blake"
2891	MASON George Robert	10 Manor Street	324 Royal Marine Engineers
2892	MASON Mathew	12 Chapel Street	14645 Pte. 10th D.L.I.
2893	MATTHEW Herbert	Bay Horse	DM2/154178 Cpl. 4th Co. M.T., A.S.C.
2894	MAUGHAN Laurance	22 Farncombe Terrace	22680 6th M.G.C.
2895	MAUGHAN George	9 Evenwood Gate	16593 L-Cpl. 3rd Dragoon Guards
2896	MAUGHAN William	22 Evenwood Gate	26/333rd Northumberland Fus.
2897	METCALFE Albert Isaac	35 Swan Steet	295867 Gnr. 22nd H. Btt.,R.G.A.
2898	METCALFE Alfred	9 Centre, Evenwood	25541 Pte. 19th D.L.I.
2899	METCALFE James Robert	50 Oaks	P.T.S. 6243 Pte., A.S.C. Rmts.
2900	METCALFE. John George	The Mill	24502 Pte. 11th D.L.I.
2901	MIDDLEMAS Robert	1 West View	45659 Pte. 15th D.L.I.
2902	MIDDLEMASS Mark	10 Stones End	252054 3rd Bp. Co. D.L.I.
2903	MORLAND Fred Adolphus	Randolph Terrace	R.N.S.A.
2904	NEASHAM Frederick Wm.	Swan Hotel	21009 3rd Dragoon Guards
2905	NEASHAM Tom	Swan Inn	216765 Gnr. R.G.A.
2906	NICHOLSON Albert James	22 West View	39463 Pte. 3rd Batt. E. Yks
2907	PARKIN Richard	43 Oaks	83650 Pte. 4th Res. N.F. Inf.
2908	PATTON Christopher	18 Oaks	62186 Pte. W. Yorks. "B" Co.
2909	PATTON George	17 Swan Street	24685 Pte. 1st Garr. B., Nth, Fus.

2910	PATTON Thomas	17 Swan Street	217090 Gnr. R.G.A.
2911	PRIESTLEY Robert	10 Evenwood Gate	61339 Driv. 13th Sig. Co. R.E.
2912	PRIESTLEY William	12 Copeland	332647 "C" Co.H.L.I.
2913	PRUDHOE Frederick	Chapel Street	580042 Cpl. 214th Div. Emp. Co.
2914	PURDY William	14 West View	J43917 A.B. "Maidstone"
2915	PURVIS Fred	22 Rochdale Street	340630 Northumberland Fus.
2916	RAINE Siddle	Alpine	750998 Gnr. R.F.A.Y. 37th T.M.B.
2917	ROBINSON Joseph	24 Centre	134690 R.F.A.
2918	ROBINSON Robert	The Green	175808 178th R.E. 4th Sec.
2919	ROE Harold	Copeland	82724 Pte. Hussars 2nd Res.
2920	ROE John William	Copeland	354132 Pte. 146th Sec., M.T., A.S.C.
2921	RUTTER Thomas Henry	9 Victoria Street	14558 4th Batt. D.L.I.
2922	RUTTER Thomas Wm.	30 Evenwood Gate	"Royal Samson"
2923	SHAW Joseph William	7 Rochdale Street	205671. 18th Corps. Signal School
2924	SHIPP Arthur William	6 Evenwood Gate	56749 Cpl. R.A.M.C.
2925	SHIPP Daniel	26 Evenwood Gate	56750 Pte. R.A.M.C.
2926	SHIPP Joseph	26 Evenwood Gate	M2/168171 Pte.12th G.H.Q. Res. MT. Co.
2927	SIMPSON John Welch	1 Chapel Street	39909 Pte. Hussars, 2nd Res.
2928	SIMPSON Robert Arthur.	Randolph Terrace	2/4th Devon Regt
2929	SMITH George Vickers	Paddock Mire	22nd Northumberland Fus.

2930	SMITH James Henry	27 Oaks	60801 Pte. "B" Co. 4th Res. Yorks. Regt. Inf.
2931	SMITH Joseph	Paddock Mire, Evenwood	54623 Pte., 4th Res. Batt. East Yorks. Regt.
2932	SMITH William	27 Oaks	104320 Pte., Res. Employ. Co.
2933	STEEL John Frederick	West View	59058 2nd A.M., R.A.F.
2934	STOKOE William	16 Evenwood Gate	214169 Gnr., 3rd S.A.R.B., R.G.A.
2935	STONEBANKS George	Farncombe Terrace	73958 Pte., 4th D.L.I.
2936	TARM Albert	3 Brookside	216750 Gnr., R.G.A.
2937	TAYLOR James Edward	57 Oaks	6234, 5th Base A.S.C. Remt. Depot
2938	TOWERS John William	6 Copeland	82963 Pte., 2nd Res. Cav. Regt.
2939	TOWERS Thomas	2 Rochdale	216748 Gnr., R.G.A.
2940	WASISTELL James Wm.	15 Rochdale Street	217180 Gnr., R.G.A.
2941	WALKER Joseph Gibson	9 Copeland	6330 Pte., 5th Guards M.G.R.
2942	WALKER Thomas Michael	9 Alexandra Terrace	30595 Pte., 5th Co. 3rd D.L.I.
2943	WALTON John William	52 Oaks	242009., 5th Batt. Nth. Fus.
2944	WATSON Arthur	16 Alexandra Terrace	M/402997 Pte., A.S.C., M.T.
2945	WATSON Harold	6 Victoria Street	73955 Pte., 4th D.L.I.
2946	WATSON Robert Wm. VictorHussars,	16 Alexandra Terrace	82220 Pte., 2nd Res.
2947	WATSON William	14 Rochdale Street	20th Lancs. Fus.
2948	WELSH Edward Watson	16 South View	129891, R.F.A.
2949	WHARTON David	Chapel Street	82712 Pte., Hussars, 2nd Res.
2950	WILKINSON Matthew	1 Farncombe Terrace	587081 Pte., Labour Corps.

2951	WILSON George	1 Accrington Terrace	26595 L-Cpl., "B" Co. L.N.
2952	WILSON Thomas Arthur	8 Rochdale Street	19469, East Yorks. Regt.
2953	WORTHY Harry	Copeland	H.M.S. "Armandale Castle"
2954	WORTHY William	Copeland	21964 Pte., 7/8th K.O.S.B.
2955	WREN Edward	8 Rochdale Street	73951 Pte., 4th Batt. D.L.I.
2956	WREN Wilfred	34 Oaks	11/37748 Pte., 7th Hussars
2957	YOUNG William	Evenwood Gate	Canadian Red Cross

APPENDIX 6

THE TOLL: DURHAM LIGHT INFANTRY

2nd
- Cant T.
- Million W.
- Heaviside W.
- Spence J. W.

5th
- Baister D.

6th
- Brown A.
- Cox G. T.
- Lee J.C.
- Pinkney J.H.
- Priestley G.
- Rushford O.
- Simpson T. W.
- Snowball W.
- Walling J.
- Wardle J.A

KITCHENER'S NEW ARMY

10th
- Graves J. C.

11th
- Dunn T. H.
- Applegarth T. W.

12th
- Maughan J.W.
- Middlemas M. G.

13th
- Raine J. H.

14th
- Wardle R.
- Maughan J.
- Earl W. E.

15th
- Metcalfe R.T.
- Towers E.
- Ellerker J.H.

18th Durham Pals
- Featherstone W.
- Million J.

20th
- Hirst F.

22nd Durham Pals
- Dinsdale W.

The First World War took a terrible toll on the D.L.I. with more than 12,600 dead and thousands wounded. The Regiment was such a part of county life that there was hardly a family that hadn't suffered. In 1922, the Regiment's officers and the Cathedral Chapter resolved to create a memorial chapel in the south transept. The Bishop of Durham, Hensley Henson dedicated the Chapel 20 October 1923.

Durham Cathedral

The Durham Light Infantry Chapel

The Book of Remembrance

More than 12,600 names fill the book for the First World War. The pages are turned daily as the books are in date order. Casualties are recorded on the date they died.

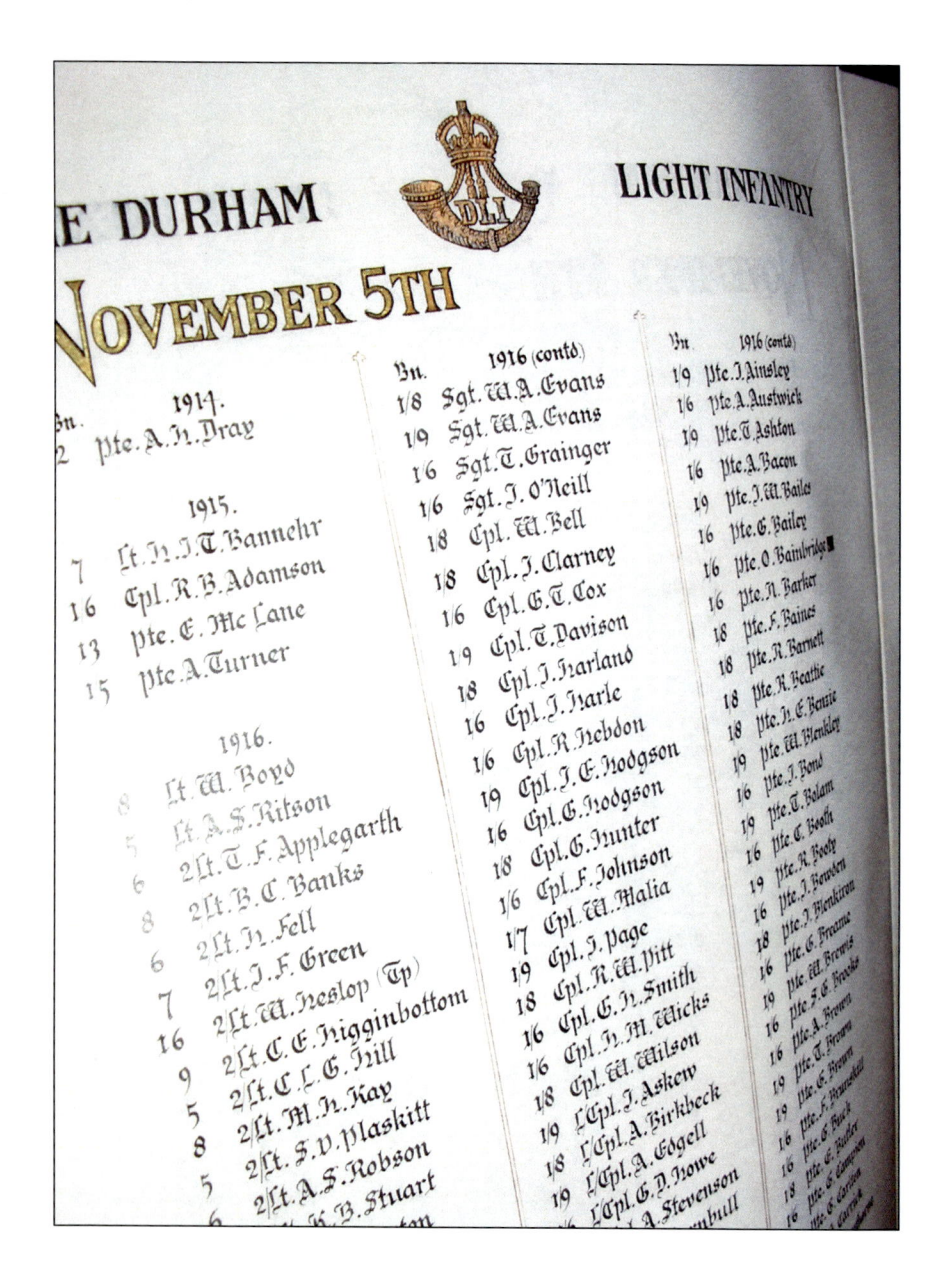

Bibliography

The classic books have been read and provide important background material:
- "The First Hundred Thousand" Ian Hay 1916 The Project Gutenberg eBook
- Ernst Junger, "Storm of Steel" 1920
- Edmund Blundon, "Undertones of War" 1928
- Robert Graves, "Goodbye to All That" 1929
- E.M. Remarque, "All Quiet on the Western Front" 1929
- Ernest Hemmingway, "A Farewell to Arms" 1929
- Siegfried Sasson, "Memoirs of an Infantry Officer" 1930
- Vera Brittan, "Testament of Youth" 1933
- Sidney Rogerson "Twelve Days at the Somme – a memoir of the trenches 1916" 1933
- Dalton Trumbo, "Johnny Got His Gun" 1939

A variety of books and articles have been read, studied and plagiarised. Particularly:
1. F.A. Mumby et al. "The Great War: a history"
2. "The World in Crisis" W.S. Churchill
3. Neil Hanson "The Unknown Soldier" 2005
4. John Keegan "The First World War" 1998
5. "The Imperial war Museum Book of 1918 Year of Victory" M. Brown 1998

6. Peter Hart "The Somme" 2005
7. "In Flanders Fields" Leon Wolff 1959
8. "11th Month11th Day 11th Hour" J.E. Persico 2004
9. Harry Moses "The Fighting Bradfords"
10. "The Durham Forces in the Field 1914-18: The Service Battalions of the Durham Light Infantry" Capt. W. Miles 1920
11. "A Short History of the Sixth Division" Major-general T.O. Marden 1920 The Project Gutenberg eBook
12. "The Story of the 6th battalion the Durham Light Infantry" Capt. R.B. Ainsworth M.C. 1919 The Project Gutenberg eBook
13. "The Fiftieth Division 1914-1918" Everard Wyrall 1939
14. "Durham Pals – 18th, 19th & 22nd Battalions of the Durham Light Infantry in the Great War" by John Sheen
15. Conyers Surtees "History of Evenwood and Eldon"
16. Evenwood Parish Magazines
17. "Evenwood's Heyday" Elsie Anderson et al and the original script prepared by John Smith
18. "The Story of the WWI Zeppelin Raid on Eldon (The Dene Valley) 5th/6th April 1916" Margaret Beith 1999
19. 1918 April Absent Voters' List – Bishop Auckland Division – Evenwood Polling District L, Parish of Evenwood and Barony
20. "The Green Howards in the Great War" Colonel H.C. Wylly CB 1926.
21. Yorkshire Regiment "Regimental Recruiting or Militia and Volunteer Artillery District"
22. The War Diary of the 5th Border Regiment
23. Government of Canada Veterans Affairs "The Canadian National Vimy Memorial"
24. "Cannock Chase" leaflet Volksbund Deutsche Kriegsgraberfursorge e. V.
25. Durham Cathedral leaflet
26. The Chapter of Durham, the D.L.I. Association leaflet
27. Carlisle Cathedral leaflet
28. The Auckland Chronicle various editions

And websites, including:

1. www.1914-1918.net "The Long, Long Trail – the British Army in the Great War of 1914-1918" Chris Baker has been an invaluable resource and many articles have been reviewed and used.
2. www.firstworldwar.com
3. www.worldwar1.co.uk/jutland3.htm
4. www.worldwar1.co.uk/outcome.html
5. www.firstworldwar.com/source/jutland_1stbritishreport.htm
6. www.firstworldwar.com/source/jutland_jellicoe.htm
7. www.1914-1918.net/Diaries/wardiary-12dli.htm – extract from the Battalion war diary which is held in the Public Record Office – document WO95/4236 (copyright Chris Baker)
8. www.historyhouse.co.uk/articles/zeppelins.html
9. www.cwgc.org/search/casualty_details.aspx?casualty
10. www.historyhouse.co.uk/articles/zeppelins.html
11. http://hubpages.com/hub/the_1916_german_zeppelin_offensive
12. www.historyhouse.co.uk/articles/zeppelins.html
13. http://en.wikipedia.org/wiki/list_of_Zeppelins
14. http://en.wikipedia.org/wiki/list_of_Zeppelins
15. cwgc.org/somme
16. www.locksley.com/greatwar/dead.htm
17. http://www.olioweb.me.uk/eshoes.htmlpages/casualty_stats.html
18. www.iwmcollections.org.uk/prisoners/essay.asp
19. www.btinternet.com/~prosearch/tomspage28.html
20. www.remuseum.org.uk
21. www.london.gazettes-online.co.uk
22. London.gazette@tso.co.uk
23. www.warpath.orbat.com/battles.htm – invaluable
24. www.dmm.org.uk/company/w031.htm
25. 1901 census
26. 1911 census

Just a few Words :: :: of Cheer :: :: from Evenwood

Fondly I think of you
　Far o'er the sea,
Humbly I pray for you, -
　God keep you free.
Loyally I wait for you
　Faithful as ever,
Loving and trustful
　The while we must sever.

MANNING

Courtesy of Colin and Winnie Priestley